Frail Riffs

Frail Riffs

The Rules of the Game, Volume 4

MICHEL LEIRIS

TRANSLATED FROM THE FRENCH BY

RICHARD SIEBURTH

YALE UNIVERSITY PRESS ■ NEW HAVEN & LONDON

A MARGELLOS
WORLD REPUBLIC OF LETTERS BOOK

The Margellos World Republic of Letters is dedicated to making literary works from around the globe available in English through translation. It brings to the English-speaking world the work of leading poets, novelists, essayists, philosophers, and playwrights from Europe, Latin America, Africa, Asia, and the Middle East to stimulate international discourse and creative exchange.

Yale University Press books may be purchased in quantity for educational, business, or promotional use. For information, please email sales.press@yale.edu (U.S. office) or sales@yaleup.co.uk (U.K. office).

Set in Electra and Nobel types by Newgen North America, Inc.
Printed in the United States of America.

Library of Congress Control Number: 2023951086
ISBN 978-0-300-26485-2 (hardcover : alk. paper)

A catalogue record for this book is available from the British Library.

This paper meets the requirements of ANSI/NISO Z39.48-1992 (Permanence of Paper).

10 9 8 7 6 5 4 3 2 1

CONTENTS

> *Que philosopher, c'est apprendre à mourir*
> — Montaigne

Frêle bruit, composed between 1966 and 1975, is the fourth and final volume of Michel Leiris's sprawling autobiography, *La Règle du jeu* — a title generally rendered into English as *The Rules of the Game*, although its French also punningly alludes to its author's search for that singular (golden) rule that might regulate and redeem the wayward writerly play (or *jeu*) of his I (or *je*) into an exemplary act of existential engagement. Its previous three volumes — *Biffures* (1948), *Fourbis* (1955), and *Fibrilles* (1966) — have already been beautifully translated by Lydia Davis under the titles *Scratches* (1991), *Scraps* (1997), and *Fibrils* (2017). Following her example, I have taken the liberty of transposing the "faint noise" of *Frêle bruit* into *Frail Riffs* — the late refrains or ostinatos of an aging soloist of the self.

Although intended to bring *The Rules of the Game* to its conclusion after thirty-five years in the making, *Frail Riffs* in fact veers off significantly from the preceding three volumes — which added up to some 850 pages in their original editions, with their increasingly unchaptered and unparagraphed prose, often composed of endlessly labyrinthine sentences, creating great serried blocks of print within which their author (much like his master, Marcel Proust) hoped to immure himself against the deadly dominion of time. *Frail Riffs*, by contrast, presents itself as a far more open and vulnerable work, its text aerated and syncopated by the introduction of generous blanks and margins, its syntax less ornately baroque. While inevitably harkening back to its earlier installments, it is also a book that inaugurates the late style on display in Leiris's subsequent gatherings of autobiographical essay fragments: *Le Ruban au cou d'Olympia* (*The Ribbon at Olympia's Throat*) and *À Cor et à cri* (*With Hue and Cry*), both written in his eighties.

Composed of 146 individual sequences, each beginning on a separate leaf, some as short as a few lines, others extending into full-blown essays, Leiris's autumnal anatomy of melancholy (or *ars moriendi*) is a deliberately hybrid work, featuring entries recycled from the secret diary he kept in his desk drawer (posthumously published as his *Journal 1922–1989*), as well as sundry anecdotes, adages, dreams, reminiscences, philosophical meditations, Walter Mittyish fantasies, bits of political reportage, travel notes, and, most notably, "pataphysical" poems devoted to what Alfred Jarry called "the science of imaginary solutions"—some in italics, the traditional French typographical code for verse, some in roman, indicating their more ambiguous slide into indented prose. Envisaging this book-to-come in late 1966—and no doubt thinking of his friend Maurice Blanchot's recent work on *le livre à venir*—Leiris wrote in his *Journal*: "A book that would neither be a private diary nor a formal work, neither an autobiographical narrative nor a work of the imagination, neither prose nor poetry, but all this at the same time. A book conceived in such a manner as to constitute an autonomous whole at whatever moments that it might be interrupted, which is to say by death. A book thus deliberately established as a work that would eventually be posthumous and as a perpetual *work in progress*."

Always entranced and terrified by the specter of his own demise—his autobiography should perhaps more properly be labeled an autothanatography—Leiris became more and more intrigued by the possibility of his own posthumousness as he advanced in years. In *Fibrils*, the third (and he believed final) volume of *The Rules of the Game*, he recounts how at the age of fifty-six he had attempted suicide in the wake of an evening of heavy drinking occasioned by a messy extramarital affair that he could not bring himself to confess (as was his usual cathartic practice) to his wife, Zette. Caught in an impossible double bind of deception and need for punitive forgiveness, he swallowed five grams of phenobarbital in her presence (an act he assured her was mere "literature") and was transported to a local hospital, where he spent three days in a coma, undergoing an emergency tracheotomy just to keep him breathing. Upon his release, still barely able to speak, scarred at the neck (and hence symbolically decapitated), he was sketched by his friend Giacometti in his bed as a recovering corpse—a Lazarus (or perhaps, more accurately, a Scheherazade) rescued from the dead.

Leiris lived on to bring *Fibrils* to a conclusion but had to admit in its final pages that at the age of sixty-five he was now stuck in his autobiography, with little more to add. He had unearthed most of his childhood and adolescent memories in *Scratches*. He had told (much to Zette's displeasure) of the great erotic adventure of his life in *Scraps*—his encounter, while stationed with the French army in the Maghreb in 1940, with Khadidja, the Persephone-like prostitute who had guided him on a ritual descent into the underworld of ecstatic sex (ruefully recalled twenty years later, at the height of the Algerian War, less as a mythical crossing of the Acheron worthy of Gérard de Nerval than as a banal colonial escapade). He had charted his political education as an anthropologist over the course of his field trips to Africa (in 1931–33 and 1945) and to the Caribbean (in 1948 and 1952), where he had encountered his idealized alter ego in the person of the poet-politician Aimé Césaire. But in *Fibrils*, faced with recounting his most recent trip, to China in 1955 as a member of a distinguished delegation of French fellow travelers (which included the documentary filmmaker Chris Marker), Leiris came up short, especially after learning of Mao's support of the Soviet Union's violent suppression of the Hungarian uprising in 1956. Disillusioned with the politics of international communism like so many of his fellow French intellectuals, he was forced to reconsider his self-image as an engaged anticolonialist whose autobiographical writing went hand in hand with his humanist service to the revolution — or, as he formulated it, whose Sartrean "original choice" involved the pursuit of an *art poétique* that would be governed by the same rule as his *savoir vivre*, thereby placing the practice of his art and the conduct of his life on the same moral plane. His recent failed suicide and all the equivocations it had entailed were there to prove that the act of writing about his life did not thereby serve to make him a better liver of that life. On the contrary.

Forced to confess at the end of *Fibrils* that he had been unable to achieve that dialectical synthesis of aesthetics and ethics that had provided the programmatic goal of *The Rules of the Game* ever since its inception, Leiris was nonetheless determined (in the words of Beckett, whose work he increasingly admired late in life) to try again, to fail again, to fail better. In any event, he simply could not conceive of going on living (or dying) without writing, that is, without engaging in what had over the course of the years become his regular and obsessive ritual of self-monitoring and self-husbandry—akin to that *souci de soi* (or "care for the self") that Foucault associates with the Stoic practice of *hypomnemata* (the taking down of memoranda or notes).

One of the vehicles for this continuous process of self-documentation was provided by the lifelong private journal he kept in a series of notebooks, their pages crowded in diary fashion with dated chronological entries and often supplemented (like an album or commonplace book) with illustrative materials: photos of actresses and cabaret dancers, movie posters, postcards, reproductions of paintings, horoscopes, travel souvenirs, clippings—in short, the bric-a-brac of a life archived as a private museum or memory bank whose various exhibits could be potentially retrieved and placed on display. In addition to this journal, Leiris accumulated a collection of *fiches* (i.e., small slips of graph paper or index cards) on which he regularly jotted down salient incidents of his life. He had developed this technique while serving as the "secretary-archivist" of the official French Dakar-Djibouti mission of 1934–35, especially employed to document the team's various objects of ethnographic investigation and then to classify these findings in special file boxes, or *fichiers*. A number of these field notes would find their way into his first-person logbook of the expedition, published in 1934 as *L'Afrique fantôme* (*Phantom Africa*); others provided the basis for his later professional (and autobiographically inspired) monographs on the secret language of the Dogon or on the theatrical performance of simulated selves in the possession cults of the Ethiopians of Gondar.

Upon his return from Africa, Leiris increasingly viewed his existence within the middle-class habitus of his own Parisian tribe as susceptible to similar techniques of documentation. His first sustained venture into self-portraiture, *L'Âge d'homme* (or *Manhood*, in Richard Howard's translation), already bears the traces of this kind of autoethnography. Described by Leiris as an experiment in surrealist collage or photomontage, the book refuses the traditional chronological retrospection of the memoir in favor of a more splintered disposition of themes (or "myths") grounded in the symptoms or complexes revealed by the psychopathology of everyday life. Rather than deal his existence out as an orderly narrative or coherent coming-of-age story, Leiris instead mentally riffles through the *fiches* of his early experiences of pleasure and pain in order to sort the history of his sexuality into a series of reoccurring straights and flushes governed by mock-Freudian face cards (Lucretia, Judith, Holofernes), all the while challenging the reader to bet as heavily as he has on this risky game of autobiographical chance. First published in 1939, *Manhood* went largely unnoticed in the fog of the Phony War. One of its few early readers was Sartre, who admitted how much his own later venture into autobiography, *The Words*, owed to Leiris's example. Another was Walter Benjamin, the author of the autobiographical fragments of *One-Way Street* and *Berlin Childhood around 1900*. In a letter to Horkheimer, Benjamin admired Leiris's deployment of imagery derived from illustrated children's books and from the kitsch of popular culture ("the folklore of the metropolis") while praising his fusion of classical tragedy with baroque allegory, but he never lived to write his intended review . . .

Manhood would have to wait until its mass paperback edition of 1966 to be consecrated as one of the canonical classics of French modernism — and it was to this prewar experiment in self-portraiture that Leiris now returned as he tried to find his way out of the dead end of *Fibrils*, published that same year. He revisited the work that had provided one of he original inspirations for *L'Âge d'homme* back in 1934: Marcel Duchamp's *Green Box*. Containing replicas of the many notes, sketches, and studies undertaken over the course of the creation of *The Bride Stripped Bare by Her Bachelors, Even*, this box was intended as a kind of portable toy that would allow its readers to playfully assemble these various materials into the purely conceptual (and aleatory) production of his as yet unexhibited artwork. (No doubt thinking of Duchamp, shortly after his suicide attempt Leiris arranged for an executor to publish a facsimile of the field notes of his life filed away in his *fichier* should he not live to complete his autobiography.)[1] The other model for his book-to-come that Leiris now discovered was the recently published edition of Mallarmé's notes toward the mythical *Book* (*Le Livre*) he had left unfinished at his death. This *Book* had been conceived by Mallarmé less as a textual object than as a public ritual carried out by an anonymous Operator who, like some Wizard of Odds, would shuffle and reshuffle the playing cards of Language (randomly retrieved from the pigeonholes of a nearby credenza) in front of a select group of spectators chosen to collaborate in the hieratic performance (or reading) of the Oeuvre as it progressively unfolded over a yearslong series of seances, eventually ushering in the millennium of the Absolute Book.

With these examples of Mallarmé and Duchamp in mind, Leiris embarked on the as yet untitled volume 4 of *The Rules of the Game* in the mid-sixties. Abandoning his previous practice of composing the various strata of his text seriatim on the bound pages of his notebooks—creating a laborious palimpsest that eventuated in a mere forty to fifty pages of finished text per year—he instead began distributing its raw drafts onto loose sheets of paper (or *feuilles volantes*) held in abeyance in folders, waiting to be subsequently

1. Denis Hollier's superb Pléiade edition of *La Règle du jeu* (2003) reproduces the actual texts penned recto/verso in a tiny hand on Leiris's file cards, allowing one to follow how he plucked these *fiches* from his *fichier* (at random?) and sorted them into unexpected puns or subject rhymes (*équations de faits*, as he called them), whose rhizomic bundles he then seamlessly wove into the intricate fabric of his final text. He consulted (and dutifully canceled) 32 *fiches* for *Biffures*, 130 for *Fourbis*, 215 for *Fibrilles*, and 130 for *Frêle bruit*. A photo of one of the file boxes of *La Règle du jeu*, which features tabs to classify its index cards under various rubrics, may be found in the exhibition catalog for *Leiris & Co* (Paris: Gallimard; Metz: Centre Pompidou-Metz, 2015).

reorganized without regard to their actual date of composition into a complex (and more spatialized) rhythm of recurrent themes or leitmotifs. At the very outset of *Frail Riffs*, he provides a number of metaphors for the pages to follow: cards put into play in a game of chance (solitaire, poker, or tarot); islands distributed into the fraternity of an archipelago (as in his idealized Antilles); constellations projected onto the sky by the mind at the moment of its shipwreck (as in Mallarmé's *A Throw of the Dice*); tiles laid down into an ever-shifting mosaic, the light stumbling on their uneven surfaces (as in Proust).

Rummaging through his *fichier* in search of material for his fourth volume, Leiris happened upon a leftover file card that he now wanted to retrieve for fuller use. The incident it related, drawn from his notebook descriptions of the Liberation of Paris in the late summer of 1944, provided a kind of primal scene, formerly repressed but now resurfacing, set in Leiris's apartment overlooking the Seine at 53 bis quai des Grands-Augustins—one of the three major topographical axes that triangulate the writing of *Frail Riffs* (the other two being his right bank office at the Musée de l'Homme and his weekend country home in Saint-Hilaire). He had bought these spacious lodgings with his wife in 1943 and (a fact discreetly left unmentioned in his autobiography) had offered it during the Occupation as a safe house to a number of members of the Resistance as well as to Jews—among whom, the celebrated art dealer Daniel-Henry Kahnweiler, a close friend of Apollinaire and Picasso, into whose family fortune Leiris had married in 1926.

Throughout his autobiography, Leiris inevitably refers to Kahnweiler as his (unnamed) brother-in-law; only after his death was it discovered that his wife, Zette, was in fact not Kahnweiler's wife's sister (as everybody pretended) but her illegitimate daughter, meaning that Kahnweiler was in reality Leiris's father-in-law. If, as Lévi-Strauss suggests, kinship systems are a kind of language that serves to define the currency (women) that makes possible systems of exchange, then Leiris's participation in the Kahnweiler family secret, that is, his rewriting of biological fact into accommodating fiction, his Oedipal canceling of the vertical relations of filiation in favor of the sheerly lateral fantasy of sororal and fraternal ties, may be read as a kind of originary family romance from which the rest of his oeuvre derives—almost as if the complicity in his wife's false identity back in the 1920s had set into motion that game of masking and unmasking, of revelation and concealment on which so much of his autobiographical writing thrives.

The episode that Leiris chose to unearth for the incipit of *Frail Riffs*, noted down in spare, Hemingwayesque prose, might just as well have been drawn from the grainy newsreels of the period or from a waking dream. He is standing at the window of his fourth-floor apartment with a group of unspecified friends (which included Jean-Paul Sartre and Simone de Beauvoir, both of whom later wrote of this same scene, as it turns out) when he suddenly catches sight of a vehicle with a red cross painted on its roof barreling down the street below, pursued by a fury of bullets fired from the nearby rooftops. Its driver apparently wounded, the car swerves into the shopwindows of the next-door publishing house of Perrin (the firm that had brought out several of Mallarmé's prose titles, we learn several pages later). As the vehicle bursts into flames, German soldiers flee from the wreckage and an argument breaks out among the armed partisans on the street below whether or not to kill them then and there, despite their pleas for mercy. One of the young partisans (on his knees, his pistol drawn) is described as a matador or puntillero about to deliver the coup de grâce—a rather uncanny comparison, especially given that the 1946 preface Leiris would add to *Manhood* was titled (at least in Richard Howard's translation) "The Autobiographer as *Torero*."

At this point, Leiris's account takes an altogether unexpected turn. Filled with horror at the scene of violence that is about to be enacted before his eyes, he retreats to the kitchen at the rear of his apartment, where, now alone and as if possessed, he proceeds to wash his hands under the sink faucet in a gesture he characterizes as purely mechanical. It is only after having come to realize the full significance of these ritual ablutions—namely, that he has been washing his hands of responsibility like a Pontius Pilate compulsively trying to cleanse himself of the sacrificial blood of Christ—that he makes his way back to the front window to resume his viewing of the operatic spectacle playing itself out below his eyes. The young partisan-torero is now in the process of finishing off one of the German soldiers, whose body lies writhing on the ground. Then calm. Then a huge explosion. The fake Red Cross vehicle had been loaded with grenades all the while.

Leiris observed in his *Journal* in 1966 that he intended this inaugural riff to provide the leading "theme" or "myth" for his book-to-come, to be followed by a series of "variations" (in the fashion of Bach's *Art of the Fugue* or Queneau's *Exercises in Style*) taking the form of commentaries or digressions that would be either documentary or speculative or lyric in inspiration. Leaving aside all the richly allegorical readings this primal scene positively invites, Leiris felt that at its core this rediscovered *fiche* presented an exemplary moment of "crisis" in which the inner world of an individual, suddenly confronted by the unexpected shock of an external event, is provoked into the performance of an automatic response of avoidance: to retreat into the private precincts of autobiography and there—camouflaged by the faint noise (or *frêle bruit*) of the kitchen faucet—to wash one's ink-stained hands of blood . . .

Frail Riffs

Rather than a logical or chronological sequence, these pages shall form—whenever completed or interrupted from without—an archipelago or constellation, an image of the spurt of blood, the deflagration of gray matter, or the final stream of vomit which my collapse (solely conceivable to me as a sudden catastrophe of this sort) shall inscribe upon the sky, fictively.

To lay them down, to move them around, to group them, like cards sorted into a winning combination. To add to them, sometimes to prolong the mosaic, sometimes to plug a gap. To do away with them, in case I (reluctantly) come to realize that the sole remedy lies in amputation. Obversely, to leave them open to interference and to accept those things (lacking as I will the time to discover and explain how they connect to the rest) that appear to occur without rhyme or reason.

If at every moment I am aware what their assemblage signifies, I remain in ignorance as to what this will indicate when suddenly set in stone—a lot my hand will not have traced, unless it be of my own accord that I have blocked the outcome, believing that the game is now over or that the match, having reached a stalemate, should be suspended.

*

August 20, 1944 . . .

Among the vehicles that were being attacked by the French Forces of the Interior lying in ambush among the various apartment buildings, we see a car coming up along the quai Saint-Michel, escorted by a trail of bullets. Unscathed, the vehicle crosses the place Saint-Michel and then enters onto the quai des Grands-Augustins. At this point, the driver no doubt having been hit, it swerves onto the sidewalk and crashes into the shopfront of Perrin Publishers. Given the red cross painted on the car's roof, I am surprised—and shocked—that the FFI was firing on it. Armed civilians are quick to surround the vehicle, which has burst into flames. Its occupants beg them: "Comrades! Mercy!!" To the side of the right front door—their only way out—a young man is kneeling, his pistol drawn to keep the two or three German soldiers from exiting the car. An argument breaks out among the FFI. Some are shouting: "Let them fry! Let them fry!" And others: "Let them have it! Let them have it!" Although the bullfight dimension of the scene (the young man on his knees with his pistol drawn, half matador, half puntillero) strikes me as the very picture of grandeur and beauty, I draw back from my window in horror and make my way to the kitchen, where, mechanically, I wash my hands under the sink faucet. But the instant the meaning of my gesture becomes clear to me (a ritual washing of the hands, like Pilate's), I turn off the faucet and return to the dining room window. With his pistol the young man is finishing off one of the Germans, who had fled the flaming car and whose body can be seen writhing on the ground. A moment of calm. Then a series of loud explosions causes the small group gathered around the car to scatter: the Red Cross vehicle was loaded with grenades, which are now detonating.

*

Parodic procurator,
poseur,
pharisee,
pettifogger,
piece of crap,
puppet,
prostitute,
puritan,
pantaloon,
poopy-pants,
pansy,
person of no consequence,
prude,
pantywaist in a sacristy,
pinhead,
pompous ass,
prig,
peppermint pastille,
preachy paralytic,
parasite,
pompous priest,
petulant pouter,
pasteurized punchinello,
poetaster,
platypus foot,

paltry Pietà,
pearl of the urinal,
philosopher doggy-style,
prudent plutocrat,
picky eater,
pissy quibbler,
prissy phony,
poster boy,
polite to a fault,
pacifist bleater,
putrid patrician,
Petronius half baked,
pure Epicurean pig,
pale pilaster.

Occupying the site of an Augustine convent that did not survive the Revolution of 1789 and very near to the La Pérouse restaurant which to this day still features private dining alcoves as it did during the Gay Nineties (one of their partitions, padded for privacy as they all were, is provided with a mirror on which, at the conclusion of an intimate repast, hands no doubt adorned with diamond rings scratched their names and the date), the apartment building in which I live is seven stories high, constructed toward the end of the reign of Napoleon III, its undistinguished architecture barely offset by a few decorative elements, notably two large female or angelic faces with the cheeks of kindly nannies placed just above the balcony that stretches the length of the third story. In the fifth-floor apartment, one of whose most attractive features is its relatively elevated view of the Seine and of the mostly ancient houses on the southern tip of the Île de la Cité, the room we call the library (although it is not the only one to contain books) was for a long time graced by a fireplace surrounded by a large frame made of sculpted wood, an ornament whose rather wretched taste vied with that of the two fake doors in the adjacent room—formerly the parlor—whose unique function it was to echo the two actual doors, still intact, whereas their replicas are now hidden behind furniture. At eye level and on either side, two identical figures made up the principal motif of this frame: heads of fauns or sileni, whose wavy beards seemed to reproduce, as if inverted, the flames absent from the unused hearth, the apartment having benefited from central heating, whose source of warmth during my residence was in turn supplied by coal, by gas, and finally by household garbage, through the system known as city heat.

Extremely cumbersome given its size, jutting out and extending up to the ceiling, the wooden frame was eliminated several years after the last war when, what with the sheer accumulation of books and the proliferation of shelving that crowded even the hallway leading to the other rooms, its walls lined with all the exposed archaic pipes whose point of origin lies in a tiny room behind the kitchen and whose point of arrival is the bathroom, we found ourselves forced, my wife's brother-in-law and I, to put up additional shelves in those areas of the room still untouched by bookcases. To tell the truth, I would have liked to have preserved this bit of decor as ugly as it was inconvenient: I was attached to its false majesty as one is attached to certain things that, though absurd, are part and parcel of the folklore that everybody, despite their better judgment, nourishes within themselves. Nonetheless, my heart was so divided between wanting to have all my books on hand and fearing I'd be overwhelmed by their mounting tide that, unable to recommend that we go after the frame with a series of sinister ablations whose surgery would have offended my obsessive need for order and unable to endorse just boxing the whole thing in (which would have been useless), I therefore made up my mind to have it eliminated altogether, thus providing a temporary solution to the problem.

In the hollow of the fireplace, now rid of its mantle, there stands a radio and record player console, a rather paltry and out-of-date instrument that is of little concern to me, since I never listen to the radio and reserve my enjoyment of opera recordings for my weekends in the country (a habit I have in the meantime given up because at Saint-Hilaire I already spend so much of my time on minor occupations such as walking the dog, a festive occasion for him and a pleasant exercise for me). Very compact (its major advantage), this little cabinet made in Germany bears the brand name SABA.

From the library—now more spacious even if more filled with books— and from the other windows, one looks out to the left onto the Pont Neuf, but even if one leans out quite far one cannot catch sight of another building that is quite close by and that also sits a few steps from the river: the Hôtel de la Monnaie, all the more important historically because it was in this vicinity that—before Louis XV had the mint built—the Hôtel de Nesle was located, with its tower so redolent of disreputable debauchery and murder. To the right, on the facing bank, one can see the spire of the Sainte-Chapelle towering over the god-awful Palais de Justice, and then, beyond the pont Saint-Michel, the two great towers and the soaring spire of the Hugoesque cathedral, revised and improved by Viollet-le-Duc, a set decorator in stone for theater pieces that bring back to life those eras when Christ was still lord.

"Didier Scholarly Books, Perrin successor," 35 quai des Grands-Augustins, later "Perrin & Co. Scholarly Books." It was here that Stéphane Mallarmé's *Verse and Prose* was first published, printed in characters whose typeface was large enough to make every line precious. Its frontispiece a lithographic portrait of Mallarmé by Whistler so transparent it seemed to consist of nothing more than cigar smoke and ash (perhaps the atmosphere of his rue de Rome Tuesday gatherings, which even without the cigars would have been smoked up by the nearby Gare de Saint-Lazare), whereas his *Piece in Summary of Vathek*—one of the bits in this collection that later provided the preface to the Englishman Beckford's tale, also brought out by the same publisher in an identical pale blue cover—seems to have been carved from ebony or black marble.

Of what sort of stone was this building built, which when I got to know it was an ancient edifice not very tall but quite rickety, with its cockeyed windows and rather oldfangled decor reminiscent of the home of some eighteenth-century alchemist or magnetizer? No doubt it was threatening to fall into ruin despite its material solidity, unless this was merely to be understood as the simple effect of the comings and goings of commerce: during the past two years, its ground floor has been undergoing renovations. Ever since the work began, there has been no indication on the construction fence of what kind of restaurant, café, boutique, or private or public sector office will take the place of this publishing house, if indeed there is anything slated to replace it.

Although I often used to look into its shop window in days gone by, I would be hard pressed to cite any other of its catalog offerings, except (if I'm not mistaken) a work by Ernest Hello and *The Great Initiates* by Édouard Schuré, about whom the only thing I know is that he was at once a great enthusiast of esotericism and a fervent admirer of Wagner, like many intellectuals of his period, the same age that saw Mallarmé alive and talking—all flame and frost—without lingering on too long in life, Mallarmé the man of the Book in which everything coalesces, the man who proved that one can simultaneously be both a soaring poet and a minor English teacher who ruffles no feathers.

*

Gothic lettering is (of course!) the Middle Ages, the barbs of stone lace-work and the cloisonné of stained-glass windows or enamels. The lovely grat-ings across which scenes of piety or chivalry can be glimpsed, caught un-awares thanks to a glance stealthily cast through the frame of a narrow window or loophole or else espied between the abundant branches and leaves of a swatch of forest.

The gratings surrounding the trees on Parisian sidewalks, heavy circular cakes cut up into quarters and occasionally uprooted by rioters. Household grates between whose curved bars the coal or peat fire brightly burns. Cages for wild beasts with their claws exposed. A trellised helmet. Ancient coats of arms or modern traceries of steel beams — a modernity now largely out of date, the style of the Crystal Palace, the Gallery of Machines, the Great Wheel, the Eiffel Tower, or all kinds of obsolete industrial constructions in the manner of Jules Verne or Robida.

Which episodes of my own history might be written in Gothic characters? I see none — unless I go back to those episodes that are purely imaginary, vi-cariously experienced during that time of life when fairy tales are cloaked in colors all the more fantastic because they exceed belief and thereby become wonders of the Marvelous, something one encounters neither in Bible stories nor in the tales of Greco-Roman mythology, and to which one more or less attends as if they were history lessons.

The other forms of writing one later discovers — Egyptian hieroglyphs, arabesques that are by definition Arab, small blocks of Hebrew or Chaldean, Chinese ideograms, Cyrillic enigmas — will be stamped with a frigidity foreign to this Gothic lettering that remains our very own despite the treatment to which it has been subjected by who knows which ironworker who, working with hammer and tongs over an open fire, complicates it without negating it, rendering it all the more rich and sensitive by supplying it with slots and saliences, with spurs and perforations, with Adam's apples and eye sockets at which the imagination grasps like a mountain climber availing himself of the slightest handhold . . .

*

Sambre snarls of brass and *Meuse* shivers of cymbals. This time involving Republicans rather than saber attacks on the Teutons and Cimbrians.

Long ago I used to adore the march of the Sambre-et-Meuse Regiment for its martial air and especially for its name. But of all the pieces of music that I had heard—most of them on the phonograph (which made them sound sour or raspy, given the poor quality of the recordings back then)—my favorite one was the "Coronation March," excerpted from Meyerbeer's opera *The Prophet,* which ends (as I was later to learn) with the explosion of a powder cellar and the burning of a palace when fortune turns against the popular prophet John of Leyden. This solemn march was executed by the musicians of the Republican Guard, which added the pageantry of gorgeous uniforms and leather bandoliers to the brilliance blasting forth from the gramophone's metallic horn. From this cylinder to which I listened so often that its grooves were nicked with whitish flecks, I have not forgotten the deep guttural tones associated with the idea of a royal coronation, akin to those of a more pagan ceremony whose wild whoops rang out from a virgin forest orchestra that later made my eardrums vibrate when *The Rite of Spring* first challenged my youthful philistinism with its astonishing savagery, whose musical excellence it would take me some time to grasp.

Ver sacrum. Is not spring the season of war par excellence? And is not war, like spring itself, always pagan? Of this point I am absolutely certain. And it is as a pure lover of the sounds and shapes of words that I observe (without trying to generalize, but moved by the pleasure I take in letting language think for me and impose its string of associations on me, above and beyond any historical or other reference points) just how evocative the *ï* in the pagan word *païen* is of things sharp, hard, and serried when it strikes my readerly eye. I therefore perceive it not as I would a consonant, but rather as a particularly shrill vowel: a Biscayan bullet, an arrow tip, a crystalline star such as those that would appear when my father's tenor voice sang out "Noël! 'Neath the starry sky . . . ," the first verse of a *Noël païen* of which he was quite fond and which, for whatever reason, I believed referred to the Gauls. Also: *ï*, a bud stridently piercing and blazing its way like the high-pitched note of a clarinet or fife.

*

Not as a druid shouting "Hey ho, New Year's mistletoe," nor as a warrior with a luxuriant head of hair and bronze collar, nor as a Gallic peasant, nor as any of those other specimens of humankind—nobility, clergy, third estate— proposed by the History of France, but as a Roman senator, this is how I prefer to envisage myself when I imagine myself living in another era.

Just your average senator, content to avoid the main stage, a character slightly concealed behind the folds of his freshly laundered toga, his hands talkative, his head shaved, shuffling about in his sandals, sharing the latest gossip with his colleagues, knitting his brows, less worried about the affairs of state—the legions in revolt or the incursions at the frontiers—than about the impossibility of predicting the emperor's next dangerous stunt. Sensitive to the latest dream that has visited his sleep, alert to the path of birds, to the unevenness of the pavement on which he has stumbled, he is afraid of blood and is no enthusiast of the circus games. Still, he puts in regular appearances at the Colosseum, for his absence would surely be noted by people of his acquaintance and defamatory rumors might well reach the ears of Caesar. What plans might a person be concocting when keeping out of sight, and isn't he already somewhat suspect for having turned his nose up at all the popular pastimes? Not a bad fellow, even if his lack of zeal makes him feel honor bound never to give a thumbs-down to a gladiator. Similarly, he finds it impossible to take pleasure in the torture of a Christian, convinced as he is that the sufferings of this unfortunate creature will redound upon him, the God of the Jews being no less irascible than the other gods.

To Pompeii—which, like the town of Timgad (a relic of the grandeur of Roman imperialism which held sway in Algeria, already a colony even back then), later struck me more like some recently ravaged Oradour than as a field of ancient ruins, and in which I felt so at home that I visited its various sites as if I had been one of their habitués, including the tavern, the brothel, the sports ground, even the Villa of the Mysteries, with its scene of whipping, an initiatory rite, so I was informed, but which to my eyes seemed to feature a woman with a backside far too tempting to be anything else than an image devised to arouse the fanciers of white skins or kisses shuddering under the rod—to Pompeii, then, which a cloud of ash destroyed without altering, he used to go every year for light recreation, claiming that he needed to get some rest from the burdens of his daily workload.

As prudent as he had been in the conduct of his life, one fine day just before he was about to turn seventy, he received word that he would have to comply with the orders of the emperor, who had for some obscure reason decided to proceed with what we would today call a purge. Trembling but trying to put a good face on things, he stretched himself out in his bathtub and, with his eyes closed, held out his two wrists to his old and faithful servant whom he had asked to open his veins. His eyes closed, tears running down his quivering cheeks, the slave, also at the end of his rope, took a well-honed blade into his hands—which he had purified by careful ablutions—and fulfilled his master's request. Then he withdrew to his hovel and, once night had fallen, proceeded to the steps of a temple to catch some sleep before making his way to the countryside, leaving his master's puzzled widow behind in the accursed villa.

Would I were possessed of the gift for hallucination of a Marcel Schwob, in order to endow this "imaginary life" with as much color and truth as if I had actually lived it, whereas the only thing (apart from the emotion) that connects me to it is onomastic in nature: the southern origins of my patronym, which would seem to derive from the langue d'oc, closer to Latin than the langue d'oïl.

*

Both likewise seated on what might have been a magistrate's curule, Pilate washes his hands of the blood of Jesus Christ, the bearded Jew, while Caesar, his head too perfectly shaven not to disdain the long moustache and streaming hair of his vanquished foe, receives Vercingetorix as the latter approaches him on horseback without spear, sword, helmet, or shield. The horse proceeds at a walk, for the warrior wants it to be known that even if he has to capitulate, he couldn't care less if his vanquisher is growing impatient. But whereas Pilate goes after Christ as a religious figure, Caesar dispatches Vercingetorix as a soldier: he drags him behind his triumphal chariot, then has him put to death.

Hereditary enemies, like the French and the Germans, whom one used to call the "Alleboches" (soon abbreviated into that foul term "Boches") or the "Prussians" (to whom one preferred the reputedly less brutal Bavarians), which then got contracted into "les Pruscos."

Long before all this, the Gallic chieftain Brennus—in truth, the *brenn*—placed his rough-hewn crude barbarian's sword onto one of the pans of the scale to add weight to the tribute he was demanding from Rome. The short-lived victory of those who, once they were colonized, furnished their foreign rulers with delicacies such as oysters and Roquefort cheese.

During my childhood, steeped as I was in catechism classes and history lessons, Gaul, no less than Judea (as much Christ's homeland as Gaul was Vercingetorix's), was never a country like any other. It seems to me that even now I still mentally pronounce its name with a slowness that sounds suspicious, inserting a pause after its closed and extended *o*, as if this word were freighted with a jumble of images that despite my having long outgrown them have nonetheless continued—undergoing a few subtractions and additions en route but more or less remaining the same—to escort this word *Gaul* ever since I left school:

the acorns of oaks;

the huts like those of colliers;

the blue wafts of smoke rising from the huts;

the pigs wandering about here and there, feeding on acorns;

the Roman rampart constructions;

the blondness and white skin of the women in their large sleeveless dresses;

the manes and thick moustaches of their male companions;

their drab, coarse clothing;

their helmets and huge military swords;

their battles fought bare chested to display their bravery;

the heavy tread of these rough-hewn tribes, more forest dwellers than country folk and who, when it came to heroism, would have as their direct descendant the Grand Ferré, this peasant represented as fighting on foot during the Hundred Years' War and whom I imagine as a kind of farrier, broad of shoulders and black of beard, striking the English as he would strike his anvil.

*

TEUTATES, three-headed terror triply thundered!

CERNUNNOS, all claw and bone, all flesh and naked nerve!

Gods with whom, mistakenly, I associated IRMENSUL—iris, mint, lily, campanula—German and not Celtic as in Bellini's *Norma*, where the priestess and the Roman who had abandoned her, now having reconciled, walk toward the funeral pyre that the Gauls had raised to propitiate the sated gods in favor of their revolt, IRMENSUL, that tree trunk or Cosmic Tree no longer to be confused with the Diana or the barbarian Venus I had imagined.

Wearers of breeches and legendary masters of the handlebar moustache, our ancestors the Gauls were so well versed in human sacrifice that they probably would have imagined that the sky would fall on all the heads they had scalped throughout the centuries if they had foreseen that their descendants, drunk on a high-mindedness as strong as hydromel, would over the course of that summer of 1944 inflict this same humiliation—thereby reviving the punishment that had already been meted out to the demon Margaret of Burgundy—on the women who were guilty of having compromised themselves with the occupiers: to have their heads shaved bald.

The shaving of the head, to wit, and not of the pubis, as logic might have suggested.

*

A phonetic cabriole suitable to a jockey who had been a steeplechase champion before distinguishing himself as a war hero: "Bob Singecop." Or the name given to the youngest of an Elephant family, one of whom, the president of the Republic, had gone missing for some time, abducted by conspirators or by foreign agents who, to make their way into his quarters, had dug a long tunnel under his palace: "Elephantinonde." Other sorts of animal names, such as Lapinot, Moutonnet, Singeonot or rather Singinesco, as well as Chien-chien, with their various nicknames, like Ecureil-reuil (who flew away but whom I suddenly remembered again when one rainy afternoon in the country I saw a red squirrel with a bushy tail scamper across the drive separating our garden from our terrace, a minor incident but one that nonetheless jogged my memory so deeply that I can say that it grabbed me far more strongly by the gut than by the heart or throat). Just like the geographical locations with which their adventures were associated — Chienville, Chatonville, Elephantinopolis — the names of these animals were dictated to my brother and me by the species to which they belonged . . . I would like to list them all and dig through my memory for the biography of each of these heroes, whose larger-than-life attributes — modestly assumed even by the major stars among them — were their bravery in all matters, their stoic courage, and their endless capacity for self-sacrifice.

As if spurred on by our need to come up with models of virtue — above and beyond the pure pleasure we took in putting our talents as narrators into competitive play — and as if we had conceived no nobler fate than to follow at least one of those paths that lead adults to the same glorious reward that a first prize bestows on a schoolboy, we together proceeded to elaborate not any old cloak-and-dagger tale or serial novel but rather an exemplary chanson de geste, an epic tale that, influenced by our childhood readings and more fundamentally by our deep attraction to animals (like the average readers to whom these kinds of works are addressed), recounted the heroic feats of these creatures whom humans are often too apt to consider their lesser brothers.

The singular reality that these names (which came to us so naturally that they seemed to belong to people we knew) conferred on those creatures they designated, so specific that we immediately sensed them as clearly defined individuals and not as mere symbols of some zoological group, the unbridled pleasure that we took in manipulating, episode after episode, these proper names that were not just labels affixed to these characters but their very flesh and blood—this was no doubt what mattered most to us. And, not immune to authorial vanity, we were especially proud to have come up with names as fascinating as those that belonged to Bob Singecop (the rider who, although human, might well have ridden his horse like a monkey [*singe*] to accelerate its stride) or to Elephantinonde, of whom I remember virtually nothing. Names that worked, names that did not just baptize these figures but gave them life.

"Elephantinonde," a lucky find on my brother's part, following upon an "Elephantinet" (which in turn had been preceded by an "Elephantin") in a more or less dynastic series of appellations of which it was the final heir, this name ending in *onde* (as melodious to our untutored ears as the female "Rosemonde" and "Esclarmonde") belonged to a character whose sole function seemed to be to act as a second Elephantinet, which would easily explain why I can recall little other than his name: "Elephantinonde," whose suffix (this bizarre syllable that, even though as much a diminutive as the suffix *-net* in "Elephantinet," tends to widen rather than narrow down the word by providing a final lingering note instead of a definitive closure) served to clearly distinguish him from his predecessor, but not to the extent that their family likeness would go unnoticed. "Elephantinonde": nothing but a word, to be sure, but a word—and here I still honor my brother's inventive genius—that has never ceased to delight me and that to this day remains an entire world unto itself.

These tales, so filled with doleful adventures yet always leading to a definitive *happy end* (with the hero basking in glory and siring children equally fearless and without reproach), eventually gave way—at least insofar as I was concerned—to several stories or sketches of stories that were less Edenic and that featured characters who were human and no longer the anthropomorphized animals that peopled the legendary cycle that my brother and I elaborated from day to day and set down in our notebooks.

Then there were the things that were no longer stories to be passed on by word of mouth or by their transcription onto the page but instead aspired to be full-fledged works—theatrical works made to be performed and that I played at composing, inspired both by the shows I had seen and by the readings to which I had now given more thought (especially the textbook by Albert Malet that explained the Middle Ages to middle schoolers): the draft of a drama titled *Brétigny*, which featured peasants from the period of the Hundred Years' War and was critical (so it seems to me) both of the French feudal lords and of the English, as well as another play that never advanced beyond its title—*The Polish Reapers*, or *Those That Die*—but was intended to portray the misfortunes of a country that my brother and I felt had been criminally wiped off the map. The exact chronology of all this escapes me, but I believe that these two attempts were preceded by an opera libretto, *Gottfried the Messenger of the Grail*, a work that was motivated—the only justification for this naïve act of plagiarism—by my desire to write my own *Lohengrin* (whereas it in fact differed from Wagner's version only by its hero's name and by the poverty of its scenes, yet despite its failure to be an improved original was nonetheless a second *Lohengrin*, different in name, different in composition, and thus fully satisfying to me, given that these minor deviations were enough to make of it a new work that I could consider the product of my own ingenuity).

In keeping with this airy-fairy Grail-mongering but now more oriented toward the sulfurous depths, there was also a *Beelzebub*, a diablerie borrowed from *Faust* that never reached fruition and that at the very most provided a pretext to dash off one or two garbled sketches in violet ink indicating the trapdoor through which Beelzebub, alias Mephistopheles, suddenly appeared onstage. This evil angel was a mere replica of Gounod's Mephisto, imagined by me in the same masked ball outfit: eyebrows raised like a cock's spurs, a provocative goatee, a cap decorated with a sinuous feather and slicing down over his forehead like a claw, a sword nervously quivering by his side, ever ready to be drawn. As for Faust, I was no doubt aware that a poet called Goethe (a name I had initially read as *Jété*, thinking I was following its pleasingly archaic German pronunciation) had composed a play about him back in olden times (certainly well before the age of powdered wigs) but one that involved too many philosophical implications to be accessible to me. Or that was only accessible to me in such a nebulous fashion that this thirster after absolute knowledge who strove to gain control over everything the earth has to offer was instead imagined by me as a young knight by the name of the faithful dog Ripeau who is made unbelievably rich by the tempter but who is then induced to commit wicked deeds that he is later led to regret when he remembers (O nightmare!) how he had once lived his life as a blameless knight and who, nearly shedding tears of blood over his sins, decides to retire to a monastery to expiate his crimes. For me back in those days, was not Good defeating the apparent victory of Evil the noblest of subject of all?

＊

In high school philosophy classes, when one begins to learn how to handle ideas the way that as a child one used to handle erector-set pieces, and when one comes to admire how the teacher—provided he be halfway competent— manages to build up and then tear apart each system concerning man or the world at large as constructed by philosophers either ancient or modern, the *association of ideas* was, among the other notions addressed by our psychology courses, the one that most interested me. Imagining this mechanism was as enthralling as witnessing an illusionist's sleight of hand: ideas intermeshing by unexpected affinities and encroaching upon each other, then bouncing off each other after a carom and then changing form, ever proliferating as they cross countless intersections and then adjust themselves in our heads like some infinite chain, each link of which gives birth to another chain . . . Armed with this capacity of ideas to attract other ideas and to connect these to yet others without the series ever coming to an end, the life of our minds appeared to know no obstacles.

In a book half humorous, half speculative, *The Testament of a Hashish Eater*, more of an apologia pro vita sua than a confession, a pharmacist who was a family friend and both a philosopher and a *hashishin* used the term *cocalinitis* to describe the hypertrophy of this mechanism (whose operations are ordinarily much poorer than can be theoretically accounted for) under the influence of this prodigious drug that could cause its user to experience an almost limitless series of random associations revelatory of various truths. This optimistic philosopher, who dreamed of spiritual euphoria and divine harmony and who had something in him of a Greek or Asiatic sage, of a me-dieval Scholastic, of a contributor to the comic *Almanac Vermot*, was a little goateed devil of a man who was also convinced that the soul was androgynous and that it was made up of two opposite but complementary principles, one of which was male, *Pandorac*, and the other of which was female, *Pandorine*.

I have never partaken of hashish, but having a definite tendency toward "cocalinitis," I have made of the association of ideas if not a technique of invention at least one of my favorite modes of interior investigation: with one idea calling up another idea, one image another image, one memory another memory, one is able to take a good look around one's self. As for my own sorry state of division—this distressing dichotomy whose two warring sides are continually lashing out at each other and getting into scrapes—perhaps I should explain that this condition of mine is the result of the turbulent co-existence within me of a Pandorac and a Pandorine, a married couple whom death shall never part even though they are rarely on easy terms. Farcical figures substituted for the ever-so-classic *animus* versus *anima* by a pharmacist's tomfoolery . . .

*

A French sociologist whose student I was and whom I would have difficulty characterizing as a "sociologist" given how much the affixing of any
kind of label onto him would mutilate him, a respected scholar who as the
son of Jews had to wear the infamous hexagram under the German Occupation, came up with the following idea: might not the fork be an invention of
man-eaters (which would authorize one to assume it was present among cannibal populations)? More than any other flesh, the meat of humans cannot be
consumed without danger; too sacred, it demands the use of an intermediary,
a means of protection as well as a luxury utensil, to be lifted into the mouth
without being touched by the fingers. The fork would therefore originally
mark the respect one owes to a certain quality of meat and the necessity of
taking a distance to avoid any sacrilegious contact between it and the hand;
perhaps the mere fact of consuming this precious product—human flesh—
represents a feast that calls for Sunday manners when it comes to enjoying
this repast.

These days in Europe and generally in the West only those with the
crudest of manners eat prepared food with their hands—except for, say,
sandwiches or cakes. One would say that to eat meat in this fashion is to
pollute the hand, to defile it, and not just to besmirch it (to handle a floury
object, for example some sweet whose powdery sugar clings to your fingers,
is far more acceptable than to dirty them with a substance more or less fatty,
be it meat or not). Similarly, when it comes to executing a deadly act, one
chooses to slip on gloves: rather than kill with a knife, you use a gun, preferably a long-range weapon and, better yet, something that blows your enemy
to bits, for this way your crime can be alleviated by the sheer nebulousness
of its anonymous victim.

And yet what elegance is demonstrated by those who eat with their fingers: seized between the thumb and the index (and possibly by the third finger), the mouthful is brought to the lips by a rapid gesture that describes a graceful parabola (as I have witnessed in Egypt and other countries of Africa). Among the most refined, this practice is then followed by the usage of a ewer, which, once the meal is finished, allows the fingers to be cleansed of their dirtiness by the fine, crystalline spurt issued forth from a receptacle inclined by a servant or some other person leaning over in the direction of the eater. It's at this point that our use of the fork seems to take on a rather vulgar appearance . . .

I, who cannot manage to eat with my fingers or to toss down a drink from a bottle without shamefully soiling myself, am I not more barbarian than those who manage to do these things effortlessly? And if I transpose this fact into the larger domain of ethics, shouldn't I reproach myself for coming up short in similar fashion? In this particular area, the fear of getting one's hands dirty in fact leads one into the worst kind of manners. Did not Lenin basically say that *one should have no fear of dirtying one's hands when working toward the revolution*—a project that is good in and of itself, given that one expects it will result in the improvement of everybody's fortunes and in equal opportunities for all, yet a project that will succeed only if one gives up one's squeamish little reservations.

Nonetheless, one needs to bear in mind that the cannibals to whom Marcel Mauss was referring in fact demonstrate (as they handle their delicately fashioned wooden forks) that the violence done to human flesh is no venal thing.

Two naked hands holding nothing, held by nothing, and reduced to nothing more than two disembodied hands washing themselves in a stream of water that flows from the faucet in the kitchen, into which the little negro girl has crept, awoken by this slight gurgle and drawn from her bed by the desire of discovering the source of the noise. This nocturnal wonder is something she witnessed with her own eyes, or claims to have witnessed, in the account of the event that she gives several years later to a cousin of hers who lives in Paris—where ghosts do not wander the streets—and who listens in terror to this tale and to others of the same ilk.

Unless she was so high strung as to be liable to mythomania, it was no doubt all the old wives' tales she had heard that had turned the head of this little girl, who, when she matured, would develop into a rather gawky mulatta, a tomboy who was quite pleasant and good natured but also quite brusque and given to temperamental outbursts, at times erupting into wild laughter, at times melting into tears, at times retreating into sullen sulks. While still in Paris, she trained her calloused hands to play Chopin and Debussy, in the hope of establishing herself as a piano teacher on the island where her relatives were awaiting her, but although she had never practiced any religion before briefly becoming an Adventist, she then dropped everything to enter the orders.

As graceful and coppery as befits her patron saint's name—a Maori Eve fashioned out of damp sea salt—this girl's cousin is now finishing up her last year of Peul at the School of Oriental Languages and hopes to be awarded a fellowship at the end of this spring to travel to Niger. After which (but this is more of a dream than a vocation) she wants to specialize in ethnography— which would allow her to enlarge her knowledge of that Africa toward which so many black or mixed-race descendants of the slave trade turn their eyes as their motherland.

Will this lovely schoolgirl prove to be more steadfast than her cousin who (how blame her?) has now already gotten fed up with theology and with the bosom of the church?

*

All the perfumes of Arabia,
all the dreams asleep or awake,
all the adventures lived or imaginary,
all the experiences born of books yet to be read or seen or heard,
all the eddies of an ocean or a glass of water,
all that might exist or not at all,
but through which one exists . . .

*

Cut off from all the hustle and bustle below my windows and with my ears shut to all the racket, am I more alive than those two stray hands that have been discovered washing themselves under a faucet in the shadows of a kitchen? But if I limit myself to looking out of my window, I am but two eyes—yet is this any better?

A solution: staking it all, to make my way down to the street below. But to give myself this kind of facelift would be even more difficult than jumping out of the window . . .

The fact remains that I am neither two hands nor two eyes; rather, a mouth that speaks, assisted by a single hand (the right one) that writes. In short, another kind of ghost, with no other occupation than this: to clank its chains while wandering from window to window, now looking out on the courtyard, now out on the street.

When the black on white of print suffices, why the black borders on death notices?

*

On the order of comedy and not of tragedy (which does not, however, mitigate their vileness), some scenes so nauseating as to make one believe one has been sullied simply by observing them:

—The spectacle, soon condemned by the commanders of the FFI but barely less revolting than the sight of Jews stamped with a yellow star just to indicate that for the Nazis they were nothing more than packages to be dispatched, of women with their heads shaved being marched along by festive crowds during the sun-drenched rejoicings of liberated Paris in 1944.

—In Sicily, under the lovely skies of Agrigento or Syracuse, a furious townsman addressing a series of slaps in the middle of the street—as if to heighten the public humiliation—to his thirteen- or fourteen-year-old son, who was dressed as if going to or returning from mass, for it was (I believe) a Sunday.

—In Paris, on the 63 bus that goes to La Muette, a woman shouting out a soliloquy at the top of her lungs, dressing down her daughter, who was sitting across from her, her face deliberately turned to the window to escape the stares of the other passengers. Vulgar to a fault, the mother (who must be the wife of some low-level employee) reproaches her young daughter for her couldn't-care-less attitude while spewing out sundry accusations and predicting that she will one day become an outcast of society, insisting ad nauseam— in the tone of a judge or a prophet pleased to be a bird of ill omen—that her moral turpitude is such that she'll later end up "all alone," you hear me, "all alone," forever condemned to solitude. The ill-tempered mother and the girl (her face blank to hide both her own shame and that caused by the uncouth behavior of her accuser) get off the bus together at the place d'Iéna or the avenue Albert-de-Mun (which runs along the tranquil gardens of the

Trocadéro), and I watch as the mother marches off, followed by her daughter, who has remained silent and who is trailing several steps behind her, like a small dog trained to stay an appropriate distance behind its master.

—In Liège, in the vicinity of the red-light district and not far from an upstanding and old-fashioned museum devoted to local folklore and urban history, a drunken adult in shirt sleeves insulting his old mother, perhaps a drunkard as well, perhaps a former prostitute and now a madame, though this hardly matters. I spontaneously took the side of the old woman being berated. But wasn't the raging adult once a son who had been humiliated in the past and who, flinging all the insults he could muster, was now taking his justified revenge?

*

August 26, 1944 . . .

Scattered shots from the rooftops force one to lie face down in the middle of the sidewalk on the street near the Étoile where, pushing my bicycle, I find myself amid the crowd that is now thinning out after having welcomed the military man who four years earlier, his voice transmitted from London, had called for resistance. The pleasure of assuming this prone position, not on a bed, not even on a carpet or a floor but as it were at earth level, at the foot of houses at least seven stories high, and not in some wooded or seaside area where lolling around on the ground would merely be the consequence of some legitimate abandoning of oneself to the charms of nature.

To be lying down, not because one is drunk or the victim of some accident but because on has deliberately chosen to do so, on one of those streets where one's normal posture is to stand up straight, whether one has a definite destination in mind or whether one is just wandering around—unless, that is, one is just standing still, waiting. Forgetting about getting myself dirty or messing up my clothes as so often threatens to happen in these situations (it being not recommended to engage in a more than pedestrian contact with public thoroughfares, no matter how clean and no matter how fine the weather), I felt quite at home with my limbs and my torso safely ensconced in the slightly worn English-style suit I was wearing. I paradoxically felt myself at once free and at peace, as if I had been released from any concern for conventions or appearances and now found myself sheltered from everything. The gunfire was of course not so sustained that one had to fear being hit by the rounds randomly shot off by the invisible snipers. This was simply the alibi that allowed one without even leaving the city to escape from the rules and regulations of its daily grind—those codes of behavior that forbid any man of reason from taking up a prone position face down on the ground, even if these days one comes across scores of hippies lounging in the street as if it were their home and deliberately obstructing a good portion of the sidewalk with their legs.

Truth be told—far from imitating the dog who lowers his muzzle so far down that he risks scraping it raw in his obsessive pursuit of that small slice of space explored by his sense of smell—I did not have my nose right to the ground but held my head slightly raised as I peered straight ahead. Part of my pleasure no doubt lay in the novelty of the angle of vision that a segment of the urban landscape offered horizontally to my eyes, for normally this was something that one saw only from a slightly elevated position, making it impossible (as was also the case here) to insert it into the urban panorama without considerable mental gymnastics—that panorama you discern from the bird's-eye perspective of an airplane (which I experienced only much later), superior in its verticality to the third platform of the Eiffel Tower, which it is rare to reach more than a single time in one's life.

No grass, no twigs, no sand, but hard asphalt, not conducive to taking a rest. In this theoretically unfavorable situation, which was not altogether without danger—why would so many other passersby have otherwise thrown themselves down on the ground, like this gentleman who was my exact neighbor on the other side of street?—it was nonetheless delicious to taste a moment of utter relaxation. No more troubles, no more questions, no more efforts to keep up appearances. Amused by my unusual perspective and entrenched behind a horizon that was very nearby (my gaze, emanating from a height no greater than that of a basement window, was pitched too low to seize very much at all), I lived without apprehension or remorse, without hope or regret, without future or past.

That day it took many detours and many wiles to avoid possible traps for my wife and myself as we made our way back, often pushing our bicycles, to our burrow on the quai des Grands-Augustins.

*

What are

— the dice, shaken by a living hand, that will take on their face only after death;

— the tunnel into which one plunges as into a molehill, leaving the normal world behind for a world without dimension that is neither life nor death and possessed of no other colors than black and white;

— the bespoke suit that one has to tailor oneself, without care for fashion and without ever being able to try it on in front of a mirror;

— the ship decked out in flags on which you embark for a more or less known destination but that takes you elsewhere than you wanted to go, unless it be to drop you off on a desert isle;

— the thing you do, not because it pleases you but because it allows you to escape from the even more unpleasant tasks you have to face;

— weighing yourself while simultaneously holding the scale and climbing onto one of its pans;

— engaging in battle with a double-edged sword that wounds the one brandishing it as much as it defends him;

— the sheer wager by which, like Barnard Palissy burning up his furniture, one uses up one's existence, well knowing that it ultimately makes little difference whether one wins or loses;

— a rat who would rather be a bat or, better yet, a swallow, and who scuttles about, scratching and itching itself in its dark hole of a kitchen, hoping for a ray of light;

— the man whose life will have been neither a tragedy nor a comedy, neither a grand opera nor a verismo drama, but who — like the father in Gustave Char-

pentier's Louise *(whose libretto was anonymously penned by Saint-Pol-Roux)* — *will have simply gone looking for his wayward daughter like a needle in the haystack;*

— *the madman who will have spent the greater part of his time stammering even more visibly than a well-educated Englishman who happens to stumble against the first-person pronoun* I?

. . . *Enigmas so obvious that takes a certain amount of artfulness to cast them into enigmas.*

*

Joan of Arc listened to voices both heavenly and infernal, the former coming to her in great sweet sweeps of sound, the latter as the bitter blarings of a brass band.

As she was going off to war, she heard her father cursing her out, for he could not stand insubordination and was truly convinced he had fathered a witch. A collabo well before his time, he soon sided with the English.

In front of the Reims cathedral, in an apparently life-size reproduction that reaches the arches, one rediscovered her facing a mighty crowd gathered there for the coronation.

Not in armor but in a long-sleeved gown with a dagger at her waist (less sexy than those modern Amazons with holsters slapping their naked thighs), she was being voluptuously kissed by Charles VII of the House of Valois in a prettily painted garden such as can be found in ancient miniatures. *Brava!*

One beheld her in prison, then dead, not burned at the stake but on a cot, mourned by her old fogey of a father and her nincompoop of a king, both standing in the middle of a stage soon to be invaded by a cohort of angels and heavenly choristers and young ballet dancers all in white.

Her legs now sheathed in ladylike tights beneath the conical candle snuffer of her short tunic, Giovanna d'Arco—that is, Verdi's Joan of Arc (derived more from Schiller than from French hagiography or history)—takes bow after bow, smiling this way and that, like a fine young woman content with her success, as hale and hearty as a canteen keeper.

In the former palais du Trocadéro, the core of which (now razed) resembled a fake Hispano-Moorish bullfighting ring, a hallway connected the
offices of the Museum of Ethnography to what was first known as the Grande
Salle des Fêtes before becoming the Théâtre Populaire. I was aware of this
hallway and made use of it (out of sheer curiosity) when the old building—
my workplace ever since I had returned from my long trip to Africa—was
completely torn down to make way for the palais de Chaillot. A bit more
"functional" (if you will), the current palais is unfortunately so worthless from
an architectural point of view that a Parisian of those days cannot look upon
this transformation without regret. To be sure, the space is more ample and
the equipment far superior, but a solemn dullness now reigns where formerly
the Trocadéro displayed its decidedly picturesque appearance—which might
rightly be called *biscornu*, given that twin towers or horned minarets of sorts
rose from either side of its enormous central rotunda, evoking an Orient that
was bogus at best.

That a more or less hidden passageway might lead from a private office
space into a theater hall—as if this huge area where people would periodically
gather to watch and listen to the events taking place on a stage that abolished
all dimensions were but the extension of the narrow quarters that someone
had imbued with their private habits—strikes me as something on the order
of a dream or a marvel. Among the tales that I have read, the one that has
most moved me is without a doubt Hoffmann's "Don Juan." The connecting
thread of this story is the corridor in a country inn that allows the occupant of
the room reserved for guests of honor to gain access to one of the boxes of the
theater where, it so happens, Mozart's *Don Giovanni* is being performed for

the traveler, supposedly Hoffmann himself, given that the tale is told in the first person.

The action of this story, insofar as I can remember, takes place in a small German town, and I experienced not exactly the same thing—for no ghostly creature so beautiful as to inspire tears crossed through the hidden passageway from the theater to visit me in my room—but rather something akin to it when I was in Milan, accompanied by my wife, a musician friend, and his female companion. The four of us were the grateful beneficiaries—not because of our good looks but because of a handsome tip—of a favor that had been granted to us, similar to the one granted to the innkeeper's boy mentioned by Hoffmann, by a Burgundian who was working as a French-language guide in the museum of La Scala.

This charming museum, only a stone's throw across a narrow street from our hotel, was filled with items documenting the commedia dell'arte and such masters of Italian opera as Verdi, and in order to visit it we couldn't refuse the services of this French-speaking guide, even if such services prove to be rather superfluous in a country where one is never at such a loss linguistically as to be unable to get by on one's own. Even so, we were wrong to imagine that this paid guide would have nothing to teach us beyond what we already knew or could easily deduce from the labels that described the items in the museum. In one of the stylish rooms (or small salons) that make up the museum, he showed us a corridor cordoned off by a thick rope, which he informed us was a passageway leading to the theater hall of La Scala. More enterprising than I, who was always too ready to imagine that any initiative I might take would prove to be useless, my wife asked our guide straightaway whether it wouldn't be possible to proceed to the theater for a visit. As I had suspected, the reply turned out to be negative: rehearsals were going on at that very moment and all visitors were therefore prohibited. Despite my wife's insistence, there was nothing to be done, and leaving behind the room that ushered into the passageway that had become all the more intriguing for us now that we knew that it led not to a dead space but rather to the preparatory commotion of a performance, we continued on our way, carefully examining all the offerings of the small museum. Having made the rounds and about to take our leave, we had already said good-bye to our guide and were no longer thinking of trying to persuade him, given how categorical his refusal had been, when our luck suddenly took a turn for the better. Our guide, a heavyset, stone-faced fellow with a moustache and the flushed features of a heavy drinker, who would later inform us that he hailed from Burgundy, invited us to come back the following day and ask for "Monsieur Gaston" in case we did not run into him directly again. It goes without saying that we took him up on his invitation and returned the following day. And this is how, one thing leading to another, we managed to listen in on the rehearsals of *Boris Godunov*, our guide having surreptitiously snuck us into the shadows of this huge empty vessel for two or three mornings in a row and installed us in a loge, but not without having instructed us mezza voce to keep quietly to the rear, claiming that he might run into serious trouble should it be discovered that eavesdroppers were hiding out in this box.

The thing I remember above all, that defining moment during which I felt that the sheer fact of theater is far richer in poetry than the pure illusion of the stage, was having heard the tenor Gino Penno—now playing the False Dimitri, but who in his former role of Charles VII in Verdi's *Joan of Arc* at the San Carlo in Naples had passionately joined his lips to those of our saint, alias Renata Tebaldi, at the the close of a long *duo d'amore*—perform in his same brazen voice the heroic aria of the revolution scene, dressed in an ordinary gray suit, wearing glasses, astride a horse.

As is well known, this revolution scene is in fact the last scene of *Boris Godunov*, and not the next-to-last one, following the practice—especially common in France—of placing it before the death of the czar, this mass murderer driven mad by remorse like Cain, Orestes, and Lady Macbeth. In the gathered figures of the peasants, the Innocent One, the three preachers, and the False Dimitri surrounded by his comrades-in-arms, one can catch an extraordinarily concentrated glimpse of the deep distress of the Russian people, crestfallen and cantankerous after the disappearance of their sovereign.

No other performance of Mussorgsky's work has impressed me as much as these fragments seized on the sly, their cast all dressed in street clothes and even their director wearing an outfit of basic black as she made all sorts of efforts to get the chorus to move this way and that, to rouse this anonymous crowd as if she were a political agitator inciting the muzhiks to shake off their torpor. Theater is a miracle when it manages to become a mirror in which the murky features of existence achieve a clearer profile, thus allowing its future audience to find itself facing a gathering of men and women who are truly alive, each endowed with their own personality, with their own desires and grievances, with their own hovels and tunnels, as opposed to merely being a crowd as neutral as a pile of stones on a demolition site.

A few years later, on the deck of a Venetian vaporetto, we saw our Monsieur Gaston again. Seated, he held on his knees a transistor radio broadcasting the Italian news—to which, in his bovine somnolence, he hardly seemed to be listening. Barely six months thereafter, upon returning to the museum of La Scala, I caught sight of him again. Leaning against the frame of the outside door and puffing on his cigarette, his face flushed and his stare blank, he no more recognized my wife and myself now than he had on the vaporetto. For us, he indeed remained "Monsieur Gaston," but what we were to him except two of the many nameless, faceless tourists he had so often seen?

*

"E poi . . . La Morte è Nulla," sings Iago at the close of his famous "Credo," first announced, then given new impetus by raucous bursts of orchestral thunder. Two words, subdued, the voice hovering in expectation, leading to the sarcastic explosion of the four following words, heavily stressed, uttered almost as if parlando.

Death and Nothing. Everything is nothing. Is this what the Russian nihilists were thinking a century ago, in the age of the knout, of the Cossacks in their astrakhan caps, of Siberian exiles, and of Tolstoy's *Resurrection?*

Nietzsche. His very name evokes the sound of half-burned logs breaching between andirons, of bundles of firewood reaching up into a pyre, or of torches quenched in water; perhaps also the sound of dried leaves crunching underfoot or of a match that has been struck and then briefly flares into a flame or else the screech of a blast of steam released by a locomotive at rest.

Like *nitchevo*, the name of Nietzsche evokes a very specific kind of tabula rasa: that crepuscular state of which Sardanapalus must have been dreaming as he lay dying in the flames of a palace filled with viands of all sorts and women writhing in their splendid nakedness, their hair disheveled, their skin streaming with sweat, some of them crazed, most of them stupefied by wine; or that inverse state to which aspired the austere act of the bomb throwers, for whom (as far as one can surmise) making a clean slate of things did not involve plunging headfirst into catastrophe with all one's worldly goods or creating a void within oneself so that reason might freely run its course, but rather entailed razing everything to the ground, leaving not a single stone standing, clearing everything away so as to build back from zero.

Nietzsche. A name full of fire and water—those twin plagues that brought down both Nineveh and Valhalla—and one that seems to set him markedly apart from this fin de siècle so jam-packed with all the crude or refined proponents of man-without-God: the decadents, whom one tends to imagine as fragile and somewhat askew, their eyes half closed, their heads slightly tilted or thrown back; the blasés, commonly held to be neurasthenic or consumptive; the viveurs, threatened by syphilis, congestion of the brain, or senile decay.

Nietzsche, and this "Nietzschéenne" (though I don't know where or how or why I came up with this female suffix) who springs to life as soon as I pronounce the adjective *Nietzschean*—which, like the adjective *Manichaean*, is but the poor masculine adjunct of a far richer female figure, perhaps somewhat ill defined and poorly remembered, yet always reinvented and gropingly revivified when called forth by the word.

This "Nietzschéenne," this Nietzche-girl, is a young sinuous creature with the distant air of a neurotic (a euphonious but vaguely derogatory term used here only to underline her exceptionality) or with the uncommunicative features of a drug addict and to whom the adjective *cosmopolitan* would well apply, less because of its useful imprecision than because there are those who are cosmopolitan by their very nature—which is true of her, even though her horizons remain definitely European, traveling as she does by express trains with services to spas and mountain and sea resorts rather than by the Trans-Siberian or by steamships headed for the far ends of the earth. In my daydreams she would appear with a head of long auburn or blond hair, sheathed down to her ankles in a tight silky dress, amid a decor impossible to describe but which I knew to be utterly luxurious, veiled by cigarette smoke (definitely Turkish) and by the fumes of aromatic spices. This image, which I have difficulty pinpointing to a precise moment of my life, I nonetheless believe to be fairly ancient. It may well have been inspired by some magazine illustration or by the cover of a cheap book whose caption or title consisted of the following two words, as sinuous as the sooty flames of a pyre: A *Nietzchéenne* . . . Not to be confused with the female student fueled by her black tea and her terrorist convictions, today she'd instead be some skinny young thing with a full head of hair and her legs and hips slipped into a tight pair of leather jeans, the thick belt looped around the waist heightening the effect of her bare belly button, a distant cousin of the deeper dimple below.

Nietzsche, demolisher of morals and smasher of idols, the man whose credo was an anti-credo, whose lightning formulas are neither rules to be set in stone like those issued by the founder of some religion nor the booming fulminations of some thunderous Jove but that instead recall the sparks sown by fireflies in the dark or cat fur charged with the electricity of a gathering storm.

Nietzsche, whom I was to read late and very little, initially prejudiced against him as I was because my Christian education could not admit of a philosopher so proud to die without remission of sin. Nietzsche, who teaches one to walk as one dances, without the need of a cane or helping hand, but of whom I have never managed to completely erase the image I had created very early on: a kind of Buddha or rather a Nordic magus who had been weirdly transplanted, surrounded by incense burners giving off the fumes of a perfume no less common but no more fulsome than Armenian paper.

Arabesques, volutes, twists, and turns, which I rediscover in the revival of the art nouveau style in certain illustrations and lettering designs of our contemporary era—an era in which the hippies and other enemies of geometric severity (in whatever shape or manner it may be found) have introduced a new aesthetics of the floral. I hesitate, however, to take this (rather casual) observation further and risk another comparison: this would involve confusing the Superman of the comic books with the one prophesied by Nietzsche—who is definitely not part of the bestiary that would include judo champions or winners of automatic rifle contests.

Nothing in all this that goes beyond the bounds of a simple impression, of the stale smell of incense in its burner . . . It is nonetheless a fact that the Nietzsche-girl—like those other images garnered from novels or plays of which I knew no more than the title (I could, for example, also mention such works as *Resurrection*, *The Moth*, or *Kings in Exile*, making a muddle of the various periods at which I learned of them)—opened vistas for me in which I glimpsed something that was slightly alarming but whose power I accepted without trying to figure out just what it involved. Today, I can admit that this marginal figure— or its ancient kernel—above all attracted me because it belonged to a zone where the noble principles drilled into me by my education no longer applied. A hybrid zone, more difficult to grasp mentally than to locate on a map, where it might be materially expressed by a constellation of places that were quite dissimilar in nature but that could nonetheless be situated with some precision, ranging from those sophisticated resorts favored by the world-weary wealthy and fallen aristocrats living a life more unhinged than sinful to those Siberias reserved for those whose behavior did not please the people in power—something that, in my utter naïveté, I could not actually understand but of which I had a vague inkling.

It was only a long time after this that a particular place-name would make its appearance—that solitary icy peak sparkling with flecks of mica and as white as a snowdrop: Sils Maria.

*

Once everything has come full circle and we therefore find ourselves hav-ing to return to the nothingness from which we emerged, would it not be a zero—a snake biting its own tail or a railroad running in a ring—that summed up our entire life? The only problem: to scribble something inside this circle that would darken its whiteness, change its emptiness into fullness, or turn its bottomless lake into an island . . . But what to scribble, given that this zero means that there exists nothing on which to ground ourselves?

*

In the beginning was the Deed. This is how Faust at the outset of Goethe's drama paraphrases the initial sentence of the Gospel of Saint John: In the beginning was the Word. There was a time when I attached a great importance to this opening monologue (which, now rereading it, I discover is far more succinct than I remembered): the internal debate of the legendary doctor as he sits in meditation in his study trying to find suitable synonyms to render the sibylline term "Word" more explicit, first coming up with the placeholder "Mind," then with "Power," before finally settling on "Deed." Introduced by Goethe into the private musings of this scholar and invited to plumb the depths of his thoughts by the various learned glosses that my oldest brother would offer for the benefit of his two younger siblings, I felt as if I had been initiated into the arcana and was doubly proud of the following: first, to have easily seized the gist of things, which was (so I thought) a definite proof of my intelligence; and second, to have been reading something that put me on an equal footing with adults, given that it was to adults and not to mere adolescents that these sorts of questions were properly addressed. But what seduced me above all was the strategy that Doctor Faust adopted in order to solve the problem at hand, proceeding as he did by three steps and gradually coming to his solution by degrees, first trying out "Mind," only to realize that this wouldn't work, then trying out "Power," only to reject it, and finally settling on "Deed," as if this word alone could capture the full truth. Even though my brother's commentaries certainly could have convinced me of the rightness of Faust's choice, I was not so much focused on the result as fascinated by the various stages by which he had arrived at it, which allowed me to observe how a philosopher follows his reasoning—just as a Marey or a Muybridge (as I was later to discover) managed to establish how horses gallop or men run by taking successive snapshots of the action. To follow the operations step by step, to be aware of the meshing of the gears, to be in on the secret not like someone watching a theater performance from the audience but rather like a spectator placed in the wings, able to observe the behind-the-scenes contriving of things that others would perceive only in their external trappings.

It was no doubt for this same reason that what I also liked about Goethe's *Faust* were its prologue in the theater director's office and its prologue in heaven: the fact that the execution of the work about to be performed should be put up for discussion in a prologue that is already part and parcel of the play itself and that the events of the tragedy as such should be foreshadowed by the superhuman backdrop of the battle between God and the power of Evil, thus providing the actual events of the play with the false bottoms of these two preparatory offstage settings, one in the theater, the other in the cosmos—all this intrigued me by its novelty and gave me as much satisfaction as if I had been witnessing the workings of some giant machine before my very eyes. That the actual play (a precious gift wrapped in several envelopes) should commence only after first stripping away the prologue in the theater (which rehearsed the various practical matters with which the performance would have to deal) and then eliminating the prologue in heaven (which theologically explained that the fictive events to follow were merely the earthly face of a larger game played out between God and his everlasting enemy and whose stakes involved either the salvation or the damnation of an exceptional creature), and that both of these prologues should in turn be preceded by a poem in which it was now the author who expressed himself lyrically in his own proper name—all these elements combined to make of *Faust* a solemn and sumptuous ceremony in which I as a reader participated at my leisure, feeling at once flattered and gratified.

Satan appearing in the guise of a poodle, a red mouse emerging from the mouth of a young and lovely witch in the midst of her song, Faust flabbergasted to recognize Margaret in the guise of a ghostly Medusa whose neck encircled by a thread of blood confirmed that her head had been cut off—these devilries filled me with delight. On the other hand, I was not pleased to discover that in the Walpurgis Night scene a number of the words chanted by the witches—some of them dirty, some of them slangy—had been replaced by three dots (a practice that is now out of date, even if this kind of bowdlerization, like other attempts to blinker us or keep us in line, has unfortunately not seen its last). What were these words? This I wanted to know, and was annoyed by being unable to find out what they were, just as I was peeved by my inability to gain access to the hidden meanings said to lurk behind all the passages freighted with symbols and allusions that I would have certainly understood had I been a few years older and therefore mature enough to venture into these scabrous realms, had I not been summarily warned off from them by "These things are not for you!" At once captivated by its love story, charmed by its fantastic or fairy-tale features, attracted by its philosophic mysteries, and hovering between pleasure and frustration depending on my success or failure in puzzling things out, it was as a child that I haphazardly leafed my way through (inspecting it rather than fully perusing it) this first part of *Faust* in the large illustrated clothbound edition that belonged to my father, unaware that it was followed by a second part, which was completely beyond my powers of comprehension at the period in question and which, later in life, I only skimmed through, finding it so overgrown with the flowers of high culture and moral parables and mystical modulations that it became a chore to read. Who would deny the poet of the two *Fausts* his passport as a man of genius? Yet one doesn't necessarily have to be mean spirited to come to the conclusion that, far from being a sprightly genius in the manner of a Mozart or of a (flashier) Picasso, he was among those who, like Wagner, are gifted with a genius so well housed, so wide ranging in its geniality that it provides one with an antidote to the vain desire to be possessed of it.

This sober visionary who in his theory of colors explored the formation of their scale by the conjugation of light and darkness—what would he think of his subsequent luminous legacy? When, borrowing from Faust's translation of the opening sentence of one of the Gospels, Goethe posited the primacy of the Deed, did he thereby intend that universal pulsation that makes all things exist or, deducing a moral law from this axiom, was he instead trying to suggest that action is the supreme virtue and that one must therefore dedicate oneself in one's deeds to keeping the world on its best course (as Faust would do in extremis as he escapes from the demon of negation)? An upper-class citizen of Weimar, did Goethe think of measuring his life in accordance with some pragmatic criterion, or did he believe, genius that he was and his glory guaranteed, that he had indeed earned his salvation?

In his final hour, Faust dreams of engaging in a useful action, carried out on a free soil among a free people. But victim of an illusion that his diabolic companion snickers at, he undertakes his public works projects only in his mind, and if his soul is saved in the end, it's only on account of his thought (i.e., his faith in the power of human effort) and not on account of his deeds. As for Goethe himself, who in *Faust* seems to make action his be-all and end-all, is it not more for his mind than for his actions that he deserves respect? He was a deployer of ideas rather than a builder or a lawgiver, and though he led a love life spiced up by his Gretchens or Helens of Sparta, he engaged in no other public activity than the honorable exercise of his duties as counselor and then as high chancellor to his grand duke. If Goethe, like Faust after all his years of wandering, had dreamed of a useful Deed, the mere dream of it would have sufficed him, eager as he was not to miss out on anything that the prodigious spectacle of the world's perpetual motion might offer him. To give shape to his dream and undergird it with his encyclopedic knowledge, to have trust in the spreading light of his own enlightened mind, this (most likely) was enough for him to attain the serenity he seems to have achieved in the end, wreathed in glory and far more stolid than the mad Nerval, the first to translate *Faust* into his tongue and of all the French Romantics the most tragically in thrall to the fatally melodious voice of the Lorelei.

*

After the challenge that Don Juan issues to society and to its laws governing the honor of women, there is also the provocation that he addresses to the Commander, daring him to come dine at his home.

First denying the moral laws and then the very existence of those powers—such as the shade of the Commander—that provide the supernatural guarantees of such laws, Don Juan, now with his back to the wall and at last forced to recognize the existence of these powers, at least denies their ability to make him bow down before them. Thus it is that he issues his final challenge, having won out because he has stood his ground to the very end, convinced that only the flames of hell will have any purchase on him.

A torero who provokes the charges of the bull, victorious in his very downfall, the ungodly Don Juan is as different from the doubt-ridden Hamlet as the two apparitions that overwhelm them differ from each other: the vengeful statue, all made of marble, and the vengeful ghost, all made of smoke. Whereas the Sevillian persists in saying no and faces up to the consequences of his negation, the Dane thinks things over, rationalizes, avoids the issue, and—too indecisive not to be defeated from the very outset—allows himself to be crushed by the role assigned to him by this Commander who, assuming the guise of his father, does not strike him down from on high but rather has risen unbidden to him from the depths: contrary to the *burlador* who welcomes his fate with open arms, Hamlet submits to his without considering it more than a dream, temporizing because he dares not wash his hands of it.

*

The spots and spatters and dribbles of blood that stain the gown of Lucia di Lammermoor are not those of her lost virginity. If there was any deflowering, it was not she who underwent it but rather the breast of the husband they wanted to force on her—a breast pierced and punctured and slashed open by the dagger that Lucia still holds in her hand as she emerges from the bridal chamber. As she makes her way down the stairs, crazed by her butchery, her fingers will lose their grip and the weapon will clatter down the steps.

In a few moments the distressed murderess will be nothing more than a bird that melodiously emits a series of piercing moans as it collides with the bars of the cage that opens out onto the courtyard and garden. Once dead, the sleepwalker will become a wandering ghost and it will be impossible to tell whether it is her gown or her winding sheet that envelops her in its whiteness.

Something that has always frightened me: the intellectual bloodstain that Isidore Ducasse inveighs against. To be sure, it is not the blood that we ourselves have spilled directly or indirectly that stains us. The fear of blood or the aversion to violence can lead us into states of inertia that we justify with arguments so specious that they can end up dirtying our hands. Moreover, is it even possible to remain spotless? To arrange things so as never to be in a position of getting one's hands dirty, is this not one of the worst offenses? Why, then, play Little Miss Perfect when it comes to the occasional necessity to sully yourself?

The nagging fact is that a spot will always be a spot and that to deny this is to demonstrate that one is already so filthy as to have no fear of defilement.

April 17, 1945, Ivory Coast . . .

It was midafternoon when my traveling companion and I arrived for our overnight stay at the forester's compound in the region of Adzopé. After we had introduced ourselves, he took us to visit the timber operation that employed Mossi tribesmen and people from Korhogo, some of whom complained to us of their working conditions (for example, they had been promised blankets, which were never delivered).

We have barely returned from the field when our driver—a very pleasant Mandingo fellow thirty or so years of age who goes by the name Lassena Fofana and whom I had at one point seen burst into laughter at the sight of an old villager woman and who, when I asked him why, had simply replied, "I laugh because of how old she is"—a dutiful husband and family man who has been driving us ever since we set out on this inspection tour, turns up in the room where my companion and I are sitting and, ever polite and ever smiling, says, "Boss, there's already a snake that's gotten into the kitchen." He asks whether he might therefore be allowed to sleep somewhere else than in the kitchen quarters he was supposed to occupy with the other servants—a request we of course granted. "Already"—Lassena Fofana's use of this word, whether deliberately or not, indicated just how uneasy he felt in this region to which he did not belong.

Before dinner, we chat with our host, a young fellow with a moustache, fairly short and commonplace, who had fought with the Free French. During this conversation, we revisit all the issues previously discussed: the mechanics of the operation, the recruitment of the workers (supplied by white intermediaries who function more or less like slave traders), their working conditions— in short, everything related to the labor problems that we are examining over the course of our investigative mission.

Around eight or eight-thirty, as we were about to sit down for dinner, very near, very loud: a huge thud. Alarmed, we went out to have a look. A huge tree, its roots undermined by the rain, had just fallen, as often happens in these parts during the spring season. As it toppled over, the tree had smashed several huts in the camp of the Korhogo workers, and then fire had broken out in these huts (or rather in these compartments, for the camp was made up not of separate huts but of rectangular structures divided into cells, each of which housed eight workers). Accident report: six dead (crushed or charred) and four wounded, whom our host will transport to Adzopé in our small van to have them treated. One of them will die on the way, unless, that is, he was already dead when they loaded him in.

Once the fire had been extinguished and corpses dragged out, our host told the Korhogo laborers that he would provide compensation to the families (about 1,000 CFA francs each) and that he would give them tomorrow off to bury their dead, and that the day after that or thereafter they could start building their new homes.

When the tree fell, the kitchen fires were all lit, and these were the flames that set the wood and straw dwellings ablaze. All this, as far as I was concerned, was just a horrible accident. But my companion—an active communist who was more attentive than I to certain practical realities—was quick to point out to me just how deeply responsible the forester was for what had just happened: he had not implemented even the most basic of safety measures by creating a broad clearing around the camp, thus avoiding the danger of falling trees. I felt quite uneasy, having now become aware of the kinds of questions this accident raised, things that made it more than the tragic consequence of a piece of bad luck.

Above and beyond the malaise that I felt at remaining so monstrously removed on the most basic human level, I now realized just how foreign appeared to me these black-skinned corpses, some of whose mouths were white with rice (the thing having happened during the workers' mealtime), in this jungle where the men, even if they did not hail from these parts, seemed to have taken on its savage near nakedness—so that when I looked upon the dead, I did not experience the lacerating vision of human corpses. As I think back on it today, they looked less like dead men than like those mannequins that had been randomly tossed into corners when they were redoing the old Trocadéro Museum of Ethnography, its directors having decided to do away with these simulated representations of racial types, old-fashioned dummies whose features were so stereotyped as to be almost comical.

The unwitting stain of racism that I wore upon me was, now that I think of it, not unrelated to the thing that tarnished my most immediate reactions to this whole event—the fact that the sight of these dead workers inspired so little horror in me, the color of their skin having somehow masked the reality of their death . . .

At Villeneuve-Loubet, in this month of August over the course of which a number of forest fires once again flared up in the Alpes-Maritimes and the Var, the spectacle—toward four in the afternoon—was that of a *Vision of Hell* such as Max Jacob describes in a volume of prose poems bearing this title in the plural: in an everyday setting where only the quality of the light evokes an apocalypse, ordinary citizens are lined up at the gates of Hell, as if attending a fair.

Tourists of all ages, local residents out on their doorsteps, youngsters who are probably camping nearby—all are waiting for what will happen next, while the police and highway patrol are trying to direct cars and trucks so as to avoid a major traffic jam. There is a burned smell to the breeze and a few flames in the distance. The castle with the square tower that was visible to the eye on our way here now stands almost obliterated by the ribbons of smoke. The quality of light resembles that of the skies cleared of smoke after a storm or, in the Caribbean, the brightness that attends the imminent arrival of a hurricane. Above all, it reminds me of the intense glow, neither day or night, that tracer flares project upon an area about to be bombed.

So it was, one night during the last war, that I saw Boulogne-Billancourt lit up by strange fireworks, just before the Allied bombs started falling. Theoretically, they were supposed to destroy the Renault factories, but in fact they mostly demolished or damaged a number of civilian dwellings—in the ruins of which, children were to be seen playing the following morning, pretending to be search and rescue teams and appearing to be having the time of their lives.

*

When Dresden, over the course of a single night at the end of the last war, was almost wiped off the face of the earth by Allied bombers, the zoo— situated in a Bois de Boulogne-like wooded area of town—was heavily damaged. Forcing their way out of their cages through the broken bars, many animals (among which, some quite consequential) sought refuge in these woods, encountering the male and female inhabitants of the city who had similarly fled there for safety. There were no incidents to report, so it is said, for the terror that reigned among man and beast alike was such that between them an earthly paradise of peace had been established. And—whether this be some romantic notion or a mere figure of speech—rumor has it that man and beast just huddled down together there, each against each.

Passing through Dresden a few years ago—which was when we became acquainted with the details of the air strike, militarily useless in everybody's opinion—we spent the night in a hotel that the guides claimed was located in the city center. But where was this center? Looking out from the hotel, all one could see were fields of weeds and trees . . . It took a while to realize that the guides were not lying or in error: this was indeed the city center—but a center that had simply vanished into thin air.

At the zoo, which we went on to visit, a huge humanoid ape was scaring the daylights out of the visitors: he was screaming and punching at the iron gate that locked him in (punches as loud as canon booms, leading one to believe that he was about to break down the gate), but this was merely his way of asking for food, and when his meal arrived all the visitors to this gallery of the zoo suddenly disappeared. Perhaps the explosion of some dim human fear that one fine day—the end of the world—the beasts might rise up in revolt?

*

Philippus Aureolus Bombastus von Hohenheim, or, for posterity, PARA-
CELSUS: the surging effervescence of salts dissolving, the spritz of seltzer
squeezed from a siphon, a match scratched and then flaring, something under
pressure now zooming into the air.

Paracelsus, your name—so awkwardly romanized—wells forth . . . Ex-
celsior! Leaping upward but also grazing the ground. You who introduced
the mineral kingdom into pharmacopoeia, who decrypted signs open only
to those illuminated by divine intuition, who perused treaties of timeless wisdom, who wore a knobbed sword inhabited by a familiar demon, O precursor,
were you not driven to gather everything up (the heterodox teachings of the
poorer classes, the secrets of artisans, the practices of those busy as gnomes in
their mine shafts, the expertise of barbers, of hangmen, of shepherds, of simple
folk and gypsies, and, why not, those other products of received knowledge,
Rimbaud's "corny paintings," "dirty books with spelling mistakes," "obsolete
operas"), to observe it all (down to the tiniest traces that nature offers to the observant eye, the folds of the skin, the creases of trees or of stones or of whatever
organizes itself into something decipherable)—in short, to collect together
every notion and every trace that offers some sort of purchase and to submit it
to the heat of an invisible focus, in this tiny portion of the microcosm that is
us, our head initially a traveling bag into which to stuff everything we gather
in the course of our wanderings, and then an alembic within which elixirs will
form into beads.

A propounder of images rather than a ponderer of ideas! A peregrine
philosopher and medical practitioner, a magister contemptuous of Latin
schoolbooks, O erratic and fantastic Paracelsus, peripatetic pataphysician par
excellence!

A passionate partisan, I should add, and so disinclined to play the Pontius Pilate that at Basel—where you taught—you publicly consigned to the flames (your way of effectuating a tabula rasa) several celebrated works whose undeserved authority you rejected.

His draft horse standing by, the carter—a figure so discredited that one always expects to see him swearing as he beats his animal—tilts the cart, having lifted its heavy backboard to release the load. At the edge of the sidewalk, half distractedly taking in the posters stuck to the walls—such as the one advertising Thermogene Cotton Wool, in which some sort of green devil is spitting out the fire generated in him by the thick cloud of wool that he is pressing to his chest— the child observes the sand pour out of the cart, thinking of all the different pleasurable things you can do with this fine, golden material:

make all sorts of sand pies (ranging from upside-down flowerpots, so pleasingly compact, to the more delicate small cakes, starfish, or shells);

plop down into it as if it were offering itself up like a mattress;

build up a little hill with your bare hands or a shovel;

plant the sandy slopes with lead soldiers or twigs, which, standing at different heights, will imitate an Alpine expedition or the assault of a fortress;

let fistfuls of it sift through your fingers;

construct a building, soon leveled by the tides or collapsed by a soundless avalanche;

risk digging a tunnel;

pretend you're someone buried with only their nose showing;

shape islands of it, as if you wanted to create miniature replicas of continents;

above all, cup your two palms tightly together and feel the fullness and the freshness—not yet feminine, but already sweet to the touch—of the mass of damp sand pressing against them.

*

Perhaps an ad for Meuse or Karcher but certainly not for Vézelise beer, these two foaming mugs carried by the young Hebe, all smiles, her blond hair tousled, her bodice laced across the white blouse that sheathes her heaving breasts, their cleavage slit down the middle as if by a razor. A brightly colored poster whose hues—ever since childhood—have barely been eroded by the action of memory.

*

Gyptis,
O my chaste goddess,
water of my life,
my Guinness good for me,
to you I toast,
my fizzy one,
my king-size one,
my more-than-naked one,
my zinc-spire,
my Venus head to toe,
my way back home!

(The Greek sailor took the cup handed to him by the Gallic lady, whose nightgown, made of a thick, white, shaggy material, masked her entire body, except
for her face, her neck, her arms, and her feet, which were left free to tan. To have
thus singled out the man who was to get her with child was not the act of some
crazed virgin, but rather that of a Cordelia whose respect for custom equaled
her care for each of the snowy hairs that framed the face of her father the king.)

*

"With a *Petibon* I'll *Fishoff* my *Bistour* into his *Cuttoli.*"

Such were the various sentences that three or four of my friends and I would invent, the principal elements of which we would cull from the honor rolls of military heroes published by the magazine *L'Illustration* in the later years of the 1914–1918 war. Each of the honorees was granted his own portrait, whether in photo ID format or somewhat smaller, together with a caption of several lines, based on what I imagine were documents supplied by his family.

A horrible circus spectacle of sorts: a scene witnessed at the outset of this same war that happened while my brother, my sister, her daughter (still a baby), and I (a kid in short pants) were making our way by rail to Biarritz, my father having decided to get us away from Paris, given the major German advance that was in progress after the disaster at Charleroi. In one of the larger railroad stations, perhaps it was Bordeaux or Bayonne, our train crossed paths with a trainful of wounded soldiers. On litters of straw, in cattle cars whose sliding doors were thrown open, lay the jacketless men in red pants, each of them wearing bandages more or less soaked with blood. How sordid these men looked, lying there as if at the scene of some filthy crime or traffic accident, or sprawled out in the stale stinking aftermath of Mardi Gras festivities.

Barely a few days after the outbreak of war, it was with considerable amusement and approbation that I witnessed a scene that now strikes me as having been just as sordid: on the rue Leconte-de-Lisle, as I remember, toward the end of the afternoon, the looting of a Maggi creamery by a crowd convinced that the Maggi Dairy Company was German and not Swiss. To preserve a memento of this event, whose ugly chauvinist inspiration completely escaped my notice as a right-thinking child, from among the debris that lay scattered all over the street I picked up a scrap of metal that might have been the fragment of a milk cannister or of a milk dispenser. For many years I kept this shapeless scrap on a shelf of my small cupboard where I tucked away precious objects: a tiny dense lump of metal that was none other than an aerolith given to me by I forget who; a minuscule lorgnette containing, it seems to me, a photographic view of the 1900 World's Fair; then other souvenirs of the war, which gradually grew in number and among which were to be found a rectangle of grayish-brown canvas that had come from a downed German airplane (with a handwritten indication of the date and time of the dogfight and the numeral of the plane), an aerial dart (a weapon that today is as prehistoric as a polished stone axe), and the cartridge of a Mauser gun.

From a distance the 1914–1918 period appears to me like a carnival where strange figures in disguise—*poilus* in their sky-blue outfits, among whose ranks there were many relatives or family friends we had known as civilians, Germans all in gray, mocked as *Boches* so as to better look down upon them as congenitally grotesque and odious creatures—would all come together beneath the gaze of the flouncy Red Cross ladies and a goodly number of other maskers with no other accessories but their moustaches, their beards, and their decorations, in order to engage in a pitched battle to the death rather than merely showering each other with confetti.

Another scene of this carnival: at the age of fifteen, trying to appear as dapper as an adult, I made my way into La Sirène, a low dive off the boulevards, as if into a house of ill repute, to feast my eyes on the dancers in their scanty skirts, who were singing the following high-minded prelude to their paltry floor show:

> From the heights of our globe
> We survey the earth below
> So much trouble in mind
> For the fate of humankind . . .

(The two final lines of this chorus of pagan divinities being sung as the rhythm sped up, as in a parade where those lagging behind break into a run to catch up with the others.)

The star of the revue, which was a mere pretext to show off the flesh of a troupe of women in enticing outfits with so-so voices, was called (I remember) Doretta, and both I and the friend who had come along with me found her quite pretty and quite elegant when we later happened to catch a glimpse of her offstage, escorted by her official benefactor or by another fellow who aspired to her favors, dressed to the nines, his plump cheeks perfectly clean shaven. For nights and even days, Doretta, a frequent subject of our conversations, became one of the succubae who gave herself up to our monastic pleasures without offering the slightest resistance.

*

When, without the slightest hug (something to which we were not inclined) or without so much as affectionately draping our arms around each
other's waist or shoulders, our hands cooperated (a simple service rendered)
in the task of bringing the other's member to orgasm, I would admire the
rigidity of his—less large but far harder than mine. It wasn't that we derived
more physical pleasure from doing together what we usually did alone, but we
enjoyed this act of sharing, for the fact that there were two of us allowed us, as
we discussed the objects of our desire—now calling them up in the flesh by
the mention of their names, now agreeing that this one should go to me and
that one to him—to intensify the presence of our imaginary mistresses, most
of whom were usually the reflection of some stage actress or of some woman
seen in the movies.

By making use of the other's hand to procure our own pleasure we two boys
were not exceeding the bounds of camaraderie. As we lusted after the women
whose features were supplied to us by our memories, our fondling of each other
went no further than this very precise act of manipulation, which involved neither my desire for him nor his for me. But the opposite occurred when over the
course of the same summer I spent what seemed an endless night in the room
of my friend's luscious sister. It was if two contrary taboos governed these two
spheres of intimacy: in the one case, I was allowed to focus on a sex that paral-
leled mine while paying no attention to the rest of the body; in the other case,
I was allowed to focus on a body (or at least on the bust, the noblest part of the
body) without my hand straying toward the sex of my accomplice.

As we lay there side by side in her bed for what seemed hours with her
underclothes slipped down just as far as necessary, I fondled the naked and
fully formed breasts of my friend's older sister while she returned the kisses I

planted on her lips, just as she had done earlier that same day when we had hidden out in a hayloft in the midst of the countryside, where, hardly more noticeable than the rumble of heat lightning, we could hear the far-off canons of war. This was no longer just a game between friends, but rather (at least as far as I was concerned) a dalliance between lovers—although a very innocent one at that, given that the bedsheet provided a boundary that had to be respected and that my hands could as a result not explore the totality of her undeflowered body, nor could any mutual rubbing of our private parts lead us into ultimate bliss.

When I returned to my room at what was still a decent hour, having followed my new companion (now clad from head to toe in her nightgown) into the garden bushes to take a piss, my timid ardor had only partially led me to give up on this little prude who blamed herself for being "sensual" but who wouldn't go back on her word. With no other playing field than the twin exuberances of her chest, our bacchanalia was to know no tomorrow, just as it had known no climax. But a bit of non-illusory flesh having finally offered itself to my hunger for femininity, this innocent night of debauchery—which had ended without any true satisfaction having been achieved—was far more intoxicating to me than the sort of thing we two boys used to do as we made ourselves come to the accompaniment of the women of our dreams.

While digging up these adolescent sexual practices, it's almost as if I've become obsessed by them, caressing these sentences that will never manage to make those naked breasts rise up again in all their vivid whiteness—the very first breasts I ever fondled.

*

Her large pale hands that she jokingly referred to as "hand-job hands" (no doubt convinced that those pitiful streetwalkers who illicitly plied their trade in the Bois de Boulogne or in the bushes of the Champs-Élysées had hands like hers, often compared to washerwomen's paddles), these strong hands as pallid as was her face (that of a tall bony girl dressed more conservatively than was usual for her profession), I remember how soft and fresh they felt as I clasped them in my sixteen- or seventeen-year-old hands, and how sexily naked they seemed under that small table where we were having drinks at the New York Bar, 5 rue Daunou, Paris.

The li'l chicken
Down in the kitchen
Going cluckety-cluck
As babe into bed gets tucked
Sweet dreams, li'l cuckoo,
Sweet dreams, li'l Coco.

Back in the days of the play *Malikoko, Negro King*, entranced as I was by the bliss of loving and allowing myself to be loved, I never so much as gave a thought to Africa, and it was surely not this lavishly staged production, whose run at the Châtelet Theater was so widely advertised, that might have driven me to dream of the Dark Continent even if I had gone to see it. Clearly this *Malikoko* character was nothing but the transposition of the classic figure of the good old cannibal with his white teeth and his top hat and his bangles on his loincloth or short skirt. Nothing there—except this rattle toy of a name, which, in our moments of puerile relaxation after spending ourselves in passion, we sometimes applied to my penis, as if it were some small personage endowed with a life of its own—yes, nothing there but this baby-talk name *Malikoko*, which so seduced my girlfriend and me as we retreated into our imaginary shelter thrown together out of heteroclite elements, such as the sheets that hovered over our fantasy of living in a private cockleshell or cocoon.

Further removed than jazz (which evoked Africa only in the person of those American Blacks who were part and parcel of the Parisian scene ever since the close of what used to be called "the war to end all wars"), more mysterious (from what I had gathered only from records), more seductive, and more likely to awaken desires in us for coconut palms, it was the sound of Hawaiian guitars—with their teary slide tones, which I only later came to realize were but a cloying syrup cooked up for tourists—that for a short time slaked my vague thirst for the exotic. After that, I fell in my dilettantish way for the allurements of Russian music, bits of which I had heard at concerts to which I had been taken, and other bits of which I had discovered both through the Russian émigré circles that were then developing in Paris and through the Chaliapin recording of *The Death of Boris Godunov* that was owned by this young woman who had basically made a grown man of me. This music pleased me. It seemed to translate the sounds of a shepherd with no other shelter but his cloak, all alone in some barren measureless expanse, or the dark radiance of an icon, or the rich colors of an Oriental market; and it was in this music that I discovered the "sensuality" pointed out by a friend, someone slightly older than I and to whom I remain grateful for having subsequently opened several windows for me. But although this music certainly set me adreaming, it did not inspire in me any idea of travel. What would I have done in a Slavic country and especially in this recently de-czared Russia in which I had not yet learned to express an interest? The question, I admit, didn't even come to mind. Did not the passionate affair into which I had launched myself for the first time constitute the most fabulous of voyages? There was no desire to be elsewhere than in the present tense: going out on the town provided opportunities for a range of new complicities with my co-conspirator rather than offering occasions to run off far away.

To be sure, the spell was eventually broken. But there was a time—and I think I can say this without falsely imputing my feelings to anybody else—when the complicities into which we retreated were like an island to us, a place inhabited only by the two of us and where all we had to do was live off the land to feed all our carnal or romantic needs. It was no doubt when this illusion began to fall apart that we were obliged, in order to keep this island as green as it was when we lived on it without a care in the world, to devise an island *myth* that might restore the sap that we dimly knew was ebbing away in us. This myth of the island to which we long subscribed (and which we never would have admitted was intended more to spur on our love than to illustrate its staying power) was grounded in a children's book, a large squarish album I had acquired after we had both caught sight of it at an exhibit of modern illustrated editions. Like those other things we went to see or hear together, the book appealed to my fledgling appetite for curios— an appetite often tentative and naïvely snobbish. Signed by an artist across whose name I would again stumble many years later—Edy Legrand—the volume bore the title of its twin protagonists, *Macao and Cosmage*, followed by a subtitle that was a pastiche of so many of the old-fashioned romances: *Or the Experience of Happiness*.

A White man—a Robinson of sorts—and a native girl [*sauvagesse*] living an Edenic life on an isle that was if not deserted at least never a port of call: such were the two heroes of this story, whose scenes were illustrated in color, showing them gathering their food (a simple task, given the proverbial generosity of nature in tropical climes), engaging in games, or (so it seems to me) getting out of trouble over the course of one of those perilous adventures that all jungle explorers seem fated to encounter. Unblemished joys under unblemished skies—until the day the steamship arrives and its captain manages to convince Macao (perhaps relying on no other argument than the industrial splendor of the ship under his command) to come aboard and make his way back to the civilized world. One of the final illustrations shows the girl he has left behind now crying hot tears upon the shore while her companion sails away, at once resigned and distraught like some Titus sacrificing his Berenice out of imperial duty.

To discover a paradise in the love of a woman with whom, physically, one can frolic about like two naked savages and yet who, ideally, can lead you into a place so exotic and so remote that it seems as if death could never come to carry you away—it was to this double-pronged desire, at once direct and fantasized, that this island myth provided a response, for it allowed this passionate affair, an oasis or isle as isolated as the trysts hosted by Cosmage (her name as eloquent as that of any Celeste, Stella, Sylvaine, or Flora), to become a complete world unto itself where I could hole up, as invulnerable as a god lording it over his *cosmos*. A utopia, to be sure, but one in which I believed or pretended to believe as I complacently sank ever deeper into a situation that I knew at heart was nothing more than a childish dream whose idyllic trappings I found reassuring. A dream expressive of a nostalgia for a perfect love that was already on the skids. A construct that was innocently partisan, willfully ignorant of our eventual end, although my far more clearheaded accomplice would occasionally allude to this fact, reproaching me for being far more sensible to the attractions that were not those of Cosmage but that pertained instead to "civilization"—namely, the appeal of all the modern art and poetry to which I was ever more eager to have access as our bonds grew looser and which she quickly came to realize (so I imagine) would soon take precedence over her.

"Macao was a wise man, but the captain was right"—this is how the story (quite ambiguously) came to a close. But if Macao in all his wisdom gives in to the reasonable counsels of the captain, doesn't this in the end mean that as praiseworthy as his wisdom might be, it reveals that faced with the hard facts of rational argument he eventually has to agree with captain, for even if the story celebrates a life lived without any need to be useful or admired, doesn't it conclude by taking the side of reason? I often dismissed the moral of this story as hypocritically bourgeois, without, however, applying it to my own case: as far as I was concerned, my own reasons were not as rationally conformist as these, and besides, there was no prior state of wisdom that I had to overcome — except a love affair that was on the rocks.

Honolulu, Waikiki, Tananarive: names that coo, inciting us to imaginary idle hours spent on sun-splashed isles; names that call out to us like sirens; names that babble far more seductively than the click of the opera hat of King Malikoko; names that work as refrains inviting us to travel to the ends of the earth; lullabies we repeat over and over again, lulled by the *farniente* they fan with the fronds of their palms. One more reason not to budge from here, if one can just be content to savor — with the right admixture of sweet melancholy — the pleasure of dreaming that one is faraway. From whatever angle I look at it, it may be that I've spent my entire life dreaming of faraway places whose colorfulness attracted me, without at any point abandoning the place in which I found myself: Mediterranean or tropical lands, where from very early on I had always taken pleasure in just passing through like a stranger and whose glamor had always haunted me, but not to the point of my leaving everything behind to take up residence in their climes; other lands that I long held up as political models (China, Cuba) but that, until I grew disenchanted with them, I praised only from a distance, after having ravenously gulped down their beauty during my visits; lands of my own climatic zone that I knew only as a vacationer but that have become my mental refuges over the past several years, the idea that I would rather be buried there than anywhere else having in a muffled-drum sort of way replaced the idea that I might make my life there (to be more exact, in Ireland and the Celtic regions of Great Britain, so rich in mournful romantic sites whose dim pearly notes or darker tessitura make me feel at once at home in my melancholy and carried away from myself); revolutionary causes that I thought might have imparted a weight to what was missing from my actions but that merely led to more or less Platonic gestures on my part and that entailed no real sacrifice of my older modes of behavior; loves without limits, for which I often thirsted in my adult years but into which I never fully plunged, instead inhabiting them only for the space of a dream, lacking as I did any true conviction.

Lands that bewitched me without uprooting me; taking sides without giving up any of my comfortable habits; loves that instead of being true loves were merely reachings after the loveliness of love during my moments of depression (rough patches that, as they multiply, will end up becoming my normal state of mind)—I wonder how much more heavily these things weighed on me than those songs we sing to ourselves or those poems we recite to ourselves in order to ward off our boredom, and whether these various attempts to get myself out of my rut were nothing more than a series of arrangements I was trying to make in my life without completely reconstructing it, like those arrangements people might make, following the advice of magazines aimed at readers of modest means, as they redecorate their homes on the cheap but with enough ingenuity to make them seem far more spacious. Honolulu, Waikiki, Tananarive: what if this poetry of names expressive of my hunger for something different were nothing but a more clever, more complicated, but hardly more efficient variant of this kind of infantile babble, what if it were nothing more than a bunch of counting rhymes I go on repeating without lifting the slightest finger? And if I set aside these words with all their redolence of exotic postcards and turn myself toward more subtle charms, I see that a major portion of what I had been searching for (to open myself onto unknown worlds through the telescoping of words) can actually be linked to the music of a book title whose preciosity involves both its play on words and the subject matter to which it alludes, the work of an author who was perhaps once well respected but who is today forgotten: *Princesses of Jade and of Yore,* a collection of stories by a French man of letters of the end of the last century who took his inspiration from the Far East of several centuries earlier, and the edition of which I remember, in its far too showy binding, as an item in my father's library, which was far too "modernist" to my taste but where I occasionally managed to satisfy my adolescent urges for books far spicier than this one in fact was.

Cosmage was in no way a princess, and even less a princess of yore, either in her actual or in her mythological form—that tropical form of which a version at once volcanic and stereotypical would be offered to the Parisian public several years later by Josephine Baker dancing at the Folies-Bergère wearing nothing but a belt of bananas. The distance between these two forms was huge. But when my rosy-cheeked little middle-class girl, who called herself a "pagan" in the *Songs of Bilitis* sense rather than in that of the ancient philosophers, slipped into the depths of the white sheets with me, this distance was erased and—at least at the outset, when it still seemed to me that our lovemaking was taking me to new continents—we lived a stainless, deathless prelapsarian life, a life I would live for a few hours on end, more nights than days. Even though these hours of apparently innocent freedom took place within the cozy artificial confines of a Passy apartment and under semiclandestine conditions, and even though I was operating under the restriction imposed by my partner which meant that our embraces would bear no fruit, I would say that these hours represented a passionate communion with nature (not the words I would have used back then) above and beyond their significance as immediate pleasure. But to speak of "nature" is perhaps to be blind or over the mark: if the body that was uniting with mine could seem to me to represent nature in its entirety, this union took place within closed quarters where discretion called for electric lighting or a protective darkness that turned our hideout into a limitless expanse empty of everything that was not us, and what's more (here the artifice gets even worse), our union was always at the very last second, if not cut off from the intensely pleasurable shudder of its conclusion, at least redirected from what should have been its natural point of arrival. No doubt because his book was addressed to children, the author of *Macao and Cosmage* did not breathe a word about the exact nature of the commerce that obtained between his two heroes, and nowhere did he intimate that the White man and the native girl could have enjoyed—had the steamship never interrupted their festivities—the happy opportunity to have many children thereafter, as at the end of fairy tales. As for the other Cosmage and the other Macao, they also placed this question between parentheses: it was understood that their coupling would remain sterile, and so practiced had they become in the ceremonies of their lovemaking that they believed they could achieve the full measure of their bliss without ever going beyond the bounds of the permissible.

After the dissolution of our union and after I had rediscovered my bearings by aligning my life with an existence that despite its highs and lows, its consonances and its dissonances, matched mine as much as Eve matched Adam while still one of his ribs, the myth of Cosmage—now differently oriented than at the outset—never fully released me from its grip.

Can one just stay at home and shut oneself up into sheer oneness or twoness as on an island? For practical reasons I had initially answered yes to this question, my eyes closed to a problem that at that point I had not even considered, at least in these terms. Was I not dazzled by the fact that after so many attempts on my part that were too timid to succeed, I had now been vouchsafed the concrete revelation of love—something of which I had known only poor ersatz versions, hardly comparable to the apparent fusion of two beings so intoxicated with each other that the rising curve of their exhilaration crested into a single moment of bliss? But if I can speak of *the experience of happiness* during this period of time, it is obvious that I thereby also discovered just how briefly this sort of happiness was bound to last. Even before I had understood that happiness had slipped through my fingers and that all I would be left with was its image (a phantom less and less capable of entrancing me), I had learned (or vaguely suspected) that the intoxications which had fueled my happiness were not in themselves sufficient to fulfill my existence; what's more, I had also received several humiliating reminders of how ill suited I was to play the role of the blithe lover ready to brave any setback or risk. The happiness that had befallen me did not possess the transfiguring powers I ascribed to it—at least this is what I felt, without being able to formulate it very clearly. But rather than seek out other amorous adventures that might renew these pleasures that were now gradually being blunted by routine and whose precariousness was further heightened by my various anxieties, and without realizing that I was thereby taking my distance on this island where I had wanted to forget all about time yet was increasingly haunted by it, knowing as I did that my lover was bound to lose her youthful charms far sooner than I was, I grew more and attached to "civilization," this hothouse modernity that was all the more contrary to the state of nature embodied by Cosmage, involving as it did (or so it seemed to me) not the glorification of things as they are but rather the ideal creation of a new world as espoused by those poets and painters associated with what was then called the avant-garde.

I was certainly not naïve enough to believe that poetry and art could offer me an equivalent to the Eden—this inviolable enclave of peace and pleasure—within which, before Macao and Cosmage entered the scene to touch up the gilding that was beginning to chip, I thought I could confine myself, but I am also fully aware that this new world of the imagination (however illusory its protections against disillusionment or its safeguards against the dangers of the real world) offered me a further asylum from the idea of death and the fragility of things in general, just as I am equally aware that the activity of writing—an activity distinct from bedroom feats but that is likewise an indoor activity, whose isle consists of a table or, more specifically, a sheet of paper—has remained my major resource, the one to which I have continued to have recourse, all the while trying to disavow the hint of the bureaucrat or the aesthete that this process inevitably tends to bring to the fore, all the while trying to find ways to discover a practice of writing that would go beyond the spirit of either of these.

As she lost the identity that I had ascribed to her at the beginning (when our bed was indeed an isle by more than the simple play of words on *lit* and *île*), Cosmage gradually became an almost abstract figure: neither her island exoticism nor the color of her skin shared anything in common with the laughing, ebony-breasted image of the young beauty that had been cynically featured on so many wall posters (in railroad stations and elsewhere) whose caption—*Enlist in the Colonial Army*—invited young men to indulge in their fantasies of cheap and easy conquests requiring nothing in return. If I today try to figure out just why the image of the ripe and healthy nature girl continues to appeal to me despite its obsolete circumstances, I think it's not simply because the image remains so linked to my past adventures of the heart, but rather because it provided a double response to the ambivalences of my feelings. Was not this image on the one hand an invitation to lead a life that was primitive and untrammeled and, on the other, a symbol of that island whose protection I have never stopped seeking out even as I applied my intellect or my passions to the search for liberation? That island, which is to say, the maternal lap represented by a woman or by the land one loves or by an ideology, or even that black hole into which one is plunged by a semisuicide by barbiturates—a true regression to fetal slumber. Yet I wonder whether by putting forward the above claim and by seeing in Cosmage's features the mask of the classic figure of the mamma or the mammy I am not fact distorting her character. What struck me then in the adventures of the White man with whom I identified and his girl Friday was the perfect friendship that reigned between them and how on their island the misplaced civilized man and the authentic "pagan" girl were joined in a loving sibling relationship to live a simple life together, a life that represented health in its most primitive state, that is *la santé première* or (as I would now call it) *la sanité primale*—which is how I had once been tempted to translate (into a gobbledygook term that I hoped would cleave quite closely to the original while also suggesting a relation to a past far more archaic than the Druids) a phrase that Walt Whitman deploys in one of the poems of *Leaves of Grass*—namely (unless some obscure dictate is tricking my memory here), "primeval sanity."

A companion too bright and breezy to qualify as a Mother Earth goddess (whose level of dignity would be ill suited to my sense of her as this woodsy Girl Scout figure prepared to deal with any challenge the forest might offer), Cosmage—the Cosmage of the children's story as reinvented by me—would probably instead be a kind of mentor to me, lacking any teacher's certificate or official qualifications yet expert in a number of basic crafts unfamiliar to me, fluent in a variety of private secrets and games, and possessed of an innate knowledge of things far deeper than my sophistries, and who thereby keeps me from getting lost in the labyrinth of false problems she enables me to see through. The color of her skin—never as anemic as ours, however hard we try to tan—would seem to indicate that she is on more intimate terms with the dark heat of nature, into whose various workings she invited me (including the final trip-up), this fresh-faced Cosmage, too pure to be dishonored even if considered an exaggerated caricature of the Malikoko show.

But even if, in keeping with the myth which (rid of its unhappy end) established the charter for our shared island love, I look upon Cosmage as a creature native to a world so natural compared to mine that I would be as foreign a visitor to its shores as to the age of gold, and even if she comes to me saying that this less suffocating world is not only real but well within my reach, even if I look upon Cosmage in this fashion and set her against a far more unsettling figure who has always fascinated me, the black Circe whose attractions include not only her animal or demonic abandon (at least so runs the stereotype) but also the exoticism of her physique and her ability to imbue me with the world of marvels in which she believes (a world not Christian and thus miraculous to me precisely because so distant from the one in which I was raised and which I cannot separate from the morals it tried to drum into me), I should nonetheless be careful not to *denature* the gracious mentor that Cosmage became to me over the course of that long and intermittent waking dream in which I idealized her to such an extent that she became the trademark image of my nature mysticism — a mysticism no less illusory than any other. The islands slipped away from under my feet (during the Spanish Civil War, when Ibiza, the least touristy of the Balearic Islands and the place where I had intended to spend a good portion of the summer, was threatened by air raids, just at the outset of the apricot harvest season), and it would be to places no longer conceived as possible retreats but as objects of sheer contemplation that I would subsequently turn the geographic mythology that I still take pleasure in conjuring up in my head. A precarious mythology at that, for the war of 1939–1945, which had initially revealed to me the beauty of the desert (where, isolated, one imagines oneself to be a speck of an island surrounded by a mineral ocean), later served to weaken my persistent belief in nature: shortly before the fall of France, as I was rattling around in a railway wagon that was part of a convoy train carrying munitions from the Allier to the Landes, I looked out at the countryside, admiring the trees in full flower and saying to myself that our defeat would never be that consequential, given that we would always have *this*; but later on, what with the Occupation and all the sordid police operations of which it was impossible to wash one's hands, I understood little by little that things could come to such a pass that even *this* — the way we looked upon *this* — might also be corrupted (tarnished, dulled, cut off at the root by all the second thoughts entangled with it). This is why, however comforted I might be by the contemplation of certain sites, I no longer believe that nature offers us the ultimate branch when all the others have been broken. Even in our own lifetimes, this branch is liable to rot out like all the rest, and this alone is enough to discredit any impulse one might have to worship it. Besides, what else is Nature but a notion dreamed up by people having nothing better to do as they idly wander around their English gardens or drink a cup of pastoral milk in their Trianons or dream of the *noble savage* at the very moment that the slave trade is going on full force? And if true Nature does indeed exist (say, as that virgin forest into which explorers love to venture), is the contact that people thereby experience not just an occasion for them to prove their power rather than an opportunity to enter into a friendship treaty?

What can I therefore salvage of the Macao and Cosmage myth, or more precisely what can I rescue from having dwelled on it at such length, for the basic story it tells is nothing more than the ever-so-hackneyed tale of an idyll lived out by two beings whose divergent origins in the end tear their union apart? If such things were susceptible to being taught, the lesson that might be drawn from this myth would be an untrammeled taste for life in all its absolute simplicity or for health in its most primal state—something one need not go looking for in other climes (as I was to discover in Africa, where I realized that a change in horizon does not necessarily entail an inner change), and something I miss the most.

If, despite my efforts to reinfuse this myth with vital relevance, I have managed only to impart to its faded lineaments the outlines of a hollow moral lesson, I must nonetheless observe that, constructed as it was out of a book aimed at very young readers, this myth allowed my accomplice and me to regress back into a childish state of enchantment (even though we didn't give a fig about kids) when we first listened to Debussy's *Children's Corner* and especially to "Golliwogg's Cake-Walk," whose title underscored its nursery rhyme ambience with an English accent that appealed to the anglophile snobbery I was back then in the habit of affecting. Thus, although I am loath to give up on it entirely, I'll have to consign this empty shell of a myth to the same dossier that contains (as "memoranda") those other motifs that have allowed me to travel abroad without so much as moving an inch, motifs that continued to cradle me even as I grew too old for baby talk: Honolulu, Waikiki, or all the Tananarives or Monomotapas of La Fontaine's fables—as well as (a quick and tricky tune filled with the peppery scent of Harlem that the Black Birds used to perform at the Moulin Rouge back in 1929) "Digadigadoo."

*

Dispensaries—like those dens in which tarot card or horoscope readings are meted out—whose prescriptions or predictions would serve to reveal everybody's *individual vice* to them, a vice with which they are certainly beset but of which in the majority of cases they are unaware and should therefore be encouraged to discover: their sexual behavior, their fleeting fantasies, their full-fledged scenarios, all the various things they devise to fuel their desires and ultimate satisfactions. These predictions would be dispensed in a sketched-out form when one is still at a pedagogically impressionable age, providing a kind of professional orientation that would allow everybody, male and female alike, to apply psychological techniques enabling them to achieve the specific love life suited to them: this one choosing to become a homosexual rather than a heterosexual, that one (or perhaps even the same one) choosing to become a sadist or a masochist, etc. Not a utopian republic, but rather a thoroughly communist society in which the second half of the motto *All for one and one for all* would now be realized, allowing the new man—apportioned, without hierarchical distinction, into endless varieties—to flower in full.

As for what I can today gather about my own particular vice—independent of any diagnostic testing I might undergo—the scenario would run as follows, and within this scenario the whole protocol of prediction would take on an important role of its own rather than merely acting as a prelude to be placed within parentheses.

In a small salon furnished in old-fashioned bourgeois style, I would consult a fortune-teller, a woman (I can't imagine this would involve a man) ripe in years, imposing in appearance, severely elegant in dress. After the cards had spoken, she would escort me to the threshold of a room where I would find my "Lady." She would belong to one of the following three types:

a fine fleshy body with creamy white skin (like certain of the nudes of Hans Baldung Grien), her hair auburn or Venetian blond, its tresses thick enough to cloak her shoulders;

a body insolently white, contrasting with the inky black of her hair, gathered up into a bun, its blackness no less black than the thick fleece below, the young woman very tall and slender yet the bulge of her hips and thighs quite pronounced in comparison to the slimness of her waist (like those "artistes" I saw one evening, almost naked and wearing black sombreros, at the Molino, a nightclub on the Paral·lel in Barcelona);

the body of a blond, sturdy enough but not too hefty, rather short and with small, almost masculine hands, dusted from head to toe with flour.

It would take a slow sorting out of the cards to indicate which of these three ladies I would encounter on this particular occasion, but the fortune-teller would not make the outcome clear except by symbols (the Moon, the Star, the Earth), or by sobriquets (the Magician, the Huntress, the Winnower), or by first names (Aurélie, Adrienne, Sylvie), or by the names of flowers (Jonquil, Dahlia, Poppy). To avoid things becoming too routine, she would each time use new, unsuspected terms, each one ever more subtle, and I would then take pleasure in solving these riddles and in recognizing, under the designation that had not succeeded in fooling me, the young woman whom I would have already met in some previous session. These three basic types were not separated into watertight compartments, and their various combinations could give rise to any number of variations, embodied by the creature on whom I would not have previously laid eyes but whom I would assimilate to one or the other of these three models, who were, as it were, the leaders of the band.

The props of the three women: a large Louis XII armchair for the first (who would be dreaming or sound asleep in her chair rather than lying down when I arrived); a couch covered in black velvet for the second; an ordinary low-slung bed for the third.

Among the three I further imagine an additional one, on a bearskin rug or on a metal shield in whose hollow she lies at rest as within a conch shell: long, very light-colored hair, eyes and skin very fair, sandals with leather straps crisscrossing their way up her calves. The names of this fourth lady: Moraine, the Traveling Peddler Woman, Gertrude, Peony. Because of that same fierce unsociability that keeps her from applying razor or deodorant to her hairy armpits, a coating of ash-gray dust—or a carapace of dried mud—sheathes her body down to her thighs, and she is scored here and there by small scars, as if while going naked in her daily life she had been scratched while wandering through the underbrush.

All this would happen in the afternoon and in closed quarters (with the curtains carefully drawn shut and artificial lighting, very subdued for the first, very harsh for the second, and as close as possible to natural daylight for the last two, with no external reminders of the current time or weather, which in any event I would have forgotten, for so focused was my attention on the sorting of the cards that everything beyond this room was erased by a stroke of indifference). And out of the blue: the likelihood that the first or the third (if not one of their doubles) would decide to die with me, with both of us taking a sleeping pill together after a few embraces and both softly slipping into the void in a shared state of bliss, with just a hint of anxiety to spice things up, nothing more.

Each of the women would equally speak in her own language (sophisticated, simple, rural, or frankly vulgar), be it French or foreign, my preference in this case leaning toward English. And furthermore, perhaps: no affected language but sheer silence from the first one; the hoarse voice of an alcoholic from the second, the tall, dark-haired one whom I see as waiting for me while she runs an electric fan all along her body or ventilates it with her sombrero to dry away even the tiniest pearls of sweat. The slightly nauseating perfume that this one would be wearing—its scent filling the heated confines of the room—would not succeed in masking the muskiness of her body odor, an odor of which the first one would be free and, in the case of the other two, would be blended with the smell of grass or forests.

During our lovemaking, no words as such, so it seems to me, but deep gasps from the first; outright dirty or simply off-color talk from the second; sweet and gentle baby talk from the third, whose thin coating of flour has been gradually wiped clean by my caresses; passionate blurts from the fourth in a language unknown to me, which serve to create a distance between us, as if the pleasure each of us was experiencing remained distinct from the person of the other.

A snatch of dialogue:

The third.—My puppy dog . . .
Me.—My sweet swallow . . .
The third.—My bundle of nerves . . .
Me.—My kissy little smithy, forge on!
The third.—Just prong me and wrong me!
(And without a further word, I prong her.)

If the scene were to involve musical accompaniment, this is what would be required (following the order of the four): a major Bellini or Verdi aria for soprano; an old ragtime for player piano; a sonatina; the waltz from the *Rosenkavalier*.

In practice, after a certain number of experiments one of the four—or one of their variants—would become my favorite, the one who, above and beyond the fortune-teller's prediction, best suited the explicit requirements of my *individual vice* and whom I would be delighted to meet even if the circumlocutions of the fortune-teller had directed me to another, which would have provided a happier and more surprising result. But perhaps my quest would have been interrupted while under way had I given in to the temptation of the sleeping pill offered to me by the first or the third, the latter perhaps being the most appropriate partner for the little drama I wanted to play out and thus ipso facto representing my favorite and final choice, so that the possibility of engaging with the others would have arisen only as a way of increasing the suspense (unless, inversely, the idea that this favorite of mine would of course eventually offer me the poison served to create a different and more aggravating kind of suspense).

Except in the case of things getting cut short in the above fashion, the session would usually come to a close with a farewell greeting. Only the second of the four would need to be paid—if only as part of the fiction—given that unlike the three others she was playing the role of the prostitute (which she did somewhat ill temperedly, at that). As for the first, I would silently kiss her feet, the nearest point of her reclining body that I could still reach as I made my way out of the door. When it came to the fourth, I would strongly press my lips against hers. But to the third I would simply smile and say, "See you soon." The last two, even though no longer girls, would clearly be the youngest of the group, whereas the second, without exactly getting on in years, would be the oldest, or at least would seem to be carrying the heaviest burden of the past upon her shoulders, given that she was a professional who had long practiced her trade.

In one way or another the gestures and words that I exchanged with these women would amount to a kind of abbreviated novel that I was writing with them, as long as it wasn't interrupted by the suicide mentioned above, if in fact this did ever occur. Is this not, after all, how novels get made? Involving characters that appear to us and take on a life of their own, dictating their conditions to us and forcing us to rise to the occasion? Indeed, as I dream of all this, without any real impulse to act upon it and without these images even stirring in me the kind of lust I might feel deep within my loins (no doubt due to the weight of my years, now so considerable that I can no longer instantly rise to the occasion), it's perhaps the kernel of a novel that I am already writing, a novel (if I ever got down to pursuing it) that would finally feature as its heroine the Earth, the Winnower, Sylvie, Poppy—that is, the third one, the least aestheticized of the lot.

These things that never happened to me and that no doubt will never happen to me, is it inadmissible that I should take such pleasure in at least making them happen on the page?

*

An eagle's pittance,
this skin
its tessitura unknown
but recognized as without blemish or opacity
whereas so many others
are just obtuse sheaths!

*

On the papal tiara (a miniature model of the Tower of Babel), the two keys are crossed like the two tibias below the skull on the pirate ensigns of the Brethren of the Coast or the flag of the Death Hussars. In Dublin, the same sign appeared to me one afternoon on the back of the dark leather jacket of a biker wearing a red and white helmet; an allusion (one might claim) to Zen philosophy and to its modern proponent, the word SUZUKI was emblazoned above it. That same day I saw in the main hall of the General Post Office—the theater of one of the first battles for independence—the bronze statue of the Celtic hero Cúchulainn, who, unhorsed and mortally wounded, was lashed upright to a rock (according to the accounts of the *fili*) so that he would be able to inspire fright in his enemies until such a moment that a raven alighted on his shoulders and started pecking at him, thus revealing him to be nothing but a corpse.

Motorcyclists parading the brand name SUZUKI or HONDA, Death Hussars, or, earlier on, the Brethren of the Coast flying their Jolly Rogers—all resemble, each in their own way, the ancient samurai of Japan, a fact that should not be all that surprising: they are all affirming their disdain for death, whether it be the death that faces them or the death they inflict on others.

As for the very ancient, very clean, very eloquent, and very holy Father, should I take at face value the insignia that heraldically links him back to all this pagan feudalism and hot-bloodedness? Tower of Babel or not, mouthpiece of morality or monument of hypocrisy, instrument of peace or engine of war, his Church—far older than the Crusades—rests not on overheated humors but on bleached bones that even the most funerary of birds will have ceased to circle once the year 2000 has been left behind, a date that once used to seem almost astronomical . . .

*

From the Augustins to the Augustines. Putting this chance encounter of terms to use, this is how I could describe, in the advertising lingo of group tours, the trip I make every Saturday (except during major vacations) between my home on the quai des Grands-Augustins to Saint-Hilaire, a village that is still rather rural thanks to its wheat fields, its watercress ponds, and its hunting reserves, even if a number of signs indicate that it will soon be no more than an outlying suburb of Paris. Was our current country home here not once upon a time a priory of Augustinian nuns?

It's now been twenty years or so that my wife and I have been coming here, but it took a number of years for the place to become what it is today: my accomplice in a tactic crucial to my mental hygiene. A periodic change of scenery, even if the different scenery always remains the same and is not more exotic than the scenery being left behind, strikes me as essential to being able (at night, in the haven of one's sheets) to turn to one side and then to the other in order to fall asleep or get back to sleep (although, inversely, this back-and-forthing can also serve to keep me awake and thus spare me from sinking into dangerous torpor).

At the Augustins, noise; at the Augustines, stillness. This difference counts for a great deal, even though I am no great enthusiast of total calm or of the silence that grows more frightening as it approaches zero. What no doubt suits me best is a small modicum of noise: just enough to allow me to latch onto something instead of feeling myself plunged into the void. At the Augustines, untroubled by all the city racket of the Augustins, I can at least have recourse to these slight sounds that splinter rather than break the silence and that enable me to lie there listening to myself without giving in to the vertigo that would inevitably ensue from the cessation of any acoustic connection to the outside world.

The view of the horizon unblocked by buildings, the meager role played by geometry in what lies before my eyes, the color far more vibrant because mostly associated with natural objects, the air obviously less polluted by the excretions of the organisms that make up the industrial realm, the interior of the house, dating back to Napoleonic times, older than the Paris apartment's — despite all these advantages (combined with the pervasive sense of peacefulness), I cannot say that I prefer my second home in the Beauce to my Parisian lodgings. Besides, too many memories attach me to Paris, which offers easy access (in itself reassuring) to far too many distractions from my worsening ruminations for me to even consider taking up residence elsewhere. The only thing that remains certain is that I like moving from one to the other of these homes and that in either one of them — be it the urban one or the rural one, the hectic one or the tranquil one — I would suffocate from anxiety were I to know I was to be stuck in the same place forever.

*

Back in the days of my dog Dine, we witnessed the following scene while taking a walk together at sunset.

In the silence of a meadow surrounded by groves of trees, a good dozen hares or wild rabbits (in any event members of the Leporidae family), almost all of them sitting stock still but some of them hopping around a bit, without any haste and without distancing themselves from the group. More or less arranged into a circle, they seemed to be engaged in an assembly or family council, and so deeply involved were they in this gathering that they did not seem to be bothered by my approach or by that of my dog, with its big black and rather menacing muzzle (at least as judged by human eyes), and decided to disperse only at the very last moment. To what purpose were they congregated there? At any rate, Dine and I would never come across anything like this again during our rambles over hill and dale, although often encountering rabbits or hares (which, being neither a country boy nor a hunter, I can never tell apart, aware only that hares tend to be bigger and have longer ears), as well as the odd partridge or pheasant.

Although I couldn't understand a word these cute rodents were saying to each other in their language (perhaps entirely made up of mime gestures), I nonetheless felt like Alice venturing into Wonderland. As for my dog, pulling on her leash with her pink chops and white teeth, she was watching this scene with me. She was a sweet-tempered dog, but I always had trouble reining in her hunting instincts—and here she was, literally frothing at the mouth.

On the palm of my hand, at the tip of my forearm stretched out horizontally as far as humanly possible, I am holding up a column of veined marble that resembles those columns painted with Renaissance decorations or later inspired by Roman frescoes. Panicked by the majestic weight of this tall shaft and by the difficulty of maintaining its equilibrium, I am ready to cry out, but, aware of my distress, my companion awakens me. Over the course of this night that took place some twenty years ago, was my hand being forced to measure the heft of the dilemma that forever burdened me, like the pan of an overweighted scale?

Somewhat earlier that same night, as I was touring an island that must have been Guadeloupe in a car driven by an acquaintance of mine, I found myself—after many twists and turns—in front of a house whose master was a white Creole: an opulent mansion with a massive wooden gate decorated with heavy ironwork. Since this immense villa lay in our path, we had to traverse its various gardens and rooms—all deserted, like those belonging to the monster in "Beauty and the Beast"—before again finding ourselves outside in front of the gate, as if we had never entered the place. It was then that we learned that it belonged to a smithy (this man of fire and iron to whom local belief ascribed so many powers) who had retired there after having made his fortune.

A fine castle dating back to buccaneer days, reminding me of the Elmina fortress on the Gold Coast, appeared to me in a dream of this same period. Having seen it perhaps mentioned or reproduced in a tourist guide or brochure, I realized with great regret that during my visit to Antigua—whose poor and derelict but strangely touching features had so appealed to me during the tour of the West Indies from which I had only recently returned—I had forgotten to visit this monument, which I subsequently recognized was similar to another marvelous seaside castle that had loomed forth in the night, another tranche of this twenty-year-old dream.

A majestic column too heavy to hold up (most likely the fragment of a palace interior), elaborate ironwork guarding the entrance to a wealthy home dating from the same period as the aristocratic residences of the Île Saint-Louis or the Marais, a castle fortress that I was too negligent to visit—what does it matter whether these various images incriminated my personal weakness or a barrier not of my making or some thoughtless blunder on my part? Isn't the negativity they all share the illustration of some farfetched desire of mine always checked halfway on its path toward satisfaction?

Many years later, as my companion and I were driving down a country road, we saw a castle (or an immense mansion) of which we could get only a momentary glimpse—unable to stop because we were not alone in the car—but which lay at a certain distance, striking us with its charm. We never again caught sight of this castle, whose very discretion seemed to make it so attractive, even though the road in question was most familiar to us, given that we often took it, season in and season out, on our weekend trips back and forth, so one can absolutely not conclude that this castle had been unmasked by the naked branches, only to be hidden again behind foliage. We nonetheless remain convinced that we did not dream this castle up, and the fact of its apparition—indubitable but never to be repeated—remains something of a mystery.

*

Will the Object be a package
wrapped in white paper
or many layers of white paper
like a Christmas gift?

Will it be a flint tasting of chocolate
although the color of café au lait?

Will it be a wax record
playing the music that astounds me
even though I've heard it before
who knows where?

Will it be a bulge
compact but porous
like the skin of sleep?

Will it be a morsel
—a smidgeon, a tidbit, a nibble—
into which I've never sunk my teeth?

In my mouth
lightning,
however tamed,
wouldn't taste better!

*

ISN'T IT?

words less brusque than endearingly solicitous, insinuating both a doubt
and the conviction that this doubt will be laid to rest.

INNIT?

brief whisper of complic-
ity inviting the other to recognize, without even the murmur of a "yes," that this
is indeed so.

SO TO SPEAK . . .

meaning that the thing mentioned is not entirely what it is, that there
exists a certain margin between what is being said and what is being intended,
and that the person addressed — in order to grasp it correctly — needs to take
this margin into account. One's getting hot, one's nearly there, yet this slight
gap needs to be signaled so that both you and the other can edge closer to the
mark.

This is something I was mulling over as I was taking my morning bath
(the water as usual far too hot), playing the sybarite while letting my mind float
as it fished for ideas or rather for words that might serve to formulate an idea
that was, as it were, still just the shadow of itself and yet, all things considered,
worth the effort to flesh out, *n'est-ce pas?*

*

Like a convict who having served his time loses his bearings upon leaving prison,

like a retiree too accustomed to the daily grind not to be embarrassed by his life of ease,

like a soldier dejected while on leave because war is all he knows,

like a monk released from his vows of chastity who discovers he is impotent,

like a sailor at a loss the moment he hits town after putting in to port,

like a woman returning to the man she left because he beat her up,

like an adult longing to be the child who couldn't wait to grow up,

like a nouveau riche unable to figure out how to blow his millions,

like a traveler learning that to visit the world is to return to where one started,

like an émigré discovering that he'll be outlawed wherever he goes,

like Lazarus in tears—at least according to Oscar Wilde—at having been resurrected,

like someone shouting "Help!" after throwing themselves into the drink,

like a head of state who regrets the time he was still struggling to take power,

like an artist dismayed to have achieved exactly what he wanted,

like a metaphysician alarmed to have finally lifted the veil of truth,

like a gambler lucky in cards but unlucky in love,

like someone distressed to be so dry eyed upon seeing a person or place he thought he would only again meet in tears,

like one or the other of these, which is to say like anybody at all.

*

This was a dream I had one June night in Baden-Baden, a spa town so ancient that in addition to its neoclassical casino and the theater where Berlioz's *Beatrice and Benedict* was performed shortly prior to the 1870 war—both edifices lining a park traversed by a rushing but duly domesticated stream, its lovely lawns dominated by trees whose dense foliage rises high above—the place also features the ruins of Roman baths that almost resemble catacombs, situated in a stray corner of the city center, now filled with all sorts of hotels (ranging from luxury to bed-and-breakfast) as well as churches (including a large Russian Orthodox slab of cake), shops, villas, and government buildings, not to mention rows of apartment houses so undistinguished and so indistinguishable as to merit no notice.

I am guilty of a theft. I'm talking this over in the street with two or three friends, and they think as I do that given the stage things have now reached, I would be best off just turning myself in. As a matter of fact, the police have already been informed of my decision. It looks for sure as if I'll be facing three months in prison.

Standing as we are in a square near the center of a large town (a major provincial city or the capital of a small northern or eastern European country), it is difficult to discover the whereabouts of the police station, even though I know there must be one around here. Along the curved perimeter of this square are a number of buildings whose charm lies in the fact that, far from being monumental, they feel so out of date, so off the beaten track. They include several small retail establishments or other shops, as well as stalls and booths, but I can see nothing that resembles a police station. After searching here and there, I see a narrow door crammed between two unassuming shops. I open it and make my way down a long and rather narrow staircase. It leads to a very spacious hall (reminiscent of a central post office), filled with various counters serviced for the most part by middle-aged ladies unremarkable in appearance. After getting shuttled from one employee to the next as I make my inquiries, I finally find myself in the presence of a tall policeman, who is clean shaven and wearing a baggy raincoat and a felt hat shoved toward the back of his head. He makes me think of those tough but decent cops who are among the classic characters of American cinema. Our conversation couldn't be more friendly.

The man leads me to the office where my interrogation is to take place. To do this, he places me (I believe) on the sort of motorized cart used to transport baggage in railway stations. In this fashion we traverse a courtyard whose shape is poorly defined, a kind of warehouse or construction site whose dimensions and level of activity are those of a huge market hall, of which he is the person in charge. This involves a great deal of organizational effort on his part, seeing as how he needs to figure out—almost as would an architect—the whole layout of the parking lots, hangars, and workshops, some of which are open air, others of which are covered by large roofs or metal or glass awnings. It's complicated but interesting, he says to me. It's like the "autumn leaves" in Marcel Proust, he adds, making a comparison that indicates that he knows I'm a writer (which of course flatters me no end), a comparison that upon awakening I didn't find too farfetched, seeing as I had earlier taken a walk in the park with its tall, leafy trees: after all, hadn't Proust somewhere observed (in a letter, I believe) that his *Remembrance of Things Past* was constructed along the lines of a cathedral (nave, transept, apse, etc.), and wasn't the more or less architectural attempt to sort things out into their compartments by someone who was at once a licensed police investigator and a human file cabinet worthy of this comparison to Proust that apparently seemed so absurd at first glance?

Before the policeman starts questioning me, it's up to me to speak: I have to go back to the beginning to confess what I have done wrong. But it's not all that simple, and eventually I no longer know exactly what crime I might have committed, even if there is no question about my guilt. This is why I ask my policeman to define theft. This question having gotten lost in the weeds, I am gradually filled with hope: I have committed no theft to which I need to confess, and it is therefore more than likely that I'll be released without even having to spend a single night in lockup. Thus encouraged, I make my way back awake without incident.

All this took place during my first phase of dreaming, and I had no difficulty returning to sleep. But when I awoke the following morning, I felt slightly queasy.

For me the thing was indeed interesting but complicated, as the police-man had said, and just as he had to figure out the overall layout of this work-place, so all the elements of this dream lingered on in my head like a cob-web that not even the light later thrown upon it by Proust's cathedral could destroy . . .

(Now, having gained distance on all this, I can come up with a clearer explanation, although one too architected to be truly satisfying: a number of activities that have to be distributed into specific areas, people who need to be shuttled from one job to the next with a minimum of delay, the vari-ous comings and goings and intertwined trajectories that need to be sorted out and predicted despite all the complexities and imperatives of time and space, and all of this made to happen without things crashing into each other—did not the whole network of actions, dates, times, and locations that took shape in the policeman's mind provide a parallel to the passionately *to-pological* cast of Proustian thought of which the moving picture of the three steeples, so beautiful because their relation to each other seems to change as the spectator follows along a certain stretch of road or a certain stretch of time, offers an illustration only a bit more graphic than those other moments reexperienced in other places and under different circumstances, as if time had merely been a vehicle to transport one's sensations from one point to the next: the same pleasurable taste experienced in Combray and in Paris, the same stumbling over an uneven paving stone in Venice and in a courtyard of the faubourg Saint-Germain, the same sound produced by the clink of a hammer checking the couplings of a train stopped in a station and by a fork or spoon on the bottom of a plate in a dining room—a trope illustrated on the historical level by all the intermarriages that prove how the times have changed and how barriers have come down, thus allowing for the ultimate interpenetration of the two social spheres respectively defined by the two cartographic "ways" of Swann and the Guermantes, which an adolescent follows on his walks?)

The memory (perhaps triggered by the old-fashioned ambience of the spa town) of *Remembrance of Things Past* was no doubt crucial to this dream, seeing as Proust is explicitly mentioned and credited in it, not only by his springtime hedge of hawthorns but by those "autumn leaves" that for Victor Hugo—another thing that occurred to me afterward—symbolized the later years of life and were therefore a transparent allusion to the flight of time. But it was a dream indebted less to the odyssey of Jean Santeuil (whose name was soon rejected by Proust because too reminiscent of those rural villages painted by the impressionists) than to the stories of Kafka, with all these offices whose outer entryways seemed to be slyly hiding from sight, all these bureaucrats befuddled by my case, all these shuttlings from one counter to the next, and this feeling of being guilty of something or another or of indeed being guilty but without being able to figure out what exactly of—other than a theft in the vaguest sense of the term—nor to understand what precise stain has tarnished me, not to mention this rather shady and almost affectionate bond that I feel with this policeman who is in fact younger than I am but who acts like an older brother.

Autumn leaves: not just a scatter of reminiscence and regret but a scurry of moments of remorse involving dirty little dusty nothings, evasions and wishy-washy hesitations, words that remained on my lips instead of being said out loud, actions that I should have taken but from which I abstained, senses of relief when alibis or ways out were offered to me, spontaneities that developed too late, as it were upon second thought, and (tiny acts of commission whose *too much* compensated for the *not enough* I was facing) desires that I quickly left unexpressed because too unworthy, sentences that I proffered merely in order to be admired by those who were listening or simply to join in their chorus, fits of pique of little consequence but petty in their intention, or, no less degrading, wretched acts of kindness that were hypocritical or without backbone—all things done without any felonious intent but perhaps even more fetid than those major crimes whose residues I have allowed to settle within me without so much as daring to cast more than a furtive glance upon them; a mounting heap of fears, given my approaching winter years, as well as a certain disgust with those fears whose weight alone would be enough to bend my back, as if the sky might at any moment fall on my head.

A yellowing decay, like the dull light of rot that shines on the final scene of *Cyrano de Bergerac* (which I so loved as a boy that I would read it to whoever wanted to listen, for example that ancient seamstress who came to work at my parents' home every week), the dying leaves lying scattered along the tree-lined paths of the convent into which the heroine has withdrawn and—food for thought—that are identified by one of her former suitors (now a duke and royal marshal) as emblematic of all those petty and ignominious deeds that sill encumber every step of the person whose ambition has been realized over time (slight obstacles that the foot hesitates to kick aside or crush and that are the cause of both melancholy and shame).

An even bigger blight: the stink of the confessional or the baptismal font that sticks to me as a result of all this wallowing in disgust and fear and remorse, a stench that no wind can waft away, a miasma fed by this chiaroscuro dream more suited to the stuffy atmosphere of the Baden-Baden spa than to the salubrious depths of the nearby Black Forest . . .

And no less in tune with all this, the sinister gallows-bird silhouette of a figure I knew would haunt these pages, but whom I am now introducing only after much hesitation: that thug who, having come up with the torture techniques he had hoped would win the "Battle of Algiers" and having been subsequently rewarded with a high-ranking military position in the Rhine region, was expected to attend (which thank God he didn't) the opening of an exhibition by a contemporary French painter (the reason we had traveled to the ex-Grand Duchy of Baden in the first place). This Punch-and-Judy puppet of a commander, this bully whose hand I swore I would never shake, come what may, a hand not of stone but of leathery meat adept at pulling stings, threatened to rejoin me in my all too comfortable hotel room, having made his way there via this dream, the musty smell of whose jail and interrogation room (as well whose difficult interpretation) had so unsettled me when I woke up the following morning—as it continued to do long thereafter, its ripple effect never fully erased.

This ill-defined misdeed, which I suspected could never be expiated because it involved a theft that implicated me to the very core, was a hole through which, if my gaze were focused and patient enough, I might observe—stratum by stratum, without, however, reaching the very bottom—my entire life (or as much as I can remember of it) toss and turn before me until I was sick to my stomach.

This misdeed—or rather this fault or flaw—the vague awareness of which always unsettles me whenever I decide to take sides or lay blame on others, is nonetheless something whose nature I can pinpoint (if only as a benchmark), given that the *grilling* to which I subject myself allows the following bit of truth to escape: beneath my futile mask of moral rectitude (typified by my noble yet inconsequential refusal to compromise myself by shaking the hand of a torturer), there lies this awful spinelessness. Which accounts not only for that indulgence in contemplative nostalgia evidenced by those "autumn leaves" that had nothing to do with the huge marketplace (or warehouse or marshaling yard) situated at the center of my dream like some switch plate pivoting toward its resolution, but also for the decision (which I didn't even make on my own) to give myself up to the authorities just to show my good faith, or for my frantic rushing from counter to counter, or for the way I went on to act like a little boy toward the policeman whom I had transformed into my mentor or even my nursemaid, with the wheels of all this getting greased by literature (my particular turf, held out to me by the policeman as an olive branch), and, as a final panning shot, the elegantly appointed salon where people of different backgrounds exchange pleasantries . . .

An accurate account, yet still too fuzzy to allow anybody to surmise just how far this spinelessness extends—which, however phony this might sound, I would gladly stiffen into marble. Yet this idea keeps on gnawing at me: deep down, I'm a total fraud.

*

Fifteen kilometers outside Milan, it's not a performance of *Aida* or of some other historical fresco exported by La Scala that is being offered but rather a veritable coliseum show where Christians will be devoured, their deaths announced by the roar of the motors being revved up to the maximum before they leap into action. The ever-intensifying din of a menagerie, as virulent as the unleashing of a sudden houvari wind in the tropics at sundown, with animals of every species pitching in: birds, mammals, batrachians, insects . . . Then, in a clap of thunder, the tightly serried start of the Grand Prix of Monza automobile race. But shortly after this moment that stuns the senses while provoking mass delirium, the pandemonium tapers off as the racing cars begin to space out on the track; then one gradually loses interest because one no longer knows—given all the early leads and staggered laps—just who is running first or running last among all these metallic cigars so gaudily colored (though lacking bands) and stamped with black numbers on white, small dirigibles whooshed along the track by the wind they create, tubular bathtubs from which heads less helmeted than mitered peep out, enviable horizontal penis sheaths like those the Bushmen (who are not just steatopygic) wear even when at rest, torpedoes whose double pairs of wheels evoke the wings that decorate the phalli of many graffiti and ancient figurative monuments of Greco-Roman antiquity.

At the edge of the cement racetrack—which though it appears completely smooth contains invisible joints that cause the cars to noticeably jolt this way and that—a fire truck, an ambulance marked with a red cross, and a cassocked priest all lined up from left to right in front of the spectator stands in a very rational ordering of the safety measures at hand: technical, medical, and, *in extremis*, spiritual.

As we followed this sacrificial trial to the end, which involved no human victims even if there were several mechanical ones (though without flames), we were especially rooting for the celebrated racer Jim Clark, somewhat the way one buys a certain product for no other reason than because one has so often come across its label in advertisements (something I once did when I ran out of toothpaste over the course of I forget which trip, buying a tube of Colgate with the passivity of a robot simply because I had long been familiar with the brand name).

Since then, the young Italian who was accompanying us died at the wheel of his car, failing to fully master the Porsche that had been given to him by his parents, who worked as art restorers in Como, where, right near the lake, there is a museum—nearly a temple—devoted to the battery and various other relics of the physicist Volta. They gave their carefree son everything he wanted, and he was as proud of his Porsche as he was of his outfits, which did not follow English fashion (then on its way out) but rather the trends (just as defensible) of his native land. His clothes were, to believe him, absolutely orthodox down to the smallest detail, each of which he had us admire, claiming that they were the dernier cri, like some salesman vaunting his merchandise as the fruit of the latest bit of industrial progress or like a teacher of night classes trying to explain the alphabet to his illiterate students.

As for the Scotsman Jim Clark, after having quit the Monza race, during which he had long held the lead, he killed himself in a subsequent event, and the press in our part of the world was unanimous in its praise: here was an extraordinary driver, never a show-off but a man of easy grace and exemplary in his conduct, as befits a sportsman who, unfamiliar with electronics, is nonetheless possessed of a fame no less far flung than that of an astronaut ready to leave his visiting card on the wilds of the moon in the form of a national banner.

*

In May 1966 . . .

On a highway in Lancashire, with the weather quite splendid, a Taunus that has just overtaken us and that has now slipped back into our lane directly ahead of us suddenly seems to be losing control. After a few zigzags, it ends up perpendicular to us and then rolls over several times.

The passengers emerge from the overturned car, apparently uninjured. But other drivers who have come to a stop as we did are helping one of the victims of the accident—a young woman—to cross over the pavement and then proceed to lay her out on the grassy shoulder, where she remains motionless. Near the Taunus, a little girl is having a fit, screaming and sobbing in front of her broken doll, which, now deprived of its semblance of life, is nothing but a junk object lying there in the middle of the road.

A young girl with flowing long brown hair—the very picture of innocence— calls for help, having left another vehicle, and, on this morning that is dressed in its Sunday best by the thinly veiled light of the sun, runs in a panic toward a telephone booth.

*

Homespun, handwoven . . .

— How far can this lead, this tendency to rebel against the trends enforced by the mechanization of life, this appreciation of things made by hand, this loathing for nylon, Dacron, Tergal, and other such textiles that huge factories turn out from A to Z, this predilection for the artisanal thing that makes me write with a fountain rather than a ballpoint pen and a with a ballpoint more readily than with a typewriter?

— Perhaps it's due to a regret for those eras when kings reigned, more specifically for those eras when people of whom one knows very little set up the menhirs of Carnac, Stonehenge, and other poorly understood monuments of stone, now tourist attractions . . .

In the Scottish Highlands, whose well-worn mountains are sepia in tone, darker on those stretches covered by heaths that have not bloomed, I fell in love with the very peaceful and lightly curved vale where, some three hundred years ago, the men of the Campbell clan (forever remembered) lured their enemies into an ambush and massacred them all. As I made my way through these highlands, so full of those peat bogs that, it would seem, give malt whiskey its rugged but succulent nose, I was filled with delight each time I came across one of those cows belonging to that (antediluvian?) breed represented by cattle whose horns are almost as large as buffalo's and who are furrier than aurochs, covered in a pelt whose strands are so long that it seems like a head of hair that has been growing for centuries to become this full and flowing.

A Scotland most romantic and, to my mind, so perfectly attuned to despondency that it induces a languor so delectable one no longer wants to leave it behind.

But this land offers you only the beauties of the past, as mere objects of contemplation. What true purchase could one find in this country that instead of opening its pathways seems to want to keep the wraps on its horizon of ancient customs, ancient bloodlines, and ancient geologies? A land folded in upon itself, not unfolded outward, whose sole reason for existing seems to be the equivocal spell cast by a mummy wrapped in bandages woven by the hands of Fates clad in their rainbow raiment, spinning their wool and linen and hemp in the off-season, *la morte-saison*.

*

Of the three cities that constitute Havana—the first of which is American, its scattered high-rises of different elevations producing the effect of irregular crenelations when contemplated from the road that runs along the city shore; the second of which is Spanish, its old houses with ironwork balconies recalling those in New Orleans at the end of the nineteenth century (if, indeed, it was houses like these that Lafcadio Hearn had meant in describing those colonial precincts that would become the original cradle of jazz); and finally this other Havana, Miramar, the banality of whose residential quarter is barely offset by its tropical flora—of these three juxtaposed cities, the first one offers to the seaside observer a profile whose denticulations evoke a modern feudal age, whereas the second presents true fortified castles, constructed as part of the port's defenses and still maintained today, for the Cuban Revolution must be ever vigilant in the face of the forces of imperialism that threaten it.

The Elmina fortress on the littoral of the Gold Coast and even the castle that I had ascribed to the island of Antigua in my dream weigh little against the massiveness of these architectural ensembles of Havana and especially those crenelations whose strange diagrams are etched against the exquisite balminess of the evening sunsets. At Elmina, the apparently unaltered presence of the fortress—the adventurous European past here rooted in a distant land—had captivated me for a long time, even though I came to realize that I might have been overinflating what was in fact a somewhat superficial emotion. As I think back on Havana, I also feel somewhat ill at ease, but in this case it has to do with something far more profound: not simply the realization that I had allowed myself to be seduced and conquered by the outward appearances of things that do not correspond to anything of value, but also the feeling that, given just how inclined I am to defeatism and fright, I am woefully ill equipped to join in the heroic project—the complete renewal of humanity—of which this capital is the hub.

I began to set all this down in writing some two weeks after my return, still in a rather peculiar state: extreme fatigue, constant need to sleep, inability to see straight, the almost physical sensation of wearing blinders that blocked out my attention to anything other than my idée fixe, which itself felt like it was some material entity pressing down upon my forehead and temples from within and keeping my brain from functioning properly; but at the same time a feeling of real fervor, of having been freshly reminted, of having come back to the surface after having been long submerged, buoyed up by joy, reinfused with youth, even though my level of fatigue, no doubt heightened by all my various current obligations, struck me as considerably greater than the amount of recuperation this kind of trip would have normally involved in the past.

Like a number of others, I had been invited to Cuba to celebrate July 26, the fourteenth anniversary of the assault (materially disastrous but rich in moral consequences) that was launched on Moncada Barracks in the very heart of Santiago by Fidel Castro and a handful of his companions, among whom two women. Under no condition should the day come that when thinking of the Cuban Revolution I feel so ashamed of myself that I mentally cross out with a stroke of the pen the precise cause of my uneasy conscience or attempt to rid myself of it by transforming it into the harmless object of a reverie. One of the worst bloodstains: to renounce a belief or kill it off because it is just too hard to reproach oneself for not having lived up to it.

Cuba, where they know how to sum everything up into a vivid allegory that can be deciphered almost instantaneously.

The 23rd Salon de Mai, sent from Paris to Havana by its organizers, had been set up near a garden that was quite unkempt and hilly in appearance, situated at the edge of one of the most traveled roadways of the city. At the request of Fidel Castro, several heifers and three or four bulls (including the mastodon brought in from Canada to procreate countless heads of cattle by artificial insemination) had been parked in the stables that lay a few meters away from the wooden pavilion—a spacious but lightweight Noah's ark readied for the occasion—that housed the works made by human hands. A few days before the exhibition, slung across the entryway like some giant poster, a huge canvas had been installed so that every artist and author invited to participate in the festivities might make a contribution. This they proceeded to do early in the evening under the lights of the projectors, and between the *Mural* in progress and the crowd gathered on the other side of La Rampa, a performance was talking place on a large stage: pieces of more or less popular music, groups of singers, all introducing the execution of a brilliant ballet danced right then and there in the street by troupes of pretty dancers, some of them white skinned, others colored, and a number of them almost naked or (in the case of the paler and taller ones) decked out as blond Nordic sailors with their bellies bare. At the opening of the exhibition that evening, not far from the book display that was also part of the event, an antiaircraft gun manned by uniformed soldiers stood pointed skyward.

Art and culture, entertainments both rural and urban, were thus gathered into a unique conglomeration that demonstrated how in our difficult times arms are necessary to protect the land and, thanks to the mural created by nearly a hundred authors working in public and not in their ivory towers, proved the necessity of a grand alliance among those who share in the general desire to see the world change. The basic message was thus conveyed by the imagery at hand: the partitions between men and their diverse occupations must be torn down; the supposed patricians of intelligence should no longer hold themselves apart from the plebeians of the same; the utilitarian sphere of work, be it for war or peace, should not in any way be seen as inferior to the sphere of play.

Regards to Cuba, Rose of the Tropics and of the Revolution was what I wrote in the space that had been allotted to me toward the top of this mural, whose composition moved upward in a spiral from the central quadrant, which had been filled in by my old friend Wilfredo Lam—the first to climb up the scaffolding with his brushes and tubes of paint, representing in his own person an abridged form of this immensity known as the "third world," given that he is a Cuban descended from a half-African mother and a Chinese father, born a mere year after my own career as a member of the drab Parisian middle class was launched.

*

Blue or red, what was the color of this house? Painted with a pigment that was too visibly synthetic, its facade was false in hue, this I remembered well. But impossible to say more than this, nor to be sure whether its ground-floor windows were decorated by iron bars—a vaguely inquisitorial note that here served to underscore the undeniable severity of this Spanish colonial–style house glimpsed while passing through a street in Santiago de Cuba on this calm afternoon, even though the town was at that point being doubly energized by the revolutionary Festival of July 26 and by the Carnival, celebrated (I'm still trying to recall in the name of what tradition) far earlier than is normally the rule.

If my memory remains hazy as to the exact look of the house, this is perhaps because it provided nothing but a frame for the real-life creature who had drawn my attention away from the rest or who had at least reduced the entire setting into a mere makeshift background. This creature, however, also remains somewhat hypothetical, even though I stared at her long enough to remember that she was sitting there motionless at the window just to the right of the front door and to recall how the two swoops of her carefully coiffed hair framed her lovely, somewhat faded mulatta face—a face that had grown more pinched with age, causing its fine features to harden into place and imparting a thin-lipped desiccation to what must have once been, in the full flush of youth, her proud and romantic air of melancholy.

Behind the paneless window that barely separated her from passersby, of what was she dreaming, this mulatta, or rather this ghost, who belonged as all phantoms do both to the world of the living and to the world of the dead, and was thus a mestiza in the fullest sense of the term, belonging as she did to two opposite realms as well as to two races? That she was alive I did not doubt for a moment, and if I mention ghosts, it's merely as an image, for the sole riddle she posed was that of her social station, which was most likely an intermediary one (the fate of most of those who by birth are located between Blacks and Whites on these islands that Africa, despite herself, helped populate), but which was perhaps more literally a median one, given that it was rumored that the demimonde recruited a good number of its professionals from this as it were equidistant category of mixed-bloods.

An undecidability analogous to my uncertainty about the exact hue of her house. This woman, who caused me to wonder whether she was there at her window for professional reasons rather than out of sheer laziness or out of the need to escape from the torrid confines of her room, was she wearing a dress that was sea green or sky blue or some other color of this sort? I am inclined to think so, or at least to hope so: the tawny skin that I remember so well would have been far better served by these colors than by mauve, pink, salmon, or yellow (her dress being, I am certain of this, of a single bright color, which excludes any other hypotheses). If her dress—probably silk or satin—was indeed a pale blue or light green or even turquoise, it's most likely that her house was red or rather darkish pink, the hue that I was in fact thinking of (or else a sort of pastel blue) when I wondered just what color the facade was, for if indeed I want to call it blue then her dress immediately turns lemon yellow. Lacking as it did any solid primary colors, it was therefore the relation *between* colors that continues not exactly to haunt me (this verb would be too strong) but rather to insistently return to mind, as if a number of lightly contrasting tints—no more than that—had been in play in this luminous but somewhat hermetic tableau whose center was occupied by the mulatta's golden-brown skin tone.

What was she doing and of what was she dreaming behind this ground-floor window that I didn't believe was meant to showcase her, her appearance rather being that of someone relatively well off and not that of some hapless creature who was forced to put herself on display every day to lure the eventual passerby into taking his pleasure with her as he wished, like some master of yesteryear with his slave? All this notwithstanding, the hypothesis that she might indeed be engaged in prostitution could not be entirely discounted. The question was simply in what capacity? Was she a demimondaine who lived in a certain luxury and who was therefore not reduced to selling herself to any paying customer, and if that indeed were the case, was she perhaps (even better) a courtesan who had retired—or even a madame, who knows?— and who was now just sitting there, dreaming of her younger days when she was so admired for the refinement of her clothes and manners, back when women of her sort would walk the streets with their heads held high, an era brought to a close by the cataclysm (worse than a cyclone) of the revolution? But as she sat there without moving, was she really thinking about all this, or is my interpretation of her simply a projection of myself, daydreaming, lost in the melancholy contemplation of the time I was wasting as I idly imagined her dreams?

Was she a bourgeoise or a demimondaine? The distinction between the two involves nuances that, in the end, cannot be resolved. What strikes me as undeniable and as the sole thing that needs to be borne in mind is that this woman — this delicate phantom — was a living anachronism who regretted (so one presumes) her existence of yore and who was watching the brave new world file by before her window with misgivings. What a carnival it all was! Who could have imagined that one day everyone would have to do their turn breaking their backs in the sugarcane fields or tiring themselves out with other peasant chores, or else doing their duty, male or female, in various militia outfits, carrying revolvers or machine guns and wearing olive-drab fatigues? O lovely lady, relic of a bygone age, and so attractive! . . . Yet does not today's society, where skin too dark and hair too frizzy no longer count against you, also feature women no less wantonly proud and beautiful? For the time being, the latter remain unsettling presences to whoever might cross their rural or urban paths, for they make one realize (like the woman in the window) how utterly elusive they are, however unmysterious they might appear or however integrated they might seem into the current lively march of events.

*

Two young black women, the more attractive of whom chatted with you while lowering her lids (a sign of politeness observed by many Africans from Africa), which imparted just a touch of slyness to her smile. Both of them wearing light blouses above the tightly fitting heavy cloth of their work pants, the former's a palish bottle green, the latter's purplish. Sticking out of their cuffed boots were the tips of the work gloves that they had stuffed in there—a little stylish touch invented to kill two birds with one stone, for it allowed them to stash the gloves away while they were taking a rest from work, a practical solution that they had managed to turn into a hint of elegance. Both these young ladies were wearing tiny straw hats that were rakishly tilted forward so that the front brims masked their foreheads while leaving most of the hair above their napes uncovered. The sun was unrelenting during this summer season, but they had reduced their head coverings to the minimum, having no doubt snipped their hats down to size from the broad Panamas that are the standard garb of Cuban peasants, whether they be working in the fields or riding along on their horses with a lasso looped around the pommel of their saddle should they need to recapture a head of cattle that had gone astray. The livelier and more petite of these two women who had so artfully transformed their rustic hats into fashion statements had stuck a small feather into the straw of hers, and this, together with the gloves peeking out from her cuffed boots, gave her the air of one of those not exactly perfidious but nonetheless fairly canny heroines whom Shakespeare in his comedies loves to portray in the disguise of a young gentleman.

Part of a composite crowd of other woman and girls (some still teenagers), these two were there to farm strawberries, asparagus, and various other fruits and vegetables that grow well only in temperate zones. A task at once delicate and arduous, to which—judging from their behavior and from the few words we were able to exchange with them and their companions over the refectory table despite the language barrier—this array of recruits, as varied in age as in color, seemed to be applying themselves with a great deal of zeal and good humor.

Whatever the old guard might find disconcerting about the current effervescence of Cuba or about the loose behavior that socialism is encouraging there, isn't it precisely in this lighthearted fashion—the sole style truly reflective of its goals—that revolution should always pursue its course: the way one loves, the way one dances, the way one turns an arduous task into a sport, as if all that mattered, both in terms of future results and in terms of the present, was to take on difficult or risky challenges and to accomplish them in beauty, once one has thrown down the gauntlet to the Evil Angel?

Formerly, there were no doubt a scattering of alligators on this very hot and humid tip of the southern coast of Cuba, but they are now found here in the thousands. As for these nasty beasts — glaucous, pustulant, treacherous, capable of arising from their stony torpor with lightning speed, armed with huge oblong jaws as powerful as harvesters that can grab and chew up everything in sight — one might have automatically thought that it would have been best to relegate them to zoos or to exterminate them outright. But here they know how to improvise and use any means to get by: this place that was once more or less prey to alligators has become a semiaquatic piece of protected land where the stench of the saurians reigns as they grow in numbers, providing their breeders with skins, a raw material that can be turned into shoes, handbags, and other articles.

To draw good from evil, to try anything that works, to increase the powers of man so that he reaches that stage where he can make use of the most minimal of resources, allowing his inner strengths to freely expand (even if this involve only monsters whose cruelty could be turned to profit, just as medicine has benefited from the noxiousness of many poisons), what other purpose would the surgery of revolution serve, if not this: to start small in order to better discover how to do things on a grand scale?

The truth, once awoken, will never fall back asleep.

Divided into three segments, this Spanish slogan by José Martí was en-
graved onto a stone plaque sunk into the sidewalk at the far end of the cool
retreat created by the overhang of a modern building that housed I forget
which service or organization, a few steps away from our Hotel Nacional, an
imposing but rather down-at-heel palace in this quarter of Havana where the
Americans had left their fabled skyscrapers behind.

An encrusted enamel portrait of José Martí, the poet and pamphleteer
of prophetic proportions whom Fidel Castro had dubbed the "Apostle" and
who was killed as an army commander fighting for independence, was placed
to the right of the inscription, supported by a curious oblique base, a kind
of elongated neck whose slight sinuosity recalled that of some mythological
snake that had slithered out of the ground crowned with a human head. The
memorial struck me as representative of the ones I had come across in many
Cuban towns, given that this portrait (which wasn't even a bust) was more or
less situated at eye level, as if it had been agreed that in this country no hero or
great man should ever exceed the stature of face-to-face dialogue.

Very realistic in its execution, the portrait represented the Apostle with
slightly hollowed cheeks, a broad forehead, and a thick moustache that dimly
reminded me—together with the sharply defined profile and the quivering
nostrils—of those features shared by so many lofty idealists of the period, men
ready to engage in all sorts of sacrifices, protagonists of that age ushered in by
Romanticism, the age during which Stéphane Mallarmé was giving a new
meaning to poetry. The type of man who is now, as it were, obsolete, but
who is worth remembering in our all too rational century, exactly the kind of

heroic figure embodied by José Martí, still so poorly known to most of us. A representative figure, moreover, who had his two feet firmly planted on the ground, envisaging as he did the likelihood of a necessary union among the peoples of Latin America and fighting as he did not just with his words but with his acts for the universal liberation of these nations. And yet a figure human enough to be known for his fondness for drink and for a love life that, so it was said, was hardly that of monk.

I have no idea what the sculptor was thinking of when he came up with the idea of so unmonumental a monument. Perhaps to show how the ideas that had fermented in this writer's head were not just airy nothings, but rather things that were solidly grounded in this undeniable reality that also provides our base—the very ground on which we make our way forward day by day?

Whatever meaning one might want to ascribe to the way in which this effigy of Martí had been executed (and it may well be that it involved nothing more than the desire to be innovative), his slogan, once read, did not fall back to sleep within me, for it forced me to realize that there were very likely other truths that had appeared to me but that I had allowed to fall back asleep simply because I was weary or skeptical of them. But this adage nevertheless awakened one cautionary realization in me, as if José Martí, giving in to pessimism and distrusting his own eloquence, had taken the word *truth* as a threat and had instead written the following: "Truth, once fallen back asleep, will never again awake."

To get to that place where poetry and revolution might blend into each other, such was the goal that in the past I had set for myself, alongside those fellow spirits who had understood that to remake the word with words or images merely entails a transformation that remains fictive, whereas what the world needs to undergo is a revolution far more real. All that I was now reading in Cuba (the sober yet illuminating words of José Martí, Fidel Castro, and Che Guevara, printed on huge billboards or sometimes painted on stones lining roads), all that I was now seeing here (the occasional soaring pylon in honor of the guerrillas set up in the entryway of a hotel and made up of stacks of crisscrossed rifles, or the occasional rural scene of agriculture or husbandry, like the surprising proliferation of white and gray fowl that covered an entire stretch of countryside), all this proved to me that, at least on this island, poetry and revolution could go hand in hand. Thus it was that, roused from my slumbers and regaining a sharper insight into the basic problems that are posed—or should be posed—to every artist and writer, I was led to conclude that even though these questions had long been blurred or dimmed from view, here they were at last coming back into focus for me, still intact.

This truth, this goal we kept in mind, had been betrayed by some or blindly embraced by others who believed the problem had been entirely solved (though it wasn't), or else it had been set aside by many who feared that its ongoing presence might somehow prove to be a false lure or be put into question by the disappointing path that socialism had taken in too many countries—yet how could I allow myself to turn away from it under the pretext that it had caused so many disappointments and that its attainment was no more than a utopian dream? Whether or not it represents an attempt to square the circle, this goal, once established, can no longer be dismissed. It would be like claiming that because two beings can never enter into total fusion with each other, love is therefore impossible, or that because one will never achieve an absolute knowledge of anything, one might just as well allow oneself to lapse into obscurantism.

For sure, I'm just a poor devil and hardly a guerrillero when it comes to moving from the plane of ideas into the rugged terrain of action. But how does this failing of mine change the basic argument? If I confess that I have absolutely no gift for the mortal combat of revolution, I am thereby criticizing myself and not the revolution. I can therefore take no pride in allowing everything to die down again, in refusing to materially help out as much as I can, in failing to contribute my rightful share, especially when it involves that which concerns me most—namely, the answer to the question: how to make poetic thought and revolutionary thought mutually reinforce each other, conjoining the former's ability to suddenly transfigure life with the latter's preparation of the path that will undo all the social shackles that restrict our lives?

Not to evade the question, not to dodge and weave, but rather to keep one's head clear by remaining faithful to a single line of thought—this is the practical lesson I learned from the teachings of José Martí. *An honest journalist is more than a king* ran another one of his adages, a simple call to keep one's mind clean and that I am here trying to translate if not literally at least in spirit—a slogan that I read on a plaque or poster in the entryway to the building that housed the offices and the printing presses of the Communist daily *Granma*, named after the small craft that had carried to shore the original eighty-three fighters whose handful of survivors would eventually become, with the support of the people, the masters of the island in less than three years.

They dealt with revolution like that Greek philosopher who demonstrated the reality of movement by the mere act of walking. They expressed their ideas by simply putting them into action. Which is the same way I want to spear-head the truth that I have so long pursued as a poet: not to merely go on and on about it but to immediately get down to work and strike sparks from it.

 . . . But if, having done this, I then say to myself that there is nothing left for me to do, this would just be another way of allowing the truth to fall asleep within me.

*

"The Revolution moves fast . . ."

So I was informed by a Cuban of Spanish ancestry, twenty years my ju-
nior. Under Batista he had been imprisoned and tortured, and later, as the
guerrilla movement was taking shape, he had joined up with Fidel in the
mountains to become the director of the rebels' radio station. His observation
was made as a rejoinder to an objection I had raised over the course of the very
brief exchange I had with the leader at two in the morning under the stars, in
the midst of a tight knot of soldiers and other foreigners such as myself who
had been gotten out of their beds by their interpreters to meet with Fidel—who
had spent the afternoon inaugurating a number of new buildings: a workers'
housing complex, a school, a dispensary, and other facilities designed to serve
the coffee plantations that were being set up on the far western tip of the island, an area that had previously been accessible only by mule paths but that
now had been opened up by new roads.

Fidel having mentioned the international cultural congress that in six
months' time would gather together representatives of various organizations
and nations in Havana, I observed that the time frame for inviting all these
writers, artists, and specialists struck me as very short indeed. I expressed this
qualm entirely out of loyalty to the Cuban Revolution and to its leader, who
turned out to be the nicest of persons (the adjective, for once, fits) and who
was, after one had witnessed his fiery oratory on the podium, surprisingly
sweet and utterly devoid of swagger despite his large build—a hulking bear
of a man, his eyes darting this way and that out of curiosity, yet who walked
with something of a waddle, almost as if intimidated by the heft of his own
bulk, and who addressed you in a very steady voice and in a Spanish that was

very clearly pronounced and melodious—in short, one immediately felt one could confide in him and freely let him know, right there and then, what was on one's mind.

When Carlos Franqui mentioned to me how fast the Revolution was moving, I initially took this to be no more than a passing quip and made little of it. Only later—given my *esprit de l'escalier*—did it occur to me that I might have rejoindered as follows: if the Revolution moved so quickly, it was because it had mobilized everybody into a common effort and could not stop to deal with formal questions, and furthermore because it had to deal with people who were living their lives at a completely different tempo—for example, those scholars and scientists who were used to making only step-by-step progress in their research and who were therefore entangled in a web of obligations from which they could not free themselves immediately. But later, on further reflection, my friend's laconic remark did not strike me as loaded with hidden irony (he was too much of a straight shooter for this), but rather with all sorts of implications with which I had to agree and which went considerably beyond the simple question of the time frame necessary to organize an international congress of this sort.

Yes, the Revolution must move fast! A question of life or death: imperialism is in full swing in Vietnam, it's setting up its military outposts everywhere, and no one has any idea what the world will look like six months from now, or, for that matter, in a few weeks. We, over whose heads no visible Damocles's sword hangs, have the luxury of not being in any hurry. But the Revolution doesn't have a minute to waste. How tarry or delay when one is working to eliminate hunger and poverty and iniquity and all the many other causes of despair and early death? And even in the domain of culture, where the challenges might seem less immediate, one cannot just take one's sweet time: culture is the mold in which minds are formed, it is the flagship that flies the national banner of prestige, it is the breeding ground of public opinion, the obstacle that stands in the way of those who would hide the brutality with which they engage in industrialized massacres in order to restore the so-called sanity of those peoples who are crazy enough to want to determine their own future without colonial protection, and seen in this light, culture is not only one of the goals of the Revolution (as a way of opening access to a society where all the capacities of humankind would open out like a fan) but also a combat strategy whose tactics demand that one *move fast* lest one be overwhelmed.

The necessary speed of the Revolution when it comes to dealing with things that cannot wait. This is the rhythm I should personally observe, applying this lesson to the limited domain of everything that I write and do, no longer content to accept myself as someone forever engaged in settling old scores or in claiming that my views or relations to the word are now out of date and in need of revision by, for example, what I now have to say about Cuba. I believe that one has to move quickly on two fronts: first, to reply to the call without delay, and second, to make oneself heard right away instead of working things to death; to strike while the iron is hot, to write not in an elaborate, polished, frigid, academic fashion but rather at a brusque and jagged pace—like a hatchet or peal of thunder—otherwise, all emotion just goes up in smoke.

Brief and easily separable from each other, the texts I am here gathering can be published before the distance between them and the private or public events that prompted them grows too great. They would greatly gain thereby. But each piece of the mosaic gradually taking shape in this fashion comes into being so slowly that it risks losing energy in the process. Instead of this far too finicky approach to writing, go for something far more incisive: an explosion of aphorisms, phrases or little batches of phrases that say a great deal in a few words and that keep the matter at hand in a state of incandescence; perhaps involving the complete explosion of syntax altogether (as a number of others have done)? A private alchemy toward which—if I ever manage to succeed—this planetary alchemy of Revolution will have led me, an alchemy fueled by the fire that causes every being and every thing to be metamorphosed.

Eppur, si muove! Galileo is said to have cried out in a burst of anger against the inquisitors (and no doubt against himself) just after he had publicly renounced his Copernican conviction as to the turning of the earth around the sun.

There are too many disrespected, humiliated people on this globe, a state of affairs that can be remedied only by a radical upheaval impossible to achieve without violence. This being the case, I stand behind the revolutionaries. I am of the revolutionary persuasion. Which does not, however, prove that I am myself a revolutionary. Bogged down in my private concerns and habits, often feeling helpless in the face of adversaries, and less inclined to butt heads than to cloak myself in a fatherly refusal to enter into the fray, I would not dare to boast about being a revolutionary without feeling myself something of an imposter. Beware of this bloodstain: to wrongly conclude that one is the product of what one thinks.

Another possible stain: to hope that the revolution will progress or spread when in fact one is doing nothing or practically nothing to hasten its outbreak in one's own surroundings. I can of course claim that it is nowhere near to breaking out here and that if it were indeed to break out I would make the right choice, but there is a gulf that separates my somewhat apprehensive state of anticipation from the impatience with which I should rightfully be burning to see it arrive. There is no point in quibbling: I am marked by this stain, one sign among many of the serious gap that exists between the way I represent the world to myself and the way I behave within it.

To distinguish between true revolutionaries and those who are merely halfheartedly or not at all engaged, a touchstone is provided by a Fidel Castro phrase everywhere cited in Cuba, spelled out in large letters: *El deber de todo revolucionario es hacer la revolución. The duty of every revolutionary is to make the revolution.* To make it: that is, to do one's utmost that it arrive as soon as possible, that it triumph, and not get bogged down in the process.

The fact remains that if I cannot in good conscience count myself among the revolutionaries, I am nonetheless not putting on an act when lending my support to them. When the hour of truth arrives, let me do better than the ancient astronomer who made a feeble attempt to save face by maintaining his certainty (almost despite himself) as to the very thing he had just solemnly denied.

A modest wish, and yet a somewhat dubious one, for one of the bloodiest mistakes one can make is to seek reassurance within the limits one has definitively assigned to one's possibilities.

*

Galileo: in the masculine, the Tuscan. In the feminine, Galilea, Galilee: the more or less mythical land of which the Gospels speak.

Galileo, a name like a jug or earthenware pot, perhaps because of the name of Gallé, this other Palissy, so famous for his art nouveau vases, gifts appropriate for weddings, birthdays, or New Year's.

Galileo, the cracking sound of a jar fracturing; Galileo with this stutter that seems to have galvanized him, far more akin to those mental and physical afflictions that gallop through our old age, galling our vision, spasming our arthritis, blocking and babbling the functions of our brain, than to those verses of "The Broken Vase" that we all had to learn, ad nauseam, galore.

*

Gondremark, this grotesque baron whose strings were pulled by Offenbach.

Gondal, an island invented in their childhood by Emily and Anne Brontë.

Gondar, where for several months I lived among Ethiopian women who roared convulsively when possessed by their master spirits.

Venice, which lends its backwaters to the Gondran company, as well as to its pinnaces, so less pointy than its gondolas.

Somewhere in Bavaria, the Wiese church, a rococo marvel.

Grund: according to Schelling, the primal ground, as opposed to essence or *Wesen*.

Gondrevise? Grondevise? Gruendewiese? A small city, not on any map, of which I dreamed one night, perhaps toward the break of dawn and almost toward the end of my slumbers . . .

Having long lain buried and only recently resurfaced, the possible model for my dream city: "Wiesengrund," the name that the philosopher and musicologist Theodor W. Adorno reduced to his middle initial, preceding his last name, and which belonged to his mother—a singer, I think.

The memory of a shared enthusiasm (the effect of an *aficion* held in common and raised to a white heat by its mutual reverberation) makes me think back fondly on this chubby fan of both Italian opera and serial music. At the house of the friend (now also deceased) with whom I had taken such pleasure in sneaking into the nearly empty hall of La Scala during a morning rehearsal, I heard him one evening sing the duet of the prisoners in their vault in the last act of *Aida*, with him performing both the soprano and the tenor parts and, half crazed with joy, accompanying himself on the piano while bobbing his head back and forth, somewhat risibly.

*

As it were watching his figure like a torero who, holding himself perfectly erect, tiptoes away to hold the bull at bay, the dog executes his war dance face to face with another dog. He rears up so high on his hind legs that you fear you might pull him over backward by yanking at his leash. So frantic are his leaps that his two paws seem to vibrate like two fiddle heads made of solid wood. The other dog backs off as the first one charges, and vice versa. Barking wildly, the two engage in their playacting. But like any number of games, this one could easily degenerate, and rather than risk falling down should a particularly violent bound cause you to lose your balance, you're better off dragging apart one of the two combatants by the leash. Turning his head toward his master, whom he has stupidly bumped into, the misunderstood canine throws him a dirty look. Which causes you to feel like some miserable wretch who admittedly might know a number of things of which this dog is unaware but who is also ignorant of so many things that he knows all too well. To judge from the dog's expression, you will always be considered a philistine when it comes to understanding this hot-blooded animal's fine art of having a good time.

This creature, in whose eyes I hope to remain a somewhat heavy-handed friend rather than a nasty impediment to all the fun he gets out of kicking up his legs, is a tawny boxer whom we call Puck, even though his official name is Pyrex. The son of Gitane and of Maki de la Banane, his paternal grandparents are Junon de Bod en Men and Elko des Bayonelles, the latter sired by Cali la Ravageuse and Boom de Karlovac.

Among dog breeds, are there feuds on the order of the Armagnacs and the Burgundians or the Montagues and the Capulets?

*

Were I to be an actor with an innate or trained talent for all the necessary skills required (major stage presence, a casual aristocratic air, a dandy's unflappability conjoined with the liveliness of a wandering minstrel, a voice as clear as a bell, free from all those fudged tremolos and other affectations that feel far too stagy), I would love to play the role of Mercutio, not because we resemble each other but rather for the opposite reason, because he embodies all it is I lack. Mercutio: the very incarnation of frivolity, someone who could care a fig for his own life.

He is neither a Montague nor a Capulet but a Scaliger [sic], thus a member of the ruling family, but fantasizing that that he belongs to the clan of Mab the Fairy Queen. Mercutio could well wash his hands of the bloody quarrel between the two rival factions of Verona. A *plague on both your houses!* he will exclaim, having refused to take either the side of his friend Romeo or the opposite side. But if these are his words, it would be because he's already been *peppered*—that is, mortally wounded by the Capulet braggart with whom he has dueled, less out of loyalty to his friend who had been provoked by this crack swordsman than out of the pleasure of having the last word and taking someone down a notch.

Scandalous Mercutio, talker of nonsense, antihero animated by no spirit of sacrifice nor by any devotion to a cause however just or unjust, but willing to risk it all for the mere hell of it.

*

Is Puck attending summer school in the kennel that this retired fair-ground entertainer, formerly the head animal trainer of the Pinder Circus, has opened on the outskirts of Étampes? Given that the gardener and his wife were taking the first portion of their vacation, we had to find a place to board our dog. On a previous occasion we had left him at an "Institute for Canine Education" in Livry-Gargan, but this time we thought it would be more convenient to find him lodgings closer to us, with an utterly unpretentious outfit where the animals—so we were told—were treated with gentle care.

Along with Puck, there were two wolfhounds (who had already been kenneled there for several days and who, like him, were not show dogs destined for exhibition), half a dozen handsome snow-colored huskies belonging to the kennel owner and still in the process of being trained, a pony, a female bear by the name of Gaby, and her two cubs, one of whom is called Michel. According to their trainer and exhibitor, a pleasant Englishwoman whose caravan is parked near the entrance to the establishment, the mother bear is fully trained, whereas the cubs are still being broken in. One has to take care when stroking the muzzles that the bears stick through the bars of the cage, for under their meek exteriors and despite the tender glances they seem to be directing in your direction, these beasts can suddenly act up.

Wearing shorts the first time we saw her and looking like some actress all dressed up for a pantomime at some Christmas party, the Englishwoman informed us that she plied her trade at "gala" events. I imagine her executing her number with a little switch in her hand, all smiles and ever so frail in her evening gown, its silver sequins sparkling against a ground of electric green or some other color that catches the light favorably and that contrasts nicely with the brown fur of her partner. I tend to imagine her addressing the latter with the formal "you" and masking her severe command of the situation with an exquisite politeness that no lord, lady, or baronet would deign to disavow.

Our sturdy Puck, named after Shakespeare's unpredictable sprite, had (so it would seem) been very well behaved, and I was tempted to ascribe his good conduct to the presence of this kind fairy, at once a flower of the traveling circus and a worthy specimen of this Britannia that has for centuries ruled the waves. We had barely made our way back home (retrieving him for the duration of the weekend) when Puck broke into the chicken coop, taking advantage of a gate that had been left open. A species of corrida ensued over the course of the next hour, moving from the courtyard to the lawn and on to the terrace. A large white hen managed to miraculously survive his ferocious attack, from which, given how amok he was running, we were unable to save her. Things were finally resolved after my brother-in-law had taken two falls, luckily without any injury to himself (but why on earth go after this innocent intruder with a rubber-tipped cane?), and after the death of a poor chicken who proved to be less valiant than the initial victim.

Afraid of being bitten, I did not intervene into the fray to save the two chickens from the jaws and paws of their assailant, and thus, despite my few feeble attempts, I became guilty of the crime that modern French law defines as *nonassistance to a person in danger*. Similarly, were not my wife and the friend who was with her also guilty of involuntary henslaughter, having left the gate to the chicken coop open without first having made sure that the dog was leashed?

One thing is sure, and no surprise here: with Puck retrieved from the traveling animal trainers, a bit of circus had come into our ancient weekend house, built on the site of a priory where Augustinian nuns had reigned until chased off by the French Revolution, itself guilty of having decapitated any number of statues on the portals of the Étampes churches.

Given that the fairgrounds people were on tour, we lodged our dog at the local veterinarian's the next time around. Rumor has it that the former menagerie manager will return to these environs to set up a new kennel in different quarters. But there has been no word about the frail Englishwoman for whom—had she so commanded me—I would have no doubt danced like a bear.

*

Let nothing petrify. Let nothing freeze. Protest without end. If it involved nothing more than this, I would gladly compose my Golden Verses, my Emerald Tablet, or my Sayings of Monelle with some of the slogans that the rebel students of 1968 wrote on the walls of the Sorbonne or on those of the other buildings that they had occupied, or even out on the streets wherever the walls came in handy.

Flares, launched with the spontaneity that the most radical among them had opposed to the bureaucratic mind-set into which revolutionary thought has almost everywhere congealed. Adages, some of which reach far beyond the witticisms of graffiti or dirty jokes or hasty scrawls on walls and that prove deeply satisfying to me, seeing as I have long tried to succeed at this kind of lapidary utterance myself.

INTELLECTUALS UNLEARN WHAT YOU ARE. No need to comment on this call to action, written in large cursive letters on one of the walls of room 343, the location on the fourth floor of the Censier university annex where the meetings of the Students-Writers Action Committee took place.

BE REALISTIC ASK FOR THE IMPOSSIBLE. No need here either for a gloss, the slogan having been generated in the same room over the course of a kind of parlor game that consisted of throwing a topic out for discussion and then finding a form for it, thanks to a series of gradual modifications suggested by all the participants.

LIFE/QUICK. Two lines in a lightly bluish red—something approaching purple—just across from the student restaurant on the rue Mazet, a stone's throw from my home. Enjambment takes the place of punctuation, and one immediately grasps the fact that QUICK here functions as an interjection, thus expressing the exclamatory desire to see what Rimbaud calls "true life" be disclosed as soon as possible. Later, I discovered this same plea reduced to the single word QUICK, as if all it took to make oneself understood was the expression of haste without any need to explain the nature of one's impatience or to weigh down the arrow's vector by specifying its target.

NO MORE CLAUDELS. In other words: enough with this mammoth gymnast of eloquence, this pride of the bourgeois status quo, sometimes disguised as a visionary shepherdess, sometimes cloaked in a mandarin version of colonial exoticism, sometimes showing off as a bookish mystic. This, at any rate, is how I see things, and I have absolutely no reason to believe that this rejection of Claudel, as posted at Nanterre, was not similarly motivated.

FLY SOAR ENJOY. This dictum struck me as more mysterious when I first read it on a Latin Quarter street and then again in several other places. But someone else whom this slogan had equally intrigued informed me that it was just a bald invitation to take LSD, "to soar" [*planer*] being merely one of the terms to which its users had recourse to describe the "trips" or the "highs" that this chemical compound offers.

BE CRUEL, inscribed on the back of the stone parapet that lines the quais of the left bank of the Seine just below the Pont des Arts—and how argue with this excellent piece of advice, given that the world in which man eats man will never be changed unless one learns to bare one's teeth.

At times a given inscription means nothing yet becomes exemplary by the way it holds the page. Thus BECOME CONCIOUS, painted in large white letters along the back of one of those classic brown benches available to pedestrians on so many Parisian sidewalks. Whether because of sheer carelessness, inability to spell, or the desire to break rules, the letter S that normally precedes the second C of the word *conscious* had been omitted from the inscription that I read as I glanced at the back of the bench that faced the boulevard Saint-Germain while on the bus that was taking me back home from the Musée de l'Homme (where things were also reaching a boil), not far from the Solférino-Bellechasse station. Several days earlier it was near this same station that my bus had crossed paths with a small parade of men and women silently marching along at a rapid clip; one of its leaders—a young man dressed in the same anonymous street clothes as his male and female companions—was flying a tiny improvised red flag that looked as if it had been ripped from the hands of some railway station master.

A THROW OF THE DICE WILL NEVER ABOLISH CHANCE. How I would love to hear the thunder and lightning of this Mallarmé maxim shouted out by a chorus, its irregular rhythm accentuated by the clapping of hands—a perfect protest slogan! But how, by the same token, pay homage to Mallarmé's ideal flower, ABSENT FROM ANY BOUQUET, if, as the protesters say, SOCIETY IS A CARNIVEROUS FLOWER?

*

May 24–25, 1968 . . .

Over the course of that night I went to the kitchen several times to turn on the sink faucet, not to wash my hands but to fill up one or the other of the following three receptacles: a plastic basin that I carefully carried down from our fifth-floor apartment to the front door of our building in order to hand it over to a young woman who, her face masked in Chinese fashion (to ward off the tear gas), had asked for some water to relay back to her companions who were manning the flimsy barricade that had been set up to block the quai just ahead of the rue Dauphine and the Pont Neuf; another plastic basin and pail, as well as the initial basin, which the girl had thoughtfully returned to me at the front door, something I had hardly expected, considering that it would have been completely normal—given everything that was going on—to have forgotten all about this lowly object, a basin. All these receptacles were period-ically emptied of their contents, as we poured them out from one of our front windows (the one in the library where we had gathered) onto the sidewalk below in an attempt to block the spread of all the dreadful tear gas that the CRS was launching at the street protesters.

It had all begun with someone shouting "Michel!" up at me as I stood there at the window with my wife and my sister-in-law, all of us curious about the rioting and the explosions of grenades below. An American female ac-quaintance of ours and a friend of hers, as well as another American woman we knew, and then a student wearing tight pants and loafers, all made their way up the stairs into our apartment. After some negotiating, I managed to convince the concierge's son to leave the front door to the building open, should there be others who needed to find their way to safety, and indeed soon thereafter three complete strangers (none of them participants in the events going on below) joined our initial group of guests: the first, a reporter from *Le Figaro* carrying a camera and wearing a white helmet to protect him from the spitefulness of the police, was telephoning in his messages from our quarters, and the other two were a young Italian tourist couple whom the police had attacked with nightsticks on their way to their hotel, but who had escaped without any visible damage.

As concerns our own safety, we experienced a few moments of nervousness when a large tanker truck that we feared might be filled with fuel came to a stop just below our windows, its passage blocked by the burning barricade. But a young man and woman carrying red flags had appointed themselves traffic cops and convinced the truck to turn around, as they did with all the cars that were just idling there.

A potential scene for a light comedy: among the strangers thrown together in a bourgeois apartment by the fortunes of war, there were several—whether rioters or not—who were never even supposed to meet.

*

Paving stones hurled, cars toppled over, fences smashed, large pipes dug up, trees cut down, flames, suffocating tear gas, the pop of grenades, the clattering of police truncheons: a spectacular sentence that flouted all the standard syntax of Paris last May. Wilder and rougher than any of the phrases written on the walls, this sentence reduced all of mine to nothing—too talky, too leaky, like water.

*

TO THE HIGHEST BIDDER:

        Bar Bear Shop
        Botcher Shop
        Booty Salon
        Delicatassassin
        Diss Cunt Store
        Dry Eye Cleaners
        Far Mare's Market
        Gross Eerie Store
        Hard To Wear Store
        Half Bakedery
        Heart Gallery
        Jew Yeller
        Lick Her Store
        Noose Peeper Stand
        Stay Shunners
        The Rift Shop
        Watch Faker
        Whore Saler

*

I REQUIRE:

  a fine sea chantey to calm those waters wherein, a wisp of smoke,
I drown;
  a wine not too heady, to laugh my woes away and get me dreaming;
  a flower nobody will have ever thrown my way;
  an hour so splendid I lose my head;
  a nothing, a breath, a nothing;
  a willow weeping all the love stories in its keeping;
  in the cistern of my head, a Salome without veils, preaching sermons
better than 7 Yohanans;
  dancing on his hind hoofs, a calf from the back of beyond, forever
golden;
  birds in my bower;
  a springtime of hope slipping its soundless love song into the heart of
Dahlila's 4,005 senses;
  a grail in need of no tale;
  a ring no child of the north could forge;
  an enchanted flute;
  a love potion;
  a kingless Ys;
  a land where the orange ever blooms.

*

FAUSTROLLIAN INVENTIONS

A phosphorescent snack to lure back your disobedient dog even in the densest of fogs.

A button you can push to simultaneously kill yourself, alert the press, and make funeral arrangements.

A machine that perfectly aligns the sheets of paper on which you sign dozens of carbon copies of your protest letters.

An armored door neither sickness nor sadness could ever pry open.

A mirror that delivers slaps when you look at yourself too long.

A bed made up with sheets that bleach both body and soul.

Deep-frozen desire, ready to eat (no guarantee).

A toilet flush that floods the whole floor or causes the entire apartment building to explode.

An insecticide that transforms a morning spider into an evening spider.

A grandfather clock (that you wind only once) marking only those hours you have wasted.

A pump that inflates you when you fall flat.

A consecrated host containing the haloed, crucified figure of a small swimmer hidden in a *galette des rois*.

A suit so slim, so tailored you need to lose weight to try it on.

*

Behind the thin sheet of mist trapped between the double-paned window,
the scrolls on the sill rinsed by rain.
Behind the dark volutes of the railing that does not parallel the line of the horizon,
the asymmetrical ironwork of the branches.
Behind the crazy limbs of the trees,
the river whose flow one cannot see.
Behind its subtle streaming toward the sea,
the cockeyed house roofs in a file.

Idling or in motion on the river's far bank,
cars or pedestrians add little to the scene
I compose or recompose into fore- and background
to get it into focus
and at the same time petrify time.

Like the body, a home has its nobler and baser parts: at its apex, the parlor (at least during the period when every bourgeois apartment boasted of one); at the very bottom, the kitchen and its counterpart, the WC, down which—in a degraded and diluvial form—is flushed whatever gets prepared in this ancillary space that is not even worthy of being counted as a "room" and whose stove and whose plebeian utensils (no matter how modern they might be) rank it below the bathroom, the design of whose various features, such as the tub and sink, are not without a certain sexy come-hitherness, even though they too are just domestic tools in the most humiliating sense of the term.

A fairy-tale Donkeyskin kitchen that often emits odors which, even if pleasing, are not always welcome, although (all things considered) its various sauces and fats and other alimentary adjunctions are less repulsive ingredients than the soap, the shaving cream, the colognes, the lotions, and the emollients whose basic purpose is to rid us of our filth and to mask—thanks to the removal of our hairs and smells (which many prefer to cover up with deodorants)—the fact that we belong to the animal kingdom.

These days kitchens often resemble laboratories or electric substations, but in our particular home the kitchen will never be what power plants are to the city: it remains altogether too rustic, its vocation depending on meats and vegetables, themselves the products of such rural activities as agriculture and cattle farming. Our kitchen is thus far closer to peasant life than to the industrial outskirts of the city, and, like the countryside, it is a place I feel ambivalent about—finding it (as do many city folk) relaxing but not wanting to live there full time; similarly, now and then I like to linger in the kitchen to raid the fridge before going to bed or to pour myself a drink of water fresher than a mountain spring, or sometimes simply to sit down and have a casual bite in the stillness of its environment, untroubled by any noise—except during the working hours of the Paris Metro offices situated across the courtyard and dominated by a tall antenna, around which, every spring, a blackbird circles in song before electing it as his perch. More than in any other refuge my home might offer, I feel at peace in this kitchen, perhaps because it houses fewer ghosts than the rooms whose walls are far more filled with the traces of my presence and, therefore, of my anxieties.

The red tiling and exhaust hood are merely memories, for the kitchen at present contains not only a stove but also its opposite, an ice box, as well as a washing machine—situated in an attached nook where the humid sheets and towels are hung out to dry like scenery in a theater and that also houses the home heating system and the laundry drying rack, the former resembling a piece of heavy artillery and the latter, hanging down from above with its various adjustable rods and tubing attached to the ceiling, resembling the airy lightness of a ship's rigging.

A kitchen—its multiple powers and discreet flames now unjustly relegated to times gone by—represents the little that remains of these former days of the *hearth*, a site that has vanished from our current dwellings, where it is no longer customary to gather around the fireplace (if such still exist) and where the "living room," despite the pole of attraction offered by the lure of its insidiously mind-numbing television screen, is now simply a place where life goes on (as its name indicates) rather than a center around which the various members of the household can all gather in daily commerce.

A kitchen that remains ageless and artisanal despite all its modern equipment, but whose unembarrassed display of pails and brooms and mops and rags and aprons and sundry utensils retains the charm of all those attics or storage closets that, like grandmas, tell so many tales to children.

*

At our country place, our housekeeper wants to get rid of the cat because she's been killing the rabbits in the woods behind the house. Only yesterday one of her one-month-old kittens was killed by the dog, who saw it sneak up on a bunch of bones on which he was preparing to feast and who took this as a threat. Dogs and cats—there were two kittens the housekeeper had discovered in the attic, into which their mother had retreated to deposit her litter—they all got along so famously that they often slept together, with the kittens occasionally pretending to suck the teats of the dog, who didn't appear to mind this at all.

Indeed, a while back we ourselves were forced to eat all our guinea hens, not because we had specifically raised them for food, but because these hens had very aggressively attacked and killed a pheasant and continued to present a considerable danger to the other fowl we were keeping in our coop. A serial massacre, as if a cloud feathered with blood had floated over our house. . .

I of course don't want to play the sob sister here, but I have to admit that this series of tiny tragedies disturbed me no end. That one should want to banish a cat because she dares prey on something bigger than a mouse (which it is, after all, her job to exterminate), that a good-natured dog should, in a moment of brutality, put to death a little friend of his just to protect his bones, that a bunch of fine-feathered fowl should display the ferocity of a raptor—all this would lead one to approve of those mystics (Brahmans or others) who are not only vegetarians always ready to turn the other cheek, but so respectful of life that they would never dare crush the bug that was biting them between their toes.

I who have long been an aficionado of bullfights and who have white-washed the horrors of the revolution in the name of the justice of its aims,

I who therefore reject the theory of nonviolence, am nonetheless unable to shake, as many others do, the idea that I belong to a world where it is the norm—for the members of each and every species—to try to dominate everybody else, not excluding the murder or the manducation of one's enemies. If this seems to sound like a disturbing contradiction, it does not exceed the no less laughable paradox of my entire existence: to take sides with the oppressed even though I belong to the class of the oppressors, to write in order to set myself free even though I am a slave to my writing and would never want to give it up, to be afraid of getting my hands bloody but to accept that my comfortable existence is built on the sweat or indeed the blood of others, to decide that life is not worth living even though I made only the feeblest attempt to end it, to go on and on about love and poetry while living the life of a bourgeois, to dream of decisive action when I know I'm a dyed-in-the wool intellectual, to refuse to believe in the supernatural while being plagued by superstitions (for example, that to predict the good is to invite evil), and, as if some invisible tribunal might require me to justify myself, to save myself as much as possible from the commission of the ultimate, unforgivable crime.

*

Living in my lines,
like a rat in his hole,
a knight in his armor,
a knife in its sheath,
a coquette in her dress,
a wine in its glass,
a prisoner behind his bars,
or an old grouch in his lair?

*

He so took me to be a friend, he so treated me as an equal (which, naïvely, delighted me no end) that our relationship became untenable in the end. No question of obeying me when he gets out of line. It's gotten to the point where I can barely keep him from lunging at people who cross our path, and I'll soon no longer have the force to restrain him.

If things keep getting worse, I'll have to stop him from bothering everybody, this friend who is far too much of friend, this excessive alter ego, and unless I decide to isolate him like someone with the plague (which would be even crueler), I will have no other choice but to sentence him to death (with a heavy heart, like the judge who, out of respect for the law, sends his own son to the guillotine, a son who has turned out badly because of the weakness his father has shown him). Whatever it costs me, I hope I'll be able to figure out how to get rid of this frightening companion while the going is still good: if he were placed into fresher and firmer hands—hands more consistent than mine, which deal with him for only part of the week—then perhaps this creature's fierce fighting disposition could be tamed and, better, trained, perhaps he could then be persuaded to change his ways.

To have to put this dog down because he is becoming far too dangerous and is now too old to be reeducated—how deeply this would wound me. I don't think I could ever wash my hands of it—hands so soft that they were led to commit the very worst of acts . . .

*

Who is neither in the head,
  nor in the heart,
  nor in the genitals,
  nor in the limbs,
and no more in the cellar than in the attic,
but who,
in a basement apartment rather than on the ground floor,
would live like a squatter
whom I could not evict lest he
—or his twin—
move back in.

Everything could perhaps be worked out if I managed to establish a line of communication with this unwelcome lodger . . . But even though he is nested in my innermost parts, his presence is so foreign to me—like some animal curled up inside me—that I wouldn't even be able to strike up a dialogue of the deaf with him.

For extended periods, this thing—so inert as to seem absent—makes me forget all about its existence. But to confront the void that is thereby created is no less revolting than to feel this thing just lingering there inside. All I can hope is that it will at long last leave its lair and rise through my throat and, once having made its way through this bottleneck, take on the shape of speech via a mutation that would more than set me free.

*

If he has so lost his head that he'll have to be committed to a country house far calmer than our own (in order to avoid having him neutered, as three different vets have recommended), it's probably because instead of having to act as my sole Horatio or Pylades, this dog has had to play a double role, like Harlequin in the service of his two masters: on weekdays, the gardener, and on weekends and during vacations, me.

But didn't he seem particularly well suited to this double role, given that his body fur was entirely fawn (at least on his front legs, sturdy as bats) and given that his muzzle (now salt and pepper) was formerly as black as those leather masks worn by clowns in their harlequin outfits?

*

Will the story of Puck end in such a way as to illustrate the fact that this name we gave him, whose lively flame seems to have marked him so adversely, also predestined him to live out a fairy tale?

Too high strung, and even more unmanageable given the state of celibacy to which he had been subjected (to have introduced a female companion into the house, so we were informed, would only have rendered him more aggressive), he was given to some animal-lover friends of ours but then had to be taken back again after he had committed several misdemeanors (having bitten a person twice, then almost having bitten someone else, then having urinated on a piece of living room furniture, then having stolen a Camembert and a quiche lorraine) and was consequently on the verge of getting castrated, which at least would have released me from the fear of having to one day deal with him the way an authoritarian regime might physically eliminate a misfit. But, as fate would have it, a former traveling showman was ready to adopt him. He had known the circus people who had previously boarded our crazy Iroquois back when he was more docile, and he was now planning to open, over toward Arpajon, a place that would be part zoo and part kennel, where Puck could be put to work as a stud.

A perfect example of how an animal may achieve greater professional success than is often the case for humans and the various trades they ply . . .

*

I assured them that I could step in and conduct the orchestra at a moment's notice, given what a music lover I was. It was—if I remember well—Verdi's *Requiem* that was to be performed. I make my way not into a concert hall but into a fairly large room longer than it is wide and arranged on an incline where the audience occupies the upper portion and the musicians are seated on the lower tiers. As I get ready to climb up on the podium, I realize that the canvas curtains that enclose it—whose cloth is rough and gray—will make it impossible for me to conduct. I have them removed. But I then realize that the podium has been set up backward: instead of facing the orchestra, I'm facing the audience. I decide that I will not proceed to conduct; one of the musicians can easily take my place, and things will work out just as well. Still, I am somewhat upset about not being able to profit from this opportunity.

A dream as clear as a mountain spring, easily interpretable without any recourse to a dream manual or a psychologist. The nature of the misfortune of which I dream matters little; what truly troubles me is my fear of becoming henceforth liable to all sorts of failures, and especially to that most crucial and most intimate of flops, the one that no inner verdict, be it intellectual or moral, can keep you from contemplating in dread.

*

The Seven of Ephesus, Sleeping Beauty, Rip van Winkle. In our nonlegendary lives, we do not reawaken after a century or two, but rather after twenty or twenty-five years or more . . . The liberation of Paris was yesterday, and I can't bring myself to imagine how the son or daughter whom my wife and I might have brought into the world back then could be of adult age today, or even a father or mother. When I mention something to someone much younger, something that I take to be part of our shared baggage of historical experiences, I always say—just to show that I am fully aware of our age difference—Well, you must have been so young that you perhaps can't remember this; but my wise note of caution often proves to be completely clueless, given that the event to which I'm alluding took place, say, ten years before my young interlocutor was even born.

Many of the objects that one chances upon in one's own home turn out to be incredibly out of date and no longer of any use at all, even though one had held on to them for immediate practical purposes: this telephone book, for example, or this booklet of train schedules, or this catalog, all of which no longer refer to anything one might seriously need, all of which have now been reduced to macabre residues, like the addresses of persons now dead left on a notecard or in a pocket agenda that has not been updated.

The same thing no doubt holds true for any number of ideas: neither swept away nor adjusted, they remain intact within us, if not forever, at least until that moment when an ancient idea rubs up against the reality of the present and produces an awful grating noise which bespeaks its anachronism and mercilessly tears away its veil.

Brutal unsealing of the eyes, earth-shattering awakening, given the disequilibrium created by the immense dead weight one had never suspected one was carrying around on one's shoulders.

*

As the Promised Land is to the Hebrews or the Land without Evil to the Guarani Indians . . . That there exists (or is taking shape) a land without blemishes or lacunae, this I need to believe. Life, otherwise, would seem a complete loss.

Even if this land were but a small island among others, the following would suffice: to know that it was a pilot capable of charting a course across God knows what misfortunes—wars, blockades, police operations, torture, blackmail, betrayal—and to recognize it if not precisely as the bearer then at least as the herald of a civilization far wiser than all of those that have taken historical or geographical place up to the present.

To want this is perhaps to count upon the coming of the Messiah. And besides, to speak of a land thus privileged, is this not immediately to invoke the Republic of Utopia? That a handful of human beings—men or women, whatever their origins—might be working toward this revolution, wouldn't this already represent a token of good luck or even (to give this a more opti- mistic turn, something I cannot resist doing) a promise?

This is my devout wish, but I'd also like to know whether these people will develop into something more than mere troublemakers and whether they will actually manage to take the reins of power while avoiding its perils, given that the more one schemes to hold on to power at all costs, the less legitimate it becomes. This would be most reassuring. But beware of falling into the disgraceful habit of using our conviction that the future already lies at hand as a way of justifying our inaction, beware of turning complacent, content to worship at the altar of such selected saints as Patrice Lumumba, Malcolm X, Che Guevara, and Ho Chi Min. We can't just allow these activists to wage their battles all on their own; to limit ourselves to merely expressing our full support for them is to retreat into a shameful version of quietism.

Paradise, Heavenly Jerusalem, El Dorado, the Land of Cockaigne, or that island that I once read about in a gorgeous illustrated book on which a shared mythology was built, that island on which (before it was visited by a steamboat bringing a reminder of the mercantile world beyond it) the white Macao was living out a perfect romance with Cosmage, his girl Friday, she with her tawny, almost naked body, a lively and shapely native girl, and he with his broad-brimmed planter's or convict's hat, loosely dressed in white linen: dreams that so resembled my dreams of a future society that I could place them in the same basket. If this were the sole dream I managed to hang on to tooth and nail, perhaps (who knows?) I might one day contribute to making it come true.

. . . But, it being admitted that this dream could become reality, who exactly are the pathfinders engaged in bringing this dream about, and should I decide to fully commit myself to the realization of this (another vexed question), are these model pathfinders really who I think they are, are they really doing the work I believe they are doing, and what exactly is this ill-defined species of work that I am labeling as "revolutionary"—which, if more fully exposed, might very well reveal itself to be incompatible with the work I personally don't want to give up on and which might perhaps even turn out to be the kind of work compromised by actions I would find it impossible not to con-demn? This monologue, whose sincerity seemed beyond doubt to me at first sight, does it merely constitute some sort of purely formal declaration—a statement of belief that commits you to nothing and thus merely serves as a precautionary performance (the way one might speak of a "bravura perfor-mance"), or is it possessed of some more useful intent? In short, does this declaration possess any meaning in and of itself, or is it just a simple set piece, a fancy series of clauses cooked up to fill the needed space on the page? A vague and pompous generalization not in the least concrete, as ac-ademic as the preliminary stitch pattern on a men's evening suit that hangs there, not yet fully tailored, on a coat stand or a valet? As I meditate upon this, pressing the nib of my pen into the paper, I have not been able—my use of the past tense is misleading here, for this lackluster string of words is only theoretically now behind me, given that, upon rereading it, I have continually been adjusting it, even to the extent of inserting this parenthesis here as a further second thought, and given that my race after words, which is just now beginning to hit its stride on this page, was already run several seasons ago (but when it comes to the writer who tells his own tale and who, wanting be truthful at all costs, adds to his telling the history of this telling, should he, if he wants to make a new start out of something he had been tempted to toss into the wastebasket and to which, having made further progress in the meantime, he now returns to file and polish even though this text had seemed untouchable because in citing it he had already consigned it to his archives, should he be so obsessively scrupulous as to limit himself to singling out and reassessing, in order to reject it or to be done with it altogether, any such sentence that seemed to relegate to the past this block of writing of which, without changing anything essential, several repeated strokes of the pen will have modified a number of the details, so that it would be henceforth difficult to argue that this block had remained substantially unaltered while at the same time not yet having become fully crystallized into something definitive and no longer subject to future change, a difficulty that logically requires that the allusion to the said passage come with some sort of explanation that, now less circumstantial, might justify the invention of a new verb tense that could simplify matters, *a nonabsolute past* or *an anticipated future* tense that would express neither the completed nor the noncompleted, but rather something incomplete that had only now been virtually brought to completion?)—to repeat, I have not been able, or per- haps, more to the point, I am not able, nor will I be able, nor will I ever have been able to make anything that is true or perceptible leap to life, I am not even able to impart facings or lapels or fancy stitchings to the evening suit hanging there with no other body to it than the ghost of a coat stand, nor am I even able to create the gleam of those scrubbed pots hanging there on a neutral kitchen wall . . . Items on show on a wall or page, or (given vol- ume) in a shopwindow or cage (planted in my head) or, better yet, in a bell- shaped display case (an object familiar to me from my museum work), not an underwater diving bell nor an aviary, but a translucent icebox, pedantic and refrigerated, whose broad surfaces of glass intersect at right angles, in- stead of being exhibited in something preferably more personal, something as openly intimate and commemorative as an attic: in one corner of the display case, a lovely little flower that popped up on the path of childhood; then its passionate blooming into a mushroom of light (say, a beautiful photo of Loïe Fuller, or the atomic explosion of the billowing swirls of a Spanish dancer); or, far closer by, the altar of melancholia (perhaps a tall jardinière or one of those prop columns used in photographs) upon which I lean as I engage in these reflections, I who over the course of several feverish days and nights would play out the following game, called forth by my current circumstances (given that I had been utterly seized by the ridiculous need to know whether, having been the recipient of some prize or special award, I might eventually enter into the honor roll of posterity, yet to be determined by a faceless, colorless jury, whose existence was therefore no more than allegorical)—namely, to imagine and to arrange my own commemorative showcase the way I might set up a Christmas crèche or a diorama.

In this space of display where chronicle and theory were supposed to meld together into myth and where the series of objects or other illustrations that typified my life were to serve a demonstrative rather than an exemplary purpose, who then was this *I*, this person I play, around whom everything was to take place? A little figurine fit to be placed on a wedding cake (taking his first Communion with candle and armband, displacing the bridegroom all decked out in black and his bride all draped in veils), it's perhaps him, this standard little cutout figure that one sees poised against a picture-postcard background of the past, pointing to a street in the heart of old Auteuil lined with drab housefronts (the sorts of places that drive one mad).

This whole display gradually emerges and spreads and takes on definition within the insomnias of night, here and there shimmering with unbelievably effulgent hues (I remember a scarf so green as to make you squint, worn around the neck by some masker or actor clad in white satin). A lengthy tale snakes its way across the entire display case, a chalky dotted line like the crumbs dropped by Tom Thumb, connecting the corner in which the small figurine has been placed to the corner where a mysterious black-and-white document lies, its pages warped and frayed, crumbling into the indescribable throes of beauty . . .

In one of the corners of the display, at the bottom of the case, the principle accessories of my first trip to Africa (a Sudanese satchel, a flyswatter, a classic pith helmet) and, not far from these, the blue revolutionary cap that I purchased in Peking for the national holiday, then the very loud shirt, a harlequin affair with a bright array of colors, that I bought for the Santiago de Cuba carnival (where the traditional festivities and the celebrations of revolution seemed to proceed hand in hand in the streets), and, here and there, turning the case into a vivarium without insects or an aquarium without fish, some tufts of that dry yellowish weed into which, over the course of our walks in the countryside, my companion Puck loves to stick his muzzle, lying on his side, wallowing on the ground, intensely snuffling this local opium, on which he gets high and from which he can be torn only once he has (as one might say) extracted his full dose—and loath to distance myself from this scene, reluctant to obliterate it by casting it into the past tense, I'm here registering this memory of Puck in the present, even though, since his initial appearance in these my written reveries, this all too imperious dog has been replaced by another one, who, I have to admit, is no more easy to handle.

Elsewhere in the display case, some ecclesiastical object of yesteryear—from the Notre-Dame d'Auteuil period of my childhood. Better yet, this secular object that my wife gave me on one of my birthdays or as a New Year's present and that is more precious to me, I know not why, than any other gift I've ever received, even though it's been a long time since I've put it to use, after having worn it every day to pin my collar together under my tie, or to fix into place those foulards one knots under one's shirt as casual vacation wear: a golden brooch—nothing special, but of British make, as befits my tastes—that I sometimes imagined as a future funerary ornament and that in my mind I caressed as a modern (extra-archaeological) f i b u l a, significant less as a piece of joinery, less as a means of clasping two opposite sides together without a gap, than as an object of pure and precious precision. Or this other token of friendship, in which my vanity as a collector takes real pride and that is like a stone marking a particularly critical moment in my life which occurred several years ago but from which I have now moved on: a cigarette lighter decorated with priapic scenes created by the man who, more than any other artist, has forever turned our vision of the world upside down by his revolutionary work, a pleasing amulet that he presented to me on the occasion of a surgical intervention into that part of the body we consider far more than a mere physical center.

Apart from the various books and office supplies and sundry paperwork (all the index cards, all the interminably revised manuscripts, all the hospital records dating from my pathetic attempt to put an end to my days), and without engaging in an intricate search for all those objects I have already mentioned without realizing that a number of them lie beyond my current reach, and apart from those trinkets (the scrapings from the bottom of a barrel that holds no scintillating treasures) that are neither works of art nor fetishes to which I would assign a particular power but that I need to have at my disposal here just to feel more assured, such as this desert rose that bears witness to my stay in the Sahara during the months of the "Phony War," or this lower jaw of a bull (La Corte 2641, killed at Nîmes on March 20, 1934, during the fifth act of a *corrida* witnessed by the friend who bestowed this trophy to me), or this starfish given to me by a surrealist fellow traveler whose passion for liberty led him to die as a martyr of the Resistance, or this piece of volcanic rock, which I cite only from memory, given that it was smashed during the renovations of my house (and probably consigned to the trash, with all the other rubble), or this dried seahorse, the sort that kids sell to tourists visiting Torcello on the long boat ride from Venice, or (making a concession to traditional superstition) these horseshoes that I tacked to the walls in the bedrooms where I sleep and write, both in Paris and in my country place—apart from these various items, to which I am today adding two images, one of which I have forgotten, even though I mentioned it some time ago, and the other an image that arrived on the scene after the initial rough draft of this text that I have so often corrected and revised and expanded that I feel an almost organic embarrassment about the discrepancy between the unfolding of its lines and the jolting rhythm of the thoughts that those lines were supposedly meant to register: the first, a flimsy pencil sketch dating from 1928 and entitled *My Life by Me* (to the left, my profile looking rightward toward a pyramid while, below, a gaze rises upward, issued from the single eye of a female profile slightly lying on its side and turned in the opposite direction of mine, its long, wavy hair in marked contrast to the hard outlines of the pyramid); the second, a photo (not in my possession) from the evening news in which I am shown at Ivry near a police van, having just been arrested, along with twenty young people whose grandfather I very well might have been, for having demonstrated in too unruly a fashion against the fact that the water and electricity had been cut in a housing project inhabited by immigrant workers from Mali after they had gone on a rent strike—apart from these various items (written or not written, fragments lifted from nature, iconographic documents, or human-made objects), most of which would be meaningful only to me or to other dreary imbibers of ink or aficionados of intellectual bric-a-brac, apart from this small and scattered handful of items, look as I may, I cannot figure out what this display case might further contain, its structure (or rather, its idea) having been suggested to me as I was recovering from a flu they claimed was Asiatic, perhaps occasioned by a period of overexertion on an exhibit that some of us at the Musée de l'Homme, together with younger volunteers, were trying to mount as a response to the street protests of the previous spring.

The theme of this exhibit was "Coming of Age," in our own as well as in other cultures, and one of my jobs (in which I was assisted by several younger friends, one of whom had been entrusted with the poetic composition of the space in which this idea would be made evident) was to come up with a display case whose nondiscursive rhetoric—in which things would speak louder than words while nonetheless eliciting their discreet support—would exhibit those ways in which the disciplining of the young and their insertion into society, either through rituals of initiation or through years in school, could often end up completely backfiring. As witnessed by some of the prime examples I had selected of exceptional breakings with the norm: Sade, Lacenaire, Rimbaud, and others whom I had personally known (Artaud, the most lucid of madmen, and Rigaut, whose vocation was suicide, the first represented by the reproduction of one of his self-portraits, in which he stares at himself as fearlessly as any draftsman in his mirror, the other represented by the photograph of the author in profile that served as the frontispiece to Rigaut's *Posthumous Papers* and by a rectangular looking glass without a frame, installed on an incline, unable to catch the reflection of any living being, given that in order to mirror oneself on its plane one would have to risk major damage to oneself after having crashed through the transparent wall of the display case with one's head or fist). These were the various spectacular exceptions to the rule of maturation that I had chosen to single out for exhibition, perhaps too extreme and too sui generis to be considered from the viewpoint of the revolution, but nonetheless striking in their idiosyncrasy (which was heightened by the isolation chambers into which they had been placed by my young friend who had designed the case). If it so happened that I was in turn to be summoned to represent a specimen of humankind, what would my curriculum vitae illustrate? Nothing out of the ordinary, despite its mixture of poetry, ethnography, and commitment to social progress; nothing, in short, that went beyond a certain openness of mind, joined by my refusal to take things for granted or to harbor any illusions about myself (praiseworthy qualities that in the end don't add up to very much, aware as I am that in order to take things to their conclusion you need to be carried away, body and soul, by an idée fixe); nothing, even if I were offered a number of second chances, that would justify my canonization or at least my inclusion in the list of illustrious *cases*. Whose destinies speak for themselves more than they need be spoken of . . .

Out of this actual display case, divided into a series of vertical pigeon-holes by large plywood panels whose deliberately sober and austere layout was designed to heighten the heterodoxy of its theme, had emerged another, fantasy display case, one of the many that I would regularly elaborate at night, creating the empty spots that would later be furnished at will, as I slid onto its brackets the thin slabs of glass shelving (chiseled, as it were, by diamonds) while my fever receded, abandoning me like a beach from which the sea retreats, leaving small islands in its wake . . .

As far as the eye can see, this beach—be it splashed by sun or rain— provides the locus of all my thirsts, all my anxieties, all my conjectures, all my litanies, all my pallid unfurlings of private standards. A desert beach, with nothing else built on it but the grass huts of my Robinsonnades.

... But —is this out of coquetry or priggery?—I pay conspicuous attention to the correct usage of verb tenses, I become conscience stricken when dealing with the tiniest lapses of grammar and spend hours trying to resolve them, playing the purist who doesn't want to be sullied by the slightest stylistic flaw and thus managing to avoid facing up to the real issue at hand. As if it constituted an end in itself that I am reluctant to abandon, day after day I waste my energy rounding out and putting the final touches on this narrative that I have already spent too much time ornamenting—patching it together, standing it up straight, and stuffing it with all sorts of random afterthoughts that in the end do more to block than to expand one's view of the horizon. Well, what it is that truly counts, my narrative as such, or rather its bedrock foundation, the things it does not say or only half says, or even sometimes the things (because still too undetected or embryonic) that can never be said at all? My cult of those figures I considered to be exceptions to the rule, comparable to the starstruck adoration of celebrities in today's culture. The desire to stay in the game, despite the ongoing temptation to get out. My intellectual and sexual hesitations as to this or that . . . And everything—for reasons often less than noble—that still impels me to temporize politically, even after I have lent my name to some public statement or signed on to causes that one couldn't possibly refuse to support: hesitations as to which of two tactics might be the better one, a dilemma all the more difficult to solve because in my pusillanimity I always shy away from the more dangerous course; it would be better to restrict myself to gathering all the information necessary to arrive at a rational rather than an emotional resolution of the debate at hand, but how boring this would be, what a waste of time! And I barely dare mention this other weakness of mine that has also cost me so much time: the minute I have agreed to run some risk, however minor it might be, my head begins to go into anxious overdrive. On the other hand, I am absolutely shameless when it comes to getting irritated with people who thoughtlessly interrupt the time I'm spending with myself with, say, their telephone calls (these days I have of course less cause to be irritated, for as I sit here revising this typescript I would be flattering myself if I still imagined myself to be the sort of person one might want to disturb) or other similar intrusions that cut into my schedule, given how I was always considered someone of good will, happy to be of whatever service. Against these interruptions I was helpless in Paris, hence my need (like a dog unwilling to give up his bone) to protect the nearly three full days per week that I would spend in the country, relaxing (not always a sure bet, because an obligation that you've managed to dodge often comes back to prey upon you, thus robbing you of the very leisure you hoped this would have guaranteed). If I really were a committed activist, ready to give up my life for the cause, I wouldn't be complaining about these minor encroachments on my time; instead, I'd be dealing with a constant stream of requests . . .

A hypocritical ploy: to register my belief in the revolution while claiming my adherence to poetry (that part of my life I pretend is too precious to be cut into), but whenever I'm writing I inevitably get lost in reflections that are far too pedestrian or in triturations of language that are far too sterile, yet any time I want to give myself over to action, I do practically nothing to bring about this revolution that, however cynical one might be, is certain to abolish the awfulness of things as they are, even if it risks ushering in (but who knows for sure?) another sort of awfulness. I may be but a mild fellow traveler of this revolution, yet I am nonetheless obsessed by it, and rather than spurring me on to thought, it merely preys upon my mind, rendering even more problematic those moments when it seems about to erupt . . .

Various ID photos that show me at different ages thumbtacked above a jumble of other items, or (perhaps a more radical and artful way of translating the idea of a life unraveling without its shape ever having been discovered), lined up side by side in chronological fashion and filling a series of cubbyholes arrayed in a band whose sole purpose is to illustrate the process of aging and that break up the inanity of a large void, this is perhaps what the outline of my private display case should involve—that is, if I were still dreaming about this poppycock project.

. . . But *you make your bed, you sleep in it,* so why kick up such a fuss about what I am in the first instance the most guilty of—namely, the fact that there has never (as it were) been a single sphere of activity in which I've paid the price that allows one to move beyond the misery of the human condition!

*

When speech is strangled by the pain it could transform.
When the male in me gags the female whose voice should be singing forth.
When the chestnut steed lumbers along like a workhorse.
When the attempt to undo the knot only makes it more difficult to untie.
When the hangover does not wait for drink to bring it on.
When the rose fades because it wished to look too fair.
When the sky becomes so thin it seems ready to break.
When the skin, now debaptized, never again feels naked.
When the torch is an oriflamme whose pole is rotten to the core.
When "Faites vos jeux" is heard as "Rien ne va plus."
When the fallen tree displays no more branches than its roots.
When the thunder turns into an upside-down umbrella.
When sorrow becomes a burning sun instead of resolving itself into rain.
When a thought taking its first steps becomes an old pair of shoes.
When the veins of marble crease the papier-mâché.
When you so ask yourself how that you forget to ask yourself why.
When your head, the only live thing left, is betrayed by the all too reasonable behavior of your sex.
When luxury is sacrificed to greed.
When in attempting to break your chains all you ever do is count their links.
When the withered leaf steps in for the spear.
When the anxiety that might invite suicide no longer leads to making love.
When the stomach is a sack instead of a temple.
When the words say midday but the acts say midnight.
When even the inside of your skull is going bald.

When the clawed replaces the manicured hand.

When the dog now barks only when hungry.

When the marriage of opposites engenders the golden mean.

When the spice so dries out it loses color.

When a firearm turns into a musical instrument.

When the bloodstain has become so oily it can no longer be seen.

When, to illuminate my now near-absent face, all that remains are these blind lines.

When the times are gone when one slipped out of one's fatigue like a snake from its skin.

When laziness becomes such a filthy thing it can no longer be rinsed away by water.

When you need to make an effort just to imagine yourself making an effort.

When you could care as little about the trace you might leave in your wake as about the name of Joan of Arc's steed.

When you blow upon what little remains of you as others blow on their fingers.

When you ask yourself which of the following arises from the other: the void within or the void without?

When life becomes so ridiculous that all you can do is joke about the death that awaits (good humoredly, and not as in "Fuck it all!" or "I'm taking a piss!").

When the tale comes to an end without the evil spell having been broken.

When I will have run out of time and no longer have the voice to cry out: "I loved Ophelia!"

When to say is no longer an empty expression, as in one could say that . . . or that is to say . . .

When the project one has decided to embark upon—to finish up once and for all—remains nothing but a projected project.

When the gulf between writing *and* doing *has become so wide that the entire dictionary tumbles in.*

When the stomatologist has placed the bridle between your teeth, and death in your oral cavity.

When no childish pleasure awaits us sooner *or* later.

When boredom becomes truly boring instead of a threatened cracking of the whip.

When, now lacking a needle, the compass can no longer panic.

When your lips are so sealed they could never let pass the final word that would allow you to die.

When the idea that there is nothing to complain about becomes another reason to complain.

When the sun beats down on its drum only with faint tappings.

When your witnesses have already died, leaving you there to duel on your own.

When, for want of fuel, your only recourse is to glide to the ground (for the love of art, given that, whatever you do, you'll end up crashing).

When you look around yourself without finding the words that used to escort you.

When I try to draw myself up to my true height, without towering any higher than my fifth-floor Paris apartment.

When death will have washed my hands, scrubbing them down to the bone.

When you can no longer can tell which there might relieve you of your disgust with here.

When this imaginary roof beam, despite all its former history, is no longer even a spider's thread.

When once the flame has died down and the earth is no more than a floor and the water is no more than something wet or something to drink and the air is this invisible thing you breathe in without so much as giving it a thought.

When, now almost entirely alone and seeing the world taking a direction opposite to the one you had hoped, you are seized with vertigo, as if standing high on a balcony whose railing has vanished into thin air.

When you realize that you are on the verge of crossing that line beyond which you find you have lost all your luggage and all your money has been stolen and you can't even remember what you did with your passport.

When the shared road takes such a fork that you realize you were not a pioneer but merely a member of the platoon of stragglers.

When you ask yourself what little tune could still be singing in your head.

When I will have finally gotten things off my chest without knowing their full extent.

When life has become so lackluster that you really have to be a bonehead to complain that one day you'll have to bid it adieu.

*

Writing, I seek shelter in the blank page, like an ostrich hiding its head in a bush, or rather as if this sheet of paper could establish a world without density, impervious to death. But isn't this world stripped of its standard three-dimensionality identical to the world of death? Thus, already posthumous, I would not be playing the ostrich but rather Gribouille, the rash fool.

Writing, paying not the least attention to my surroundings, not even to the furnishings of this room in which I live and work, I wash my hands of all the filth that fouls the world. But in so doing, I only get more ink on my fingers. What subterfuge would allow me to avoid even these stains?

A rash Gribouille or a cautious Pilate, or both at once, this is who I am when I think I'm playing my cards right by writing and when, much like my dog Puck standing on his hind legs, I stagger through my sacred dance with an earnestness that should make me laugh.

*

Message in a bottle,
Rabelais's divine bottle,
ink bottle,
Leyden bottle?

*

    I am so little possessed of authority or consistency that when it comes to the most ordinary of challenges I cannot measure up even to this modest victory: to somehow get this dog to listen to me, he who is so friendly to everyone else but so obstreperous to me (who is, because nominally his master, the major target of his humors).

    We race around in silly fantasias, I running after him brandishing his leather leash and he advancing and retreating or looping away to escape or leaping or flattening himself against the ground with a menacing air, always staying just out of reach (but not too far, for he would like to see this game go on forever). Such is the full extent of my attempt to police the movements of my new dog, Typhon, a boxer with a fairly dark striped coat, set off by socks and plastron of white, as well as a long streak that cuts vertically down his brow and then zigzags to the right cheek of his muzzle.

    In the company of this creature given over to licking, nibbling, wagging his docked tail, lifting or lowering his cropped ears, gazing pensively, twirling around, scampering about, raking my chest with his powerful forelegs (whose nails sometimes dig into my arms), in the company of this quadruped for whom a can of dog food is the high point of the day, providing his sense of smell with as many delights as I experience by my sense of sight or hearing, in the company of this garrulous beast who raises his voice when he wants to go outdoors and play, or else (if I'm trying to rein him in) to tell me *Just go ahead and try* or *I'll never let you get away with this*, of this mammal who grumbles when in need and who emits a sigh of relief when he has finally found a comfortable position in which to sleep, in all this I feel myself to be in the company of a being who resembles me and who, precisely because his reactions are prompter and his language simpler and his entire life briefer (even though there's a good chance I'll beat him to the finish line), represents (even though laughter, that most human of traits, is absent from his repertoire) a condensed version of what it is I am, a synopsis that I cannot contemplate without emotion, for the foreshortened biography of this creature (who will reach adulthood having maintained the sort of innocence one tends to attribute to children) seems to demonstrate to me, stripped of all embellishment and immediately legible at first sight, what it simply means to exist. Similarly, all our little conflicts appear to provide a summary version of my own struggles. I keep on rehashing the fact that I can't get him under control—which is perhaps all for the better, but nonetheless symptomatic . . .

To thrash around in the void. To pretend. To place as many barriers as possible between what is real and what is me, who is better suited to saying rather than doing and who prefers a literary mode of expression—because more distanced—to direct speech. And who tends to put on airs, well knowing (which is fairly grotesque) that there is nothing (or very little) behind them. Like someone whose voice is driven into a falsetto out of sheer anger, pitching his rage an octave too high because it would seem too controlled if kept low. Will I one day be unmasked? Will I fall to pieces under the eyes of those who know me? Will my writerly efforts to escape from this bind prove to be just another way of eluding detection and of delaying the obvious failure that was only too predictable from the very start?

For some time now, every morning before I absorb this gelcap (a philter whose solid state renders it almost imponderable) that allows me to bear up more or less bravely, especially when afflicted by something so inarticulate as to resist the provisional relief that words might provide, and that supplies me with the sole means of dissolving a sadness so nagging that its sobs can no longer be offset by orgasms, every morning (or almost) I inwardly melt into tears, mourning my effusions of yore and suffering all the more because in losing these I have lost the only true recourse against the suffering that their loss has inflicted on me.

True tears would no doubt be preferable to this private meltdown, a kind of inner seasickness betrayed only by the sour or sullen look on my face. If they poured forth freely, these tears would at least be possessed of some sort of veracity and would simply be what they are: namely, a sign of misery, and not the poisonous miasma of this measureless swamp created within me by the fictive humidity of my immaterial tears.

My physique (I have always seen myself as a cutout figure, unimproved by any regular exercise, someone who, were he a silhouette used for target practice, would fit into the less than virile outline of a lozenge rather than into a trapezoid whose broad shoulders would gradually taper off below, in Egyptian fashion) makes of me a nonviolent person, someone who will never know how to raise his voice into a tone of command, someone who could never crack a whip, someone who, if he doesn't want to build his life on a lie, needs to come to terms with the fact that his vocation lies in nonviolence.

But how espouse nonviolence without completely giving in to a world more and more dominated by the discourse of ogres, robots, newsprint thugs, and brainwashers?

*

The past few nights filled not even with images but with all sorts of murky thoughts turning on the idea of *making ends meet.*

"To make ends meet," not in the figurative language of a housewife trying to manage her budget, but literally: to force two separate things to bind together, the way a spacecraft that has just taken off from the surface of the moon (where its occupants, bounding around in their space suits, have finished making their observations and gathering their samples) now needs to dock with the other spacecraft, still in orbit.

Make which ends meet? No doubt, at this very moment, how to reconcile the governing idea of a text I am in the process of writing on Picasso with a subsequent realization that would seem to undercut my basic thesis, which means that I will have to revise, adjust, accommodate, or simply begin the thing all over again, but on what basis? More generally—in my own life and in this current work, which, having lost its urgency as the guide on which the direction of my life depended, now instead serves as its *Guide bleu* (offering a panorama or a reflection on the order of Pausanias's *Description of Greece*, said to be the most ancient example of a Baedeker), and with the help of which other readers, should they be curious, will be able to map out my life—to make these two absolutely opposite ends meet: social commitment on the one hand and, on the other, poetry, a stranger to all calculation and morality.

In my half sleep, the idea (less an idea than an imaginary course of action) of making ends meet took on various guises, involving any number of pairings that could be put into play or different operations that could be undertaken, all of which would be recognized as feasible conjunctures upon waking. All this, so complex and (as mentioned) so murky that I don't even feel I can reconstruct it. But I do remember that one of these dilemmas turned on the decision—I forget its precise terms—that the rock singer Johnny Hallyday had to face when he had to choose between two possible paths his musical career might take, one of which would have excluded the other and which he would have done better to combine, just as I in my own way never managed to stop mulling things over and, even though I was convinced I was almost getting there, never succeeded in conjoining one end to the other.

To make ends meet? Basically: to overcome those difficulties that exceed the scale of space travel and to succeed (if just barely) at ridding myself of this double-mindedness I hide under my hat—which forever makes me fall between two stools.

*

A random game involving
　　a pear sliced in two,
　　chalk and cheese,
　　somewhat but not too much,
　　a step forward a step back,
　　to cut losses to buy back,
　　obedience and rage,
　　highs and lows,
　　flames and extinguishers,
　　openings and retreats,
　　confessions and retractions,
　　Scottish showers,
　　reason and unreason,
　　hope and despair,
　　civic center and ghoulish dungeon,
　　affirmation and negation . . .
A tight game, no doubt. As happens when playing a double game.

*

"Arrigo Boito": a proud name, rugged as a rock, belonging to the librettist of the two Verdi works based on Shakespeare, *Othello* and *Falstaff*—and above all the name of the composer of *Mephistopheles*, an opera whose author was unknown to me but of whose existence I was aware ever since childhood, when I attended it one Sunday afternoon in the San Carlo theater in Naples, the standing-room-only crowd perhaps the result of the "working class" ticket prices advertised on the posters.

Driven by the same ambition as Goethe's—to marry classicism with Romanticism, Greek antiquity with the late Middle Ages—Boito fearlessly wanted to pack everything into this work, whose title honors the devilish acolyte whom God punished for his overweening pride, and this he wanted to achieve not only by blending Verdi with Wagner, Italian with German opera, but by bringing together the first and second parts of *Faust*, without omitting the "Prologue in Heaven," in which, after a pale scrim of clouds has lifted, the bass who sings the part of the Spirit of Evil launches his tenebrous voice into a tune that will be echoed by a choir of angels. In his voracious attempt to adapt all of *Faust*, Boito's initial version even included the "Prologue in the Theater," which he then had to cut in the subsequent version, whose spectacular effects still proved very expensive to stage. A whopping undertaking, whose creative frenzy is so overwhelming that one cannot decide whether in the end it is a work of beauty or simply an oddity. An undertaking that, after its initial scandal, never quite met with great success, this monster of a *Mephistopheles* was rarely performed abroad, even though it continued to attract decent audiences in its native Italy.

Was it Boito (who shied away from nothing) or was it the director of this San Carlo production who had decided that in the Walpurgis Night scene Mephistopheles would briefly hold aloft an enormous translucid ball in which any student of symbols would immediately recognize the earthly sphere, this metaphysical allusion being accompanied by the entrance of the corps de ballet, all suited up in white skeleton bones? Was it the respect for his source text or was it some pataphysical demon that drove Boito to light this scene with torrid Mediterranean light, featuring Faust and Mephistopheles dressed in medieval jerkins, shoulder to shoulder with ballerinas in Greek tunics and a Helen of Sparta (performed that day by an opulent brunet, half Circe, half gypsy) decked out in an ample gown with marmoreal pleats? But it's without irony that I want to evoke the opera's apotheosis (the way I might unabashedly recount an erotic episode inserted into a baroque dream): the last temptation of Faust, in which, as the scenery dissolves behind him, Mephistopheles presents him with a raft of half-naked females, who (once Faust has triumphed) then turn into a no less voluptuous congeries of women disguised as angels and equipped with long trumpets, a living cluster of bodies recalling those crazy sculptures in the Italian churches decorated by Bernini and other artists of the same period.

Even though by nature and by method I tend to think too big and to stretch my wings too wide, I sometimes tell myself that, bubbling over with the same creativity and willing to take on the same risks as the composer and librettist of *Mephistopheles*, I would one day like to stage an opera of this sort. Incorrigible Boito, whose final work—completed by others and performed when he could no longer hear a thing—was a *Nero* during which, like the fiddler emperor himself, one could be exhilarated (or so I imagine) by the hugely popular spectacle of Rome going up in flames!

*

"This innocence that lies too heavy on my breast . . ."

This is Orestes speaking in Racine's *Andromache* at the point when his love for Hermione has caused him to abandon his duties as the ambassador of the Greeks and to engage in a course of action that will eventually result in murder, leading to his disfavor in the eyes of the gods, a disfavor from which he had long suffered without really deserving it. How stupid to be innocent, given that one can be punished without committing a single crime!

But innocence is not a thing that one can easily rid oneself of. In polluting himself with blood, Orestes remains doubly innocent: his act is an error, resented by the woman whom he had hoped to satisfy by killing a king, and—still too much a novice to be a killer without remorse—he becomes the prey of the Furies.

Innocent from the very outset or guilty from the very outset, I shall never be rid of the idea of sin, convinced though I may be that I have freed myself from it, and this naïve conviction accounts for the fact that, be it in the domain of love, pure action, or literature, I have never been able to triumphantly do as I like without being assaulted by the Furies, so eager to rob me of any chance of victory.

As a lover (a subject that I find it difficult to permanently consign to the past), I bridle at the idea of adultery—the violation of an oath—just as I bridle at the eventuality of all the lies, large and small, that I will have to come up with. As a revolutionary (even if this ever so hackneyed term does not imply that one's primary raison d'être is the Revolution), I want to act, but—whether out of the fear of making a mistake or simply out of the fear of fear—whatever I do I only half do, unable to commit myself all the way and unable to simply cut my losses to avoid having a guilty conscience. As a writer, I hope no longer to confuse the white page with the confessional, but it is still to no avail that I try to honor a sentence I once noted down in the hope that it might help me sort things out: *Why insist on speaking nothing but the truth when so many things happen merely in the head or heart?* But this is not enough to rid me of my mania for truth, of my stern need to be sincere and exact to a fault: so heavy is its purchase on me and so deeply anchored in me are my fears of all the Erinyes-to-come that when I just want to let my pen go its own way, my imagination goes mum, for my heart is not in it.

Haunted in advance by all these phantoms who tear at me and slow my progress, am I anything other than a ham Orestes, his strings maliciously pulled by a Molière rather than a Racine?

(During my troubled periods, I sometimes liked to dream of myself as a Racinian Orestes, torn asunder by his furies. Too tragic to agree with the frightened Pierrot figure that I in fact was, a puppet in a moon-colored cloak and no muscle-bound hero. I therefore had to let the role go. But to rid myself of Orestes and Racine would involve ridding myself of the *weight of innocence*, something I wouldn't have imagined without them and an idea powerful enough to help me throw off my yoke and to allow me to create the foundation for this fragile edifice of lines I intend to let stand, committed as I am as a working writer not to destroy what it is I produce. Wanting to rectify things but reluctant to sacrifice Racine and his Orestes, I simply changed the lighting a bit, removing the purple glow in which this evocation of the Atreides was bathed and shifting my projector away from noble Racine to our officially recognized master of comedy, Molière, another leading light of the century of the Sun King and another of the classics we studied at school. In this I am a total conformist, an industrious student of my lessons in French literature, sworn to revere both unity and dignity of tone. But if I was so attached to the classics, it was also out of my purely childish desire to escape criticism and to acquire confidence by identifying with Orestes; pursued by a troupe of female monsters as lovely as a swarm of bees, he seemed to speak for me in the empyrean of high culture. But if I now still identify with Orestes, it would be only to parody my own empathy for him by declaiming—less out of madness than out of utter disorientation—his famous line, to which I give myself without qualification:

"And at last I bring her my heart on which to feed.")

*

That which one should forever leave unnamed, that which one should barely mention, even by periphrase . . .

A helmet of invisibility, hiding only tears.

A magic ring, changing a soul in despair into a sole to be repaired.

A perpetual lamp, illuminating only its own tomb.

A pilgrim's staff, knottier than a marshal's baton.

A sorcerer's wand, revealing everything it cannot plumb.

A crystal ball, so transparent that you can see in it only what you imagine.

A flying carpet, careering through time and space like a weaver's shuttle.

A knife that simultaneously stabs you and your attacker in the belly.

An arrow that pierces your flank without having to circle the earth.

A sword that cuts through a Gordian knot with a permanent deferment from the draft.

A billboard in front of a vacant lot on which it would be a good idea not to lay your eyes.

A candle whose flame flickers down the minute you place it in a holder.

A sphinx every answer to whom lands you in the lion's den.

A church without cross or vane, without baptismal font or tabernacle.

A burrow hollowed in the void to flee the void of that other burrow, hollowed out since time knows when.

A stone that transforms the undrinkable into potable gold.

*

A kind of huge spike—a cylinder or a parallelepiped beveled at one end—cast in a metal (or other substance) that shades toward black and that I know to be extraordinarily dense. Slanting at a forty-five-degree angle from the lower left to the upper right, with its beveled edge turned upward, it is placed in a milieu that is fairly solid but less compact and less dark than the body that lives within it (and this is all that I can say about it, for the question as to the exact nature of milieu did not come up when this object first appeared to me).

It was the incomparable *density* of this spike that made it so much more than a mere signifier of beauty—not the "equivalent" or "symptom" of beauty, but hiding within itself something that kept it slightly at a distance from being just that. Neither an allusion to, nor a symbol of, nor a substitute for beauty, this object was, in and of itself, *beauty*. There were no memorable events in this dream. Just this obsessive image of a spike, reinforced by what I imagined to be its immense weight and providing the kernel of all sorts of confused and fleeting thoughts.

Though this was not its ultimate source, this dream was occasioned by a conversation I had had with a young Caribbean friend of mine who, after finishing her studies at the École des langues orientales, was now working on a thesis about the aesthetic sense of the Woodabe herdsmen, relatives of the Peuls of Niger. As I saw it, she hadn't managed to effectively lay out the various facts and oral interviews that she had gathered to demonstrate just how sensitive to beauty these nomads in fact are despite the poverty of their artistic displays, nor had she managed to set out in a clear and concise fashion what beauty might mean to them. That very morning, I had met with her to give her thesis a second critical going-over, and all day long the theme of our two exchanges had continued to preoccupy me.

Despite its light dusting of sleep, in my dream I was no doubt wondering about the Woodabe's idea of beauty, something that still needed to be defined, and I was also thinking, insofar as my young friend was concerned, that the cornerstone of her argument was still too lacking in solidity or density to make it convincing. Throwing all pedantry to the wind and avoiding the staidness of ethnography, I think that at root this image that constituted the entirety of my dream was the concretization of something that I viscerally and urgently desire, while at the same time providing an incarnation of that golden rule I had interiorized yet now also realized I would never be fully able to follow, a reminder that the quality I wanted to achieve in my writing—the area of my current concern—was precisely the *cold ardor* that this dream object allowed me to recognize in all its beauty and density and whose very materiality, whether or not the product of metallurgy, evoked the idea of something tightly textured and worked by fire. In short, a dream image (without putting too fine a point on the logic it suggested) that could be said to illustrate a lack, in the form not of a hole but of a solid shape deeply encased within itself, the very thing of which we need to assure ourselves and the absence of which causes us such unbearable pain.

All other reasons aside, what I am above all looking for in my writings—independent of my desire to provide a few building blocks for a new ideology—is a kind of transfiguring focus on pain. And I hope that in the more exceptional moments of these acts of writing, which basically involve my responses to a lack, I reach the point where the very expression of this lack becomes inseparable from its possession . . .

Such are the incandescent (but ever so sporadic, ever so uncertain) moments that give me the same pleasure as this dream, so beautiful (to my eyes at least) in its concision and its density, enough to make me believe that here at one fell swoop and in unmediated fashion I was now face to face with *something on the order of the black idol—imaginary, of course—that could fill the void left by the absence of the god—now reduced to ashes, of course—that was once a fetish before becoming a puppet.*

*

How did nickel, this common metal, make its way into the adjective *nickelé*?

As a child I adored this word for its glint, its neatness, its rarity. Qualities absent from nickel coins, but here offered to the eye and ear by a silvery whistle, its shrillness conveying the quick cascade of helmet, breastplate, and trumpet in a cavalry parade. The same quality that as a young man I would appreciate in bars (with their intensely shiny bottles and glasses, their ice buckets and shakers free from condensation, their streamlined furnishings, their woodwork so waxed it was no longer wood) and in the acid sheen of jazz instruments (the slickness of a lacquered piano, the banjos, the brass, the hailstones on the drums). Qualities that I now more and more want to achieve in my writing, after having strayed so far afield from them . . .

Perhaps I would look upon death with a clearer eye if instead of being so fouled with filth, it instead fell as cleanly as a guillotine blade, resembling this hard, smooth, unnickable surface that I used to associate with the word *nickelé*—rotating like a lighthouse or a revolving door and emitting the same icy bolts of lightning as that starry silk top hat I am just as happy never to have owned.

*

In his tailcoat, patent leather shoes, and white tie, the image of the *noctambule*—almost that of Fantomas, were his black wolf not missing—still sets me to dreaming, a trace of my childhood in Auteuil, when the goings-on along the boulevards seemed as fabulous to me as the Thousand and One Nights. A twentieth-century version of the libertine in his red high heels, or of the Byronic debauchee drinking punch from a skull, or of Milord l'Arsouille or Dorian Gray cruising low dives. An embodiment of those pleasures one offers oneself, burning the candle at both ends while all the honest folk lie abed. I imagine a witches' sabbath where this insect in his black-and-white carapace, an outfit suitable for both celebration and mourning, would be rubbing shoulders with gamblers tempting their fate until dawn, leaving their tables only once they had made their fortune (soon to be unmade) or else ended up flat broke, or frequenting theater actors now stepping out of their roles in the dark and catching a late supper rather than dining out, or mingling with prostitutes engaged in changing night into day and day into night or with those drug addicts to whom it makes absolutely no difference what the sun or the moon might be shining down upon.

If I attach such a poetic value to this figure of the night owl, it's not only because he is located on the reverse side of daily life, but also because he thereby goes against the grain of the dominant morality that insists that one regulate one's acts in the name of some higher ideal, a morality that therefore cannot tolerate any periods of idleness in which the full spectrum of illusion and temptation might open up before one's eyes, a morality that always demands that things be planned out in advance, as opposed to those ephemeral joys that descend upon you as if you had just unexpectedly won a bet in a card game—all those poetic moments that come out of nowhere. And if the silhouette of this *noctambule*, all gussied up for his night out on the town, still exercises such a sway over my imagination, it's no doubt because what I see in him is not an effigy of wealth at its most sovereign and complacent, but rather a symbol of luxury in the truest sense, which involves throwing away all the money one has (or doesn't have), wasting one's time, and ruining one's health on worthless things while all the solid burghers out there are stuffing themselves with sleep.

As far as hoodlums are concerned, the night owl is protected from their attacks by his pocket derringer, his sword cane, and his expert knowledge of boxing or jujitsu; as concerns ragpickers, he likes to slum it with them by inviting them to a bottle of rotgut at the local bar; as concerns streetwalkers, he occasionally picks them up and, hiding behind an opaque mask, makes love to them in a trashy hotel room, on whose chest of drawers he will have deposited his top hat or else, in his great haste, he will have tossed it on an armchair—all these provide the foils for this figure who takes on his full meaning only via his encounters with the demimonde.

He is not even a character out of novel, for he is just a silhouette without depth, whom I can barely bring to life by evoking the errancies of Wilde's hero as an example. As a sadist, he besmirches those less fortunate with his luxury; as a masochist, he exposes himself to the injuries or dirty tricks provoked by his displays of luxury—a luxury he does not hesitate (so scandalously) to drag through the mud. Embodying both elegance and perdition, he oscillates between the princely pleasure-seeker and the disillusioned dandy, a Hamlet whose dressiness imparts just a touch of the macabre to him, and whose further caricature might be found in the figure of Baron Samedi—in Haitian voodoo lore the patron spirit of cemeteries—all decked out in his Sunday finery.

An anachronism, this nightbird dressed to the nines perhaps goes on living within me only because so untimely, so obsolete. In the end, he remains primarily valid as a stereotype illustrating everything that is offbeat or *warped* about the poet, pursued as he is by a cortege of demons, if indeed it be true that in his vocation to go beyond all bounds he needs to make the acquaintance of the darker powers. Otherwise he would just end up serving the Good, observing the iron rule of utility and common sense, whereas his artistry demands that he also play the role of the whore, of the histrio, of the madman profiting from his folly, or of the magician forever part charlatan rather than priest or leader—this great lord and outcast cloaked in the magic he pulls from his pockets, a treasure beyond measure yet also palpably a farce. As my desire to "change life" (Rimbaud) became more lucidly insistent, my former ideals became less absolute and the project of bettering our common condition began to outpace my private need to rebel against morality or to escape from it altogether by systematically compromising myself with Evil (or at least what my years of catechism had taught me to consider as such).

The word infinite *can be fittingly uttered only by a young gentlemen of the Louis XIII era, dressed in furs and blond of hair.* I think of this statement of Mallarmé's whenever I try to explain to myself the aura that still surrounds this young gentleman with his clean-shaven face, wearing his tailcoat, his patent leather shoes, and his white tie, for whom the nightclubs of Montmartre seemed to provide substitutes for the castles of the Louis XIII period just as the ennui he could not dispel seemed to act a substitute for the infinite.

*

To weep bluely,
to laugh yellowly,
to rage redly

To love violetly, indigoly, greenly, orangely.

To dream whitely,
to scream blackly.

*

If by shoring up my memory my writings keep me from dissolving, the role they thereby serve becomes utterly worthless the minute they too escape my recollection, as is the case today.

A black swan, this: the unforgettable brief turn of phrase that might capture—in distilled form—everything essential . . .

*

Did this prefigure, charged with a meaning of which I was unaware, what would later come to define not merely a phase but an entire aspect of my life?

When I was very young and my sister would tell me about the "egg dance" scene in the comic opera *Mignon* (whose libretto was indirectly inspired by an episode in Goethe's *Wilhelm Meister*), I was filled with sympathy and, believing that I might one day have to undergo this trial myself, seized by anxiety. There was this poor little girl, a captive of the Gypsies who were eager to earn a few pennies by putting her on display, made to dance around this tiny space strewn with eggs without breaking a single one of them and, should she fail, threatened with punishment once the audience had left and no one would witness the cruel beating she would receive.

I certainly do not run the risk of this kind of physical punishment, for when I fail at some feat, the only person who whips or beats me back into shape is me. But even in my sleep, I am forever pursued by the fear that I will foul up the inner acrobatics required by my number.

*

In the Amsterdam neighborhood where the sailors go out on the town, not far from the old Jewish Quarter and the Rembrandt House, there are two pickup joints, one right next to the other: the Butterfly Concert and the Café Traviata, their facades both brightly lit. In Copenhagen, right near a public garden, sitting on a rock where she seems to be taking a rest after emerging from the sea, is the Little Mermaid of the Andersen tale, as large as life and now almost a pilgrimage site: cars come to a stop, pedestrians approach, and Japanese and other Asian tourists can be seen earnestly snapping pictures of this little nude whose girlish body is presented in all its simple freshness and whose nonhuman half is so faithfully reproduced that one can almost count its fish scales. At Longjumeau, cast in bronze, the dashing little Coachman stands there in his conical hat (in the *Courrier de Lyon* style) and his top boots, a somewhat forgotten character from an old opera but who remains there firmly anchored on his plinth like a local celebrity. In many plazas de toros in the South of France, the "Overture" to *Carmen* is blared out not as a symphonic composition but as an authentically Spanish piece of bullfighting music that accompanies the parade of brightly spangled participants. Such are the effects of glory! And which artist or writer wouldn't want to have at least one of his works, even if displayed in the cramped confines of a provincial town, achieve the legendary status of the works of Andersen, Bizet, Verdi, Puccini, or this other author whose name escapes me: the composer of *The Postilion of Longjumeau*, a comic opera no doubt famous in its day but which remains a mere title to me (I have never seen it performed, and if I happen to have heard fragments of it, I probably had no idea to what they belonged).

That a work of whatever sort should leave the sphere of art and join up with life, bravo! But there is better yet. Sometimes the brainchild of a novelist, a playwright, or an opera composer acquires such credibility that one almost forgets that at the outset the thing was largely if not entirely fictional. The locus that provided the theatrical setting for an action that was more or less imaginary (be it a complete fabrication or borrowed from tradition) is in turn transformed into a genuinely historical site, as if this action, now rendered true, had henceforth planted its solid roots in a topological ground that was thereby transfigured.

Thus it is when in Marseilles one visits the dungeon of the count of Monte-Cristo (the jewel of the château d'If), or when in Nagasaki the house of Madame Butterfly. Just as in Rome you can visit the terrace of the Sant'Angelo castle—the very one from which La Tosca, pursued by henchmen, threw herself into the void—and also see the wall where Mario Cavaradossi was shot to death. In Sicily, in the town of Vizzini, they sell postcards that picture the square where the church and the peasant dwelling stand facing each other, just as they do in the stage setting of *Cavalleria rusticana*. In the forest of Fontainebleau there is a path that runs between a double row of rocks meant to evoke the megaliths of Celtic landscapes, a path that is called "Norma's Way." In Venice, the gondoliers on the Grand Canal will point out to their passengers Desdemona's house, a tiny Renaissance palazzo two rooms of which the management of the Grand Hotel (which annexed it several years ago) has furnished in period decor. In Mantua there is not only a so-called Casa Rigoletto near the ducal palace, but also another building that Hugo's very French play *The King Amuses Himself* inspired Verdi to create: namely, the Sparafucile inn, situated on the other side of the river. Sheep graze around this decrepit building, but nothing about it, other than its isolated setting and its romantic allure as a ruin, could remind one of the sinister cutthroat Paris inn that the criminal, named Saltadil by Hugo, ran with his sister. In Verona, Shakespearean drama has taken pride of place in several areas of the city: Friar Laurence's cloister, destroyed by bombs during the Second World War but since reconstructed, where they house doves whose whiteness inspires the tender gazes of honeymoon couples apparently unaware of the flagrant brand-newness of the monument; the chapel (a baroque one, by the way) where the aged friar married the two lovers in secret; Juliet's tomb and, in another neighborhood, her balcony (on the second floor of a building that houses the offices of the chamber of commerce); and elsewhere, Romeo's house, the latest of these tourist attractions, as a skeptical citizen informed me when I was visiting Verona. In Denmark, at Helsingør (Hamlet's Elsinore), the fortress is equipped

with a "battery" some two or three centuries old, and it is commonly acknowl-
edged that it was upon these ramparts (which don't even date back to the
Elizabethan Age) that the ghost of the murdered father wandered in search
of vengeance; a sentinel is posted on these ramparts, and when a visitor appears he presents his arms with such gravity and righteousness that the latter
is convinced that he is being saluted (in a long-ago era that was already the
distant past for Shakespeare) as some Marcellus or Bernardo, or even as the
heroic princeling himself, his friend Horatio, or his father's ghost. Finally, at
Leipzig, Auerbach's Inn, which today owes its fame to Goethe's *Faust*, was
the locus for a curiously circular game that played itself out in the following
order: a painting, a legend rooted in a precise place, a play, then a painting
again. The interior walls of this inn are decorated with large, relatively recent
compositions that illustrate various episodes drawn from the first and second
parts of Goethe's drama, which (as everybody knows) was built on the legend
of Doctor Faust and one of whose early scenes shows this philosopher who was
so eager to know the world now visiting this cellar tavern and joining in with
the revelers who are drinking all the wines their hearts could desire, magically
offered to them by his demonic companion. If Goethe, on whom so many
artists and musicians in turn would build, took this low-life detail supplied by
folklore as the basis for his scene, this aspect of the Faust legend in fact had
its (as it were, chance) origins in a work of art, for as the modern tourist who
lunches or dines at Auerbach's Inn will learn upon reading the brief history
of the place appended to the menu, the pictorial tradition on which Goethe
based his drunken revels was as follows: at some previous point, a painter who
was trying to publicize the place had decided to show Doctor Faust, who was
already something of a mythological hero, making merry in the tavern like
some Bacchus astride a barrel. As it turns out, this part of Faust's legend grew
out of an artwork, and not the other way around: because some ingenious
painter had the idea of including him in a mural on these cellar walls, it
became a folk tradition that Faust had indeed gone carousing at Auerbach's.
Then, with Goethe, there is a return to a professional playwright's handling
of this scene, which in turn generated all the mediocre academic paintings
which I inspected, not without a certain malicious pleasure, the single time
that I took a meal at this celebrated establishment.

Art, legend, reality . . . I here note down these words in their alphabetical
order, not knowing which laws of precedence should govern their enumera-
tion. If the (merely picturesque) reality of a tavern in Leipzig wears the halo of
legend, it owes this aggrandizement to a mural that was conceived primarily
for promotional purposes, something on the order of a billboard or a poster;

but this halo would never have expanded if Goethe's art had not been visited upon it. Taken up by Shakespeare, the story of Juliet became so real as to end up as a tomb, one that in fact most likely belonged to a young girl of Verona, whose name remains unknown. Without the dramatis persona who perpetuated the memory of Macbeth, a king whose reign would otherwise have been relegated to the dust of chronicles, would the traveler to Inverness think of climbing the hill near the railway station to visit the residential area that is said to house one of the castles of this usurper, a fortress of which not a single stone remains but that seems to mark this location as tenaciously as the spot of blood on Lady Macbeth's hand? But then again, just as one sells one's soul to the devil in exchange for fortune or power, perhaps Shakespeare did in fact trade his own existence for the life that so miraculously animates his creations. So profuse was his genius that many came to doubt his very identity, wondering how so modest an actor could be possessed of such outsize talents. Isn't it therefore possible that Shakespeare himself, this incredible creator of a plethora of characters so fantastically alive, might have begun to doubt his own existence?

But this reality that a work of art can end up assuming—as an invention that has henceforth entered into the realm of fact, regardless of its original time or place, and whose contours are far firmer than the figure of its inventor—is just a catchpenny reality: a bit of raw material mostly made up of smoke and mirrors, on which our dreams alight, investing it with the glamour of a diamond.

But here's a jewel that's far more real, for the dreams it inspires seem to inhere in its very nature: this manatee in the Dakar zoo, sloshing around in a pool that seems to have been especially dug to its size, vague in its dimensions, as if it had not yet completely emerged from its primeval slime, a kind of huge tadpole still in the process of maturing, an awkward giant, more mossy than scaly or furry, in fact a mammal, kindred cousin to the seal, and perhaps the progenitor of the sirens, the undines, and the rusalki, known in Africa as a "sea mother" because believed to be a genius of the waters capable of transforming herself into a seductive long-haired maiden fatal to those—fisherman and others—who dare disturb the peace of her backwater pools.

A flawless masterpiece that owes nothing to dream or invention, because it provides such a true image of its own defunct yet fascinating reality: embalmed like a saint and preserved in the cool of his mausoleum on Moscow's Red Square, Lenin lies there in his black workaday suit, a titan with no more legendary accoutrements than a minor office manager.

*

This piece of writing, too waxed, too polished to allow my cry to crackle forth!

This memoir that so poorly mends the tatters of my memory!

This plural essay in which I again and again try to open many a door with many a key!

Sort out, caress, marry the words together; at times dissect them, twist them, break them apart. Not to seduce them or mock them, but as a way—needless to say, an illusory way—of appeasing, of turning around, of putting a stop to something inevitable. As a way—despite all its weaknesses, all its blemishes, all its lacunae—of conveying the fact that somewhere within ourselves it still might be possible to get a grip on things . . .

If this did not involve asking for the moon (for there are afflictions that nothing can cure and that only poetry can help you come to terms with), what I would hope for—in some future I shall never know—is the establishment of a society in which birds of my feather, should such still exist, would no longer have to have recourse to these sorts of subterfuges.

*

At the Ideal Hotel the chambermaids do not speak your language yet still manage to pamper you with their chatter. And if the switchboard operator, far more competent in these matters, doesn't have the time to engage even in the briefest of chats, her voice is so sweet that the few words she does exchange with you count as much as a long and tender conversation.

At the hotel's restaurant, where unaccompanied guests who don't want to eat alone can take advantage of a *table d'hôte* (more or less large according to the number of diners but invariably round to facilitate conversation), there is no need to study the menu: at lunch or dinner, the "chef's surprise" will be delivered straight to your table, whether private or not, observing your dietary restrictions if necessary, with you always being perfectly content with what you have been served.

At the Ideal Hotel you'll believe that the entire staff is on holiday just as you are. Smiles all around, the service so smooth and so quietly efficient that it would be an insult not to ask to be waited upon.

Whatever floor your room might be located on and whatever side your windows might face, at the Ideal Hotel you will always have a clear view of the sky—whether it be in the hotel's modern and perfectly well-appointed wing or in its historical landmark portion, which is all the more sought after because it is so pleasantly run down and because within its confines space has been so gratuitously wasted on large rooms that seem to serve no precise purpose and on unlikely hidden nooks and crannies, the whole strange building cut up by unexpected changes in level and featuring tall windows behind which silhouettes occasionally float by, causing the locals to imagine it is haunted by all sorts of White Ladies, Surly Monks, and Bloody Nuns. So that you might enjoy the perfect peace of this corner of the universe so untroubled by earthquakes, floods, tornadoes, and forest fires, the hotel's concierge is careful to deliver your mail to you only upon your express written consent; and if he does so, it will be only in dribs and drabs, so afraid is he of becoming the bearer of bad news.

In this establishment whose peace would be disturbed if the echoes of wars, revolutions, and other disturbances were allowed to interrupt its calm, there is hardly a newspaper to be seen. There's an out-of-the-way room that does indeed contain a television, but it is sought out only by those who are bored or incorrigible—those who wander around without ever finding a spot to settle down or those eager for their latest dose of antiseptically filtered news.

At the Ideal Hotel, if you open the drawer of your bedside table you will find not a Bible but some unknown or little-known work that you are certain never to have read and whose discovery fills you with delight. Otherwise, however late the hour, you can always have access to the hotel library, whose manager (so expert a psychologist that he or she can immediately recognize what it is you might require by the tone of your voice on the telephone) will be all too glad to make a recommendation.

In this hotel you will find the reading room filled with magazines you can agreeably leaf through, as well as everything you might need for writing: standard fountain pens, ballpoint pens, typewriters with a variety of keyboards, stationery in all sorts of formats, weights, and colors (with or without letter-head), and even the butcher paper favored by snobs, as well as a full panoply of postcards so alluring as to make you want to visit all the nearby surroundings and thus extend your stay. In addition, a sizable gathering of dictionaries and grammar manuals to allow you to avoid spelling mistakes in whatever language it is you are writing.

At the Ideal Hotel, all the recreational activities have been provided for, be they on an individual or group basis, tailored to the specific tastes of the guest (who is presumed to be enough of a grown-up to attend to his or her carnal diversions without any help). Without your having to formulate your slightest desire, room service will deliver your breakfast and announce the day's program, a program appropriate to everything that is known about you, deduced from a sample of your handwriting (taken from the form you filled out when checking in) that has been expertly analyzed by a graphologist. This program, as judiciously constructed as any preestablished sequence of activities could be, is announced to you in such a pleasant fashion that never for a second would you think of taking advantage of the freedom that you enjoy (of course!) to decline the proposal.

On the grounds of the Ideal Hotel or in its nearby surroundings, guests are free to engage in their favorite games or athletic activities. The swimming pool, however, presents a problem that has not yet been resolved: for those wanting to use the pool, it would of course be better to have it just next to the hotel, but then how hide from view those individuals whose swimming outfits might be perceived by the rest of the guests as aesthetically violating the propriety of the place, or else as obscene reminders of what they see when looking at themselves stark naked in the mirror?

Also still under study is the disposition of the gyms dedicated to both physical and spiritual exercises: Swedish gymnastics and yoga, for example, as well as whirling dervish dances and all the various practices of trance and meditation.

At the Ideal Hotel, the discotheque is open all night, and everyone considers it quite normal if an insomniac in his dressing gown and pajamas should drop by its bar to get dead drunk, several members of the staff being on duty should the need arise to transport him on a stretcher to the recovery room, from which they will then escort him back to his suite even if he insists on returning to the bar (a measure taken for no doubt paternalistic motives but executed with such finesse that none of the involved would think of taking any offense).

At the Ideal Hotel, should a nightmare cause you to cry out in fright, nobody will hear, for your room has been so well insulated that your neighbors will never have to wash their hands when faced with what might occur within its four walls. But the following morning, if you so wish, you are free to recount your bad dream to the concierge when handing over your key. The longtime beneficiary of a corporate Pentecost that enables him to speak in every tongue of the Tower of Babel over which he stands guard and therefore gifted with an extraordinary ability to tune in to his clients, he will listen to you and perhaps gratify you with some sympathetic or witty insight into your dream, or perhaps he will cite a proverb from his homeland that will help you unlock its meaning. This shepherd of a flock that is less heterogeneous at root than it appears to be on the surface has no equal when it comes to comforting, regardless of the person's nationality or faith, someone who has lost huge sums at the gambling tables and to dissuading him from committing suicide, an accident that would do great harm to the hotel's good name—as would any death, for that matter, hence all the efforts to throw a veil of secrecy over this eventuality and all the diplomatic maneuvers to make sure that the nearest of kin, should there be any in residence, behave themselves in the unobtrusive manner one fully expects from people of their breeding.

At the Ideal Hotel, tipping is not permitted, but you can express your friendly appreciation—tactfully, neither too much nor too little, just enough not to appear too distant or too bent on popularity—by recognizing those small services that went above and beyond your expectations.

As for your bill, you can settle it whensoever you wish, if you are a frequent guest or the friend of one, and upon its payment the establishment will extend its thanks as if this constituted an outright gift, no matter how ordinary a client you might be.

The Ideal Hotel is a place in which you would like to spend your entire life, free from all cares and remorse. But if, nothing having called you away, you prolong your stay beyond several weeks, the hotel management will see to it that you are gently reminded—by telling you how pleased it is at the prospect of new arrivals or, somewhat more subtly, by placing a bouquet of flowers in your room identical to the one that welcomed you when you first registered—that you would have to be a complete egotist to refuse to give up your place to a subsequent guest. Should you prove tone deaf to all these requests or should you obstinately ignore them even as you are being presented with the guest book on whose pages everyone is democratically invited to leave behind a few thoughts upon signing out, you risk returning to your room one evening and seeing that all its closets have been emptied and all your suitcases have been packed. And if, still recalcitrant, you decide to unpack your suitcases and put everything back where it was, a narcotic shot will be administered to you by a nurse so ingeniously disguised and so charming and so expert that you won't even know what hit you, and you won't again regain consciousness (or perhaps not?) until you find yourself in the airplane taking you back home, unless—and this is a transmigration sometimes accorded to first-class guests, albeit a mere reprieve that allows you to take one step back in order to leap forward—it turns out that you have woken up in a hotel that is part of the same chain but that is a thousand leagues away from the first one, in a place you never had any intention of going.

By an agreement negotiated in advance, a similar shot could be administered to any individual who might prefer to sleep like a log rather than suffer the throes of a parenthesis that was ineluctably coming to an end.

Relatively simple when involving the stubbornness of merely a single traveler, the question becomes far more complicated should a couple be involved, and even more so if that couple should have children (given that the shots will have to be administered to several patients without awakening anybody's suspicions). The method to be employed in these cases is still under study: perhaps a squad of trained nurses all operating in concert?

*

When Whites as a race finally also come to be considered as nothing more than "overgrown children."

When CEOs are now history, like pharaohs.

When woman (on what mantlepiece?) is no more than the pendant of man.

When the noblest of jobs is to be a cop.

When soldiers come to be extras in musicals.

When priests are content to act merely as undertakers.

When the mad become court fools adulated by entire kingdoms of kings.

When bandits seem no more than incorrigible brats.

When workers and peasants come to blows only in sport.

When whores come to be saints, bringing consolation to the lonely.

When death is no longer a bigger deal than birth.

When those we call "poets" are relabeled "long-term mercy killers."

When everybody speaks according to their own dictionary, certain to be understood.

When coupling to procreate becomes the most extreme of vices.

When love will be made everywhere, except in bed.

When ads tease your desire without offering any product in return.

When the wind rose replaces the red star as hammer and sickle did the cross.

*

I don't remember how the author of a piece I read in *Le Monde* one or two years ago, one of whose sentences especially struck me, had described (if in fact he did describe it) the room in which this torero, an old acquaintance of his, received him shortly after having performed his farewell corrida, where, as the sole matador featured that day, he had put the sword to six toros. I see, at the very heart of Madrid, a very large and somber high-ceilinged room, a decor fit for the musings of a Philip II helpless against the vapors of his night-time solitude—such as Verdi shows him in *Don Carlos*, dreaming amid the wood-paneled walls of his Escorial chambers—or fit for the brooding of an Igitur, standing there like a faint ramrod *i* in his tights and seeming to be uttering "To be or not to be" in his timeless presence as a single shadow summing up all the midnight that surrounds him . . .

When the sportswriter asked the bullfighter what he was now going to do after his retirement, the latter had replied: "I will have to learn to be nothing anymore." A lesser figure than his older brother Manolo—who had been felled by a deadly sickness before retirement age—Antonio Bienvenida had left behind him the memory of a very elegant and knowledgeable torero, and in fact the image of the success he had been at his very best should certainly prove to be lasting, given how beautiful his final performance turned out to be. Not only did he insist on delivering all the coups de grâce himself, but in addition—according to the sportswriter's article—he had dealt with his six adversaries with extraordinary skill and insistence as he brought his career to a glorious and definitive close; there was therefore no reason to suspect that he might wrongly return to the ring a few years later, either because he needed the money or out of some nostalgia for the fight or because of public demand.

From here on in, he would no longer be anybody any longer, and he would have to get used to the fact. A crepuscular insight on his part, along the lines of (or so it might seem) "I am nothing but dust" — a notion probably familiar to this Spanish Catholic, and a practicing one at that (like most of the members of his profession), whom one can well imagine crossing himself to ward off misfortune each time he entered the plaza. But to say of oneself that one will have to get used to being nothing, is this not to maintain that one once was something — and doesn't this suggest something other than a simple resignation to the fate one shares with everyone else, doesn't this instead point to the overweening pride of someone who knows he has now rejoined the common ranks but who will never forget that there was a time when he occupied a place well beyond the ordinary run?

No doubt that in saying these words Antonio Bienvenida thought he was merely being modest or devoutly Christian. But weren't his thoughts, at some deeper level, turned elsewhere? The wheel of fortune, whose whims can make of you a king who has been dethroned, a criminal who has been absolved, a leader who has been dismissed, or a traitor who has been rehabilitated. The world as a closed field in which even the strongest of combatants will someday see his star fade. A place in which inconstancy and fantasy rule behind the scenes. A marionette theater in which all the characters — serious or comic — speak in borrowed voices and, as they await their withdrawal into the shadows, strut and fret their hour upon the stage as chance would dictate. Despite the initial moments of confusion, the knell is tolled by the Bible verse's ironic view of the way things will turn out for anybody who dares think of himself as a king raised upon a shield.

It was quite graciously, as befitted a man whose trade had made of him a prince, that this celebrity had agreed to become no more than a random individual. Tucked away in a closet were his array of suits of lights, and hanging on his walls as trophies the heads of several of the bulls that had earned him his fame in his early years, and in addition to these (one well imagines), stacks of newspapers and photos — all bearing witness to the artist he once was. But bearing witness only to himself and his kin, in the confines of his home. Consigned to the mists of memory by those who celebrated him, he would soon be no more than an ancestor figure, still loved and respected by his immediate entourage but nevertheless having lost his halo, someone of whom one no longer expected anything, neither victory nor the actual bloody consequences of the menace he faced. The worst, perhaps: to be somebody to whom nothing more can happen, except to die in one's bed or by pure accident, or to fall the anonymous victim to who knows what cataclysm.

But to be this man no longer in the running, for whom the wheel of fortune has now turned and for whom the only thing left is to descend the stairway of the years—to no longer be anything, in the sense that Antonio Bienvenida meant it, still involves being a great deal. The ultimate decline—which artists of every kind all have to admit as a possibility—would involve the following:

to no longer be able to live on in memory;

to no longer exist behind one's eyes or in the hollows of one's ears;

to be even less than alone;

to no longer have a today, yesterday, or tomorrow;

to no longer be in debt, having returned everything you were loaned;

having seized the tangent on the face of the clock, to discover by chance—in that whiteness where all colors cancel each other out—a spotless innocence that lies even beyond the reach of the village idiot, an innocence in which one exists (if indeed one still vicariously exists in the minds of a few others) without knowing or doing or feeling anything;

hypothetically, to speak behind the scenes, or rather by traces, to the past—as long as such traces exist, whatever the forms they might take;

to manifest oneself only via one's archives (which will then also turn to dust and thus be duly forgotten by one and all);

to be seen from the angle that one would have refused when one was alive (as if rabbits were sitting in your judgment), and then to be no longer seen at all;

to deteriorate by stages, the final one involving the absence of any intelligible residue, accompanied by the absence of anybody aware of anything at all.

Thus, to no longer exist on one's own or by an intermediary. To be beyond the verb *to be* and even the adverb *beyond*, with all the workings of language abolished—not even any of those shrieks or tattered shreds of words or roars or meows captured by the electronic jungle—now that there is nobody left to express anything whatsoever. To have reached the point that resists all toponymy (including this attempt to describe it, if only to achieve some sort of abstract mastery over it), the point that could be emblematized—the phantom coat of arms of a phantom city—only by a zero shorn of its two syllables and of the circle that provides its image. And at the very end of this long downward spiral, to say an all too lucid farewell to one's virility and to all those who, now left behind on the other side, might have allowed one to cross the sharp edge of death with less terror

—the loss, one by one, of those who understood you implicitly, struggling for breath in the attempt to make oneself understood,

everything that one once loved (or practiced) in all its newness now turning into obsolete folklore,

ruination of desire, bundled up like a mummy in its bandages or cut off from its deepest springs,

physical decay,

a level of disintegration of meaning that at every moment one discovers a snag in one's head that one anxiously hopes will be mended (a hole dug by a name one has forgotten, a word escaping and then returning too late to say what one wanted to say), one's eyes similarly diminished and unable to get a direct purchase on things (but instead creating a distance from them by the fog they interpose), the eyelids heavy with uneasy sleep, one's thoughts all rusty and functioning only intermittently, giving one the sensation that they will soon run down completely—

to have reached, stage by stage, the outer limit of the *hereafter*, that intense inane into which this fallen world, the faithless custodian of our remains, will have deposited us: a void with no witnesses, a silence uninterrupted by the buzz of a single fly, and in which the fact of having been a somebody or a nobody makes no more difference to the hypothetical observer than those equations erased from the blackboard by a sponge or those traces left in the empty air by a bullfighter's passes of the cape or other suertes in a now deserted arena . . .

But it seems rather unlikely that the words uttered by Antonio Bienvenida over the course of a casual interview were intended as a bitter invitation to engage in a Hamletic meditation on that coming wasteland bereft even of the sand that would make of it a veritable desert. If his statement *I will have to learn to be nothing anymore* can teach us anything without forcing the issue, would it not mean that one should act as if nothing were instead of going to pieces, difficult though it might be—for someone who was or thought of himself as a star—to fall back into the shadow of a life without éclat or—for someone who wants to see things even more clearly—to know that you won't even be a memory or a fossilized bit of detritus when this world (or whatever inconceivable realm that replaces it) no longer contains anything whatsoever that might be susceptible to identification?

Was he speaking of learning to be nothing anymore because he was in fact aware of how difficult it would be to master this? Would financial difficulties or the simple lure of money have any effect on his decision? Would he give in to nostalgia, or would he, out of sheer courtesy, briefly come out of retirement just to ritually consecrate some younger matador? I read in *Le Figaro* that the day after tomorrow, on August 5, 1973, in Málaga, Antonio Bienvenida will take part in an official corrida with two younger members of the Miguelín and Campuzano teams.

October 8, 1975: I hear on the radio that Antonio Bienvenida has died, wounded by the horn of a bull during a training session.

"Training session"—this surprised me. But I later learned that the retired torero had been the victim an accident—a piece of pure bad luck—that had occurred over the course of a *tienta*, an event in which the young bulls and breeding cows are tested for their aggression and selected for their aptitude for the ring.

*

If we were climbing plants or candles on a Christmas tree!

If our tongues were spears and our hearts as red as those on playing cards!

If our souls, given over to words, were flowers in our mouths!

If our life and our death could be sung as an opera!

If sorrow were to joy as pepper is to salt!

If the rumples of an unmade bed at waking were as cheerful as the froth of Champagne poured into a glass!

If the words I appropriate from the common treasure could by contagion prove everlasting!

If our flesh could fully rise into the illuminations of eroticism, instead of gradually fogging up into the obscenity of a corpse!

*

With the helmet of Clorinda, whom he has mortally wounded over the course of a long hand-to-hand combat with this adversary whose gender was never revealed, Tancred scoops up the water with which he will now baptize his victim, whom he has just discovered to be a woman, near the tower in flames, and who with a faltering voice has asked him to make of her a Christian.

For this Crusader encountering an Infidel, the breasts bared by the chink in her armor must have been of the same order as those that appeared to Siegfried as he awakened Brunhild while lifting the breastplate that covered her as she slept at the center of the circle of fire. But in both cases the realization came too late, proving that the hearts of brave heroes are as devastated by love as by sorrow and shame.

For Tasso, the author of this poem, and for Monteverdi who set it to music, was not love an indiscriminate slaughter that literally translated the cruel allegory of warfare as well as the more ironic allegory of concealment?

*

Although made of the same mettle as the Amazons, the woman who dealt me the final stab wound or *descabello* in our one-on-one mortal combat (and this is hardly a metaphor, given that the only life that remains to me is that of a phantom) is no femme fatale nor virago. Rather than a *señorita torera* or regular horsewoman, she resembles an Anglo-Saxon schoolteacher, all the more enticing because somewhat affected and high strung, less out of the need to display her intelligence than out of her desire to seduce. As I try to connect this slender image to something out of my past, I discover (somewhat arbitrarily but with conviction, seeing as how I can raise this image to the dignity of a myth only by grounding it in some earlier memory) that it bears a vague resemblance to a charming English teacher of mine at the Berlitz School, who I think took turns with another instructor who was a far taller brunet and—apparently—something of pathetic spinster.

Wounded as I am, I resent the woman who wounded me by her contact. But was it indeed she who delivered the blow? Or was I not, as our friendship reached its highest pitch, a bull already half dead whom even the most expert of matadors would be unable to lure into the final passes of his *faena?* Bogged down in the physical fatigue of my body, a prisoner of all those responsibilities real or imaginary that were multiplying day by day, lacking the strength to untangle the web of false pretexts that, instead of radically changing my way of life, I had woven just to play out my paltry game in this affair . . . Without being able to see (far from it!) the true cause of my shortcomings, I cast the blame on my tendency to wallow in my private obsessions, my endless checking of the calendar or clock, my constant self-evaluations and projections, all of which served to distract me from paying full attention to what lay before my very eyes or to consider the place or time that I should have dutifully observed as a fully devoted lover. But if, leaving all this deceptiveness aside, I dare look at the situation directly, it becomes clear to me that all this was owing to a severe two-way split involving on the one hand the body of the other, perceived less as the intense presence of a subject on whom one is dying to make one's mark but more as a piece of delicate machinery that will generate shared pleasure only if subjected to a requisite series of maneuvers (caresses carefully distributed here and here, presumably leading up to the final embrace, as opposed to a fierce frontal assault involving a flood of indistinguishable caresses), and on the other hand involving my own body, never entirely placed within parentheses but nonetheless sensed (a depressing realization) as better nourished than need be, its belly too protruding, its chest too fleshy, a body without muscles or nerves, sheathed by a fragile layer of emotive skin, and all this coming at the expense of the very thing that lay far deeper and that was supposed to stand up straight to the task at hand, erasing all the rest. A skewed perspective, admittedly, which only illustrates the specious manner in which I dwell on details instead of letting myself get fully carried away by the whole and giving myself over to the passionate arousal that would very likely do away with the obstacle altogether. (As for this obstacle, I would prefer it to be above all mental, something that it was therefore in my power to remove, something therefore less humiliating to explain because it had to do with my head rather than with my sex, so disincarnated, so spectral, so abstract even as it quietly struggles to rise to the occasion. But even if this were the reason, to what should the fault be ascribed? To a lack of ardor, an inability to abandon myself, a small-mindedness more shameful than all the physical embarrassments brought on by age? Yet: *If I wanted to* . . . By saying this, I think I've found a way out, even as I forget that my deeper flaw might involve my inability to *want* and that, moreover, it is in order to create this condition of wanting—to awaken my desire rather than satisfy it—that I have in the end affected the behavior of a man afflicted by poor sleep.)

Even during the time when her image obsessed me, there was not a single night that she came to visit me in my dreams. And yet during that first conversation as we sat side by side on the 63 bus (normally my reading room, outside those encounters I'm unable or unwilling to avoid, giving in to the lazy drift of mental associations or letting my eye wander freely over the other riders or the streets flowing by), didn't we speak of the various dreams that had visited her—and about this woman from another era she had met in a distant country and whose motherly shadow haunted her memory? Her dreams and her hauntings revealed that she too was someone anxious and wounded, despite the energy that seemed to be indicated by her hands, small but well chiseled and with broadly defined veins—an energy that I later came to admire, even if its cutting edges did much to slash apart the stag at bay that I played before being forced to beat my retreat.

Eager to provide a portrait of her, yet aware that by saying too much about her I would only encourage gossip (something to be avoided like grease stains or kitchen smells), I'm looking for the word that might discreetly restitute her presence, this hardness of hers (or rather, the hardness of the wall into which I crashed) that calls to mind the name of the agate stone or that of Agathe, which well befits her preciousness, in both the best and the worst sense: her makeup, her affectations, her sometimes frumpy and sometimes elegant ways of dressing, but also her well-scrubbed clarity of outline, her watchwork precision, and her elusiveness—like that of some intangible salamander slithering its way from one hemisphere to another, finding free passage everywhere. "Agathe," the name reminds me of her eyes and seems to (phonetically) express the incursion of an Agave or a Judith into the candor of a chaste virgin's chamber.

Imaginary bits of dialogue, addressed to her now that my fate had already been sealed:

(*as a courtier*)

—No, my dear . . . I look upon you as I would look upon a very pretty stone.

(*as a besotted lover*)

—At what point would you like me to play your bleating lamb, unable as I am to play your wolf?

The final rejoinder, invented when the whole thing seemed viewed through a telescope:

(*as the Good Lord's angel*)

—You who have for a second time unsealed my eyes by showing me that a world once marvelously open to me would now be forever closed!

*

Neither alone nor not alone,
neither with all nor with some,
neither here nor there,
neither inside nor outside,
neither dead nor alive,
neither somebody nor nobody,
neither me nor him,
neither hot nor cold.

Unintentionally, I touch the left edge of my left foot (shod) to the right edge of her right foot (equally shod). She explains to me that having her foot touched this way, even if it merely entail one sole grazing another, is a phobia of hers. Taking this explanation into account, I withdraw my foot but feel physically ill at ease because we are seated quite close together and I'm somewhat afraid that the situation will repeat itself, to her great displeasure. And yet she does not protest the fact that my right palm (naked) has now been resting for some time on the top of one of her hands (no more gloved than mine), which is lying on her thigh nearest to me.

This is taking place on the deck of a ship or in some open-air area (perhaps lit up like a café at dusk with lanterns, candelabras, and other light sources shimmering through the foliage) over the course of an organized cruise that is now coming to an end. She and I have known each other for a number of years but have seen each other only very occasionally, but a more tender friendship seems to have now developed, even if it is far from being the kind of flirtatious situation that, once the trip was over, might lead to a closer relationship: what never happened in the past will certainly not happen now. To say my good-byes to her, I invite her to have dinner with the little group with whom my wife and I have been traveling.

But the plan doesn't work out, because she apprises me that she is among the passengers who will be making the return journey later that day. She tells me she was informed of this only at the very last minute and in the most the offhand and discourteous manner, and I conclude from this that my own departure will follow somewhat thereafter, given that I had not been apprised of any information of this sort. Although I am sad to see her leave so soon,

I'm happy to know that I still have some time ahead of me—probably until tomorrow—to prepare my return, to get used to the fact that the party is now over, and, once having come to terms with this fact, to deal with a number of small matters on which I confer more importance than they deserve: to retrieve the items that I had thoughtlessly sent out to be laundered, to pack up my belongings, to inspect the cabin to see that nothing has been left behind, etc.

To depart is to die a bit, as the old saying goes. And I think that it is in the light of this pearl of wisdom that while looking back on this frivolous dream in which I am taking a trip and discovering the sweetness of friendship in the process, I begin to understand just why—even though none of its details exceed the comfortable bounds of a romance novel fit for the young girls of yesteryear—I can't clear my mind of the sinister hue that this dream has taken on (for no particular rhyme or reason, it should be added).

When (out of sheer laziness or fatigue?) my head comes to a standstill, apparently emptied of ideas, I often try to reorganize my library—filled with books of various sorts and formats, magazines and journals, catalogs and other publications (including what earlier centuries might have called lampoons or broadsheets, etc.). Though time consuming, it's a worthwhile activity: whether purchased or received in the mail or given as gifts, so much printed matter has accumulated here in our home in Paris or in our countryside place that we can no longer keep up with it, my brother-in-law having deliberately decided to avoid the issue altogether and I never having had the courage to dive in and to proceed to the serious business of finally winnowing things out . . .

A mechanical way of keeping oneself occupied, in which the material practice of bricolage is substituted for that other mode of bricolage which I call *my work*, even though I hope that by some sort of sympathetic magic the former will eventually translate into the latter. Or perhaps I am driven by the dim need to manipulate cultural objects, seeing as I am intellectually in no condition to produce any of these myself and, more specifically, because I cannot muster even the level of attention required to engage in the perusal of those objects in my possession? In the long term, I suppose I'll be able to say to myself that I will have handled, leafed through, and organized as well as possible (by rearranging the shelves or by transporting items from one residence to the other) all these various things that I may have not read but that I have somewhat absorbed during this process. Given that the void I observe within me represents a kind of death, aren't all my outward activities merely the imitation of someone who is "putting his affairs in order" because he senses his end is nearing?

*

The spot of blood. Not the blood that sullies you, but the blood you spatter on the face of others: Van Gogh making a gift of his severed ear to a woman in a whorehouse. (It's not onto this woman that this madman wanted his blood to spurt in order to wash himself clean of who knows what, but rather it is we who are splashed in the face by it, we who are the chefs and gastronomes of works of art, even if we refuse to consider ourselves aesthetes.)

Yellow suns, black sun, and the nonchemical red of this blood spot . . .

*

In the game called art (however one might want to justify this activity), you have to catch the thing, nail it down, but in a roundabout way, leaping this way and that, now and then suspending the action, like a cat playing with a mouse. In comparison to the dog—a stolid middle-class citizen or, if you prefer, a mere commoner bulldozing his way ahead—the cat is (as is often remarked) an aristocrat and an artist.

The beauty of bullfights, the beauty of cockfights. When I compare them, I am taken aback by the far greater atrocity of the cat-and-mouse game—certainly as grand a game as these others, but one I can't bear to watch, perhaps because its victim is so utterly innocuous.

I suppose this likening of art to a cat playing with a mouse is a bit facile, for when I initially came up with the comparison I was only thinking of the deft feline gestures of the cat while forgetting that this bit of chamber music (however elegant and discreet) is predicated on the torture of a very small creature whom one could hold in the palm of one's hand, a massacre dribbled out in droplets, as it were, so pocket sized as to further inspire horror.

Besides, to imagine that in the act of writing or painting one might achieve the cruel sovereignty of the cat, is this not to engage in a ridiculous bit of braggadocio by casually comparing the domain of art to a blood sport?

What's more, given that my strategy entails avoiding major scratches rather than dealing a mortal blow, I should probably compare myself not to the cat but to the mouse—if I insisted on seeing things from a tragic point of view.

*

Grain that gets ground, animal that gets caught in a trap—to be the plaything of two absolutely contrary motions: wanting to slow down the grind and grip of time, yet simultaneously giving in to the opposite impulse, constantly wanting it to flow so swiftly that every day you look forward to in dread will quickly come and go.

*

To the shipwreck of one's advancing years should be added the more historically significant wreckage of the civilization to which (like it or not) one
belongs, together with the loss of one's illusions (the ultimate wreckage, this?)
about the more transparent light of the civilization that might replace it. That
one should experience old age in a double or triple fashion, this is more (I
dare say) than I can bear. Yet the fact is: I *am* bearing it, for I'm neither mad
(at least so it seems to me) nor dead by my own hand.

It should be noted that a good number of my hours will have been spent in a basement, for my office at the Musée de l'Homme—this tiny room that has been allotted to me even though I am officially retired, given that (anything can happen!) I am considered by the outfit as something of a venerable feather in its cap—is situated at a slightly lower level than the gardens of the Trocadéro.

Sitting at my desk and turning my head to the left, I can see—beyond the protective iron bars of the window—the upper half of the Eiffel Tower, half hidden by a small assortment of trees whose names I have still not mastered, just as (too much of a city dweller, no doubt) I am unable to master the names of almost all trees. Among the ebbs and the flows of the task that I had assigned myself—namely, to undermine the foundations of our Western arrogance by using ethnology to give every culture its rightful due—what better place to undertake this in than this sunken lair, which, like its adjoining office, opens onto a larger but very cluttered area—the "Department of Black Africa," served, like the neighboring premises, by a slightly curved and artificially lit hallway dominated at one end by the candle-colored octagon of the clock situated to the right of the (often broken-down) lift and at whose other end lies, shrouded in darkness, a freight elevator whose creaking cabin is sturdy enough to transport heavy loads or large numbers of passengers.

People sometimes feel sorry for me for not having a better office. But the truth is that I have been on the whole perfectly content with this quiet work space, appreciative of the fact that it offers an alternative to my home office, not so much because it provides a different space but because it supplies a locus where other ideas become active, for it is as rare for me to play the ethnographer at home as it is for me to play the writer between these four walls—two of which, facing each other, are taken up by the door and by the window that sits halfway above the heating pipes, while the two other walls, to the right and left, are free of any functional furnishings. On one of these, across from the desk where I most often sit, there hangs a mask from Mali, featuring three antelope horns and covered with glued-on decorations (shells, gaming chips, European pocket mirrors), whereas the lower part of the mask, in the shape of an upside-down ogive, is made entirely of wood. On the facing wall hangs a nineteenth-century painting that reproduces a Pompeian fresco from the Naples museum representing a scene having to do with the mysteries of Isis, no doubt a faithful copy as its artist (probably intending just to create a documentary reproduction) saw it, but done in an old-fashioned style so kitschy and so pompous that it seems as distant from us today as it was from its original, all of which lends this work a certain charm as something doubly anachronistic, at once scholarly and naïve.

It's only after having weighed all my choices that I decided to hang these two objects on my office walls. I was sentimentally attached to the first of these: it was a mask I had acquired at the outset of my first field trip to Africa and that I had personally inventoried on an index card. As for the other, I had saved it from the flames when the former Trocadéro Museum of Ethnography became the new Musée de l'Homme and the decision was made to rid its collections of all the old-fashioned items that now seemed so silly. In any event, these two objects could be taken as emblematic of the work I do as a specialist in one of the disciplines housed in this institution to which I commute several times each week. If, above and beyond the value it holds for me as a souvenir, the mask so enchants me, it's because its borrowings from Europe (tacky mirrors, gaming chips) introduce a baroque note of exoticism in reverse while leaving intact its completely African character, bespeaking as they do the casual use the sculptor made of our products of industry; far from being influenced by Europe, he was engaged in making the mask into something truly African, something capable of imparting a nobleness to cheap trinkets by associating them with the striking simplicity of carved wood, thus creating an object that would eventually enter into the orbit of local rites. In opposite fashion, the painting on my wall conveys not the same unexpected heightening of its raw materials as the mask but rather their derisory debasement (on the order of those "idiotic paintings" or "obsolete operas" of which Rimbaud speaks). What attracts me to the gentle patina of this copy are several specific details, among them a nearly naked negro crowned with foliage dancing on a small stage that no doubt serves as the entrance to the temple at the base of whose steps there kneels a nubile female celebrant all clothed in rich veils and shaking a sistrum in the direction of the dancer, near the altar at which two large birds are picking and on which a holocaust seems to be burning. A mockery of a picture and, what's more, a nose thumbed at the scientific study of cultures—because if a well-intentioned copyist can manage to transform this lovely vestige of Rome into a mock-up for a wretched staging of *The Enchanted Flute*, this leads us to conclude that we may be doing the very same thing when we work as observers of societies far from our own: we may well believe that we have painted a portrait of them that is quite accurate, but perhaps our mode of interpretation is doomed to produce an image that will appear just as mawkish once this mode again changes.

Irony certainly plays its part in the somewhat uneasy pleasure I take in the three-horned mask and in the painting rescued from the flames. In the case of the mask, the irony derives from what some might consider to be the degradation involved in introducing worthless pieces of European junk into its composition, but this speaks to me far more subtly than if the piece possessed the purity of an antique untouched by the waywardness of a madman's bells. As for the Isis scene, its power derives not only from the level of doubt it awakens via analogy but from the bizarre blend of the comic and the serious that it immediately puts into play, with its naïvely parodic features amusing me like a carnival while at the same time causing me to feel something of the grandeur of the mysteries of Isis in a disguise that allows me to be touched by them without being held back by the fear that I might thereby be indulging in vacuous mysticism. Knowing this, someone analyzing my service record at the Musée de l'Homme might well ask himself why, during the period when I was still officially engaged in fieldwork, my preferred area of research involved the Antilles, the place where Africa and Europe flow into each other, giving rise to any number of curious cultural hybrids—and also why I have been so drawn to the study of cults in which the adepts in their trance states imitate gods, engaging in a kind of living theater played out without the slightest proscenium separating actors from spectators, any of whom could presumably be visited by a god at any moment, thus making it possible for the ethnographer himself, driven by his attraction to what lies *elsewhere* while remaining respectably rationalist, to become a wholehearted participant who, without abandoning his role as a observer and without changing the color of his skin, finds himself playing just as much of a role in these pieces of theater as anybody else.

Inasmuch as I have had the opportunity to freely choose the fields and the themes of my ethnographic research, I have oriented myself to those objects of study that seemed to harbor the kind of intrinsic irony that so appealed to me. That two cultures seem to have commingled in a suspect yet alluring embrace only in order to give a more marked lie to each other, that one might invite the gods to appear in epiphanies that take on the guise of masquerades, all this satisfies my deep need to intermix the *yes* with the *no*, to admit of things only by continually throwing them into question, to be attracted less to a beauty that is sublime than to a beauty that seems to denigrate itself, a beauty whose very slightness is all the more heartbreaking, or, obversely, to a beauty whose tragic outrageousness violates good taste with such cynicism and candor that it cheers you up—a deep need that at times would seem to indicate (far more than my coquettish resistance to wholehearted enthusiasm) my perverse inclination to take pleasure only in ambiguity or in paradox, and at other times would seem to be sanctified by the idea that the marriage of contraries is the highest summit one can metaphysically achieve.

Yes and *no*. As to these two locations of very different kinds of activities between which I generally commute by the 63 bus (more of a pleasure outing than a chore), would one of them represent the "yes" and the other the "no"? If I appreciate the back-and-forthing between the work I engage in at home and my work at the Musée de l'Homme, it is perhaps partially as someone who hopes to win back on red what he has lost on black, but partially because of the constant irony that this alternation implies: to take my distance from ethnology while engaging in my literary work or vice versa (although upon closer examination of my workdays, even this scheme is too theoretical to merit a monolithic *yes*), to change course according to my schedule but always to make detours between the two, even if the ethnographic research that formerly called me abroad has now been reduced to the cold management of documents or the brittle labors of scholarship.

*

Back then it was the council of rabbits or hares that my dog Dine so desperately wanted to join. Now it is Typhon who is straining at his leash as he rears up and lets out a long moan at the sight of a charming ballet that is playing itself out in the nearby underbrush.

Disappearing and then reappearing until their final flight takes them away from us, a hare and (I imagine) his doe scamper after each other, circle around each other, and come to a stop, facing off as if to engage in combat (their forepaws lifted in kind of boxing stance). Vanishing behind the bushes, returning in a flash, briefly taking up their stations for new rounds of fighting—all this commotion (which went on for a number of minutes) seemed to me merely an example of witty badinage, whereas the dog probably saw it as some crazed pitched battle between two foes into which, had he been free, he would have thrown himself to finish both off.

Cruel aesthete that I was, I quietly awaited the end of this performance, caring little about the Tantalus-like torture that I was inflicting on my companion as I stood there, unaware that he was no mere dilettante capable of enjoying the graciousness of this pas de deux.

*

Even when this short scene is not omitted (which is often done, under the ludicrous pretext that it contributes nothing to the action), they remain invisible, and if one hears them, they're barely audible, or my memory of the scene is so vague that I can't even decide whether their whispers came from the wings before briefly blending into the sounds rising from the orchestra pit.

Imitation rocks (so light they would make you dizzy if you tried to lift them), trees so flat and hollow that they never needed trimming, faded leaves, a fine cloud of dust that one imagines rose from the boards every time even the lightest of steps would tread upon them—the exactness of detail hardly matters: all these outmoded trappings of the Salon d'Automne serve to frame the tiny cross-dressed character moving this way and that in the fake half light and whose age, like whose sex, escapes precise definition.

While searching for a lost toy, how taken this child was by the herd of animals (invisible to us) whom it avidly watched and listened to as they huddled against each other at dusk. But how worried it was when they all fell silent!

I am all of this at once: this anxious child, this invisible shepherd who can answer its questions only sub rosa, and this herd of lost sheep who—in act 4 of *Pelléas and Mélisande*—stop bleating and fall completely still, aware that the path they've been told to follow this evening is not the path that usually leads back to their pens.

＊

Just as a world of worry can enter into me through the needle's eye of a
minor task at hand (a letter to write, a telephone call to make, a minor action
I must take, a short errand I must run), making it seem that I attach a huge
importance to these trivial matters that become so obsessive that I think everything depends on them, so on the other hand my anxiety can seem entirely
dispelled by something no less infinitesimally small: the sight of a location that
moves me for reasons that escape me, a fleeting encounter, a chance event
with no fuller implications than anything a flâneur might happen across along
his way . . . What is amazing is the disproportion between the immensity of
this anxiety and the utter triviality of the things or events that either trigger it
or relieve it, as if their quantitative value didn't even enter into play, but rather
only those beneficial or detrimental qualities that have absolutely no bearing
on anything that might add up to an explanation.

For a long time, I was granted a moment of pure happiness (everything
that was weighing upon me chased away by a sweet and almost imperceptible
ripple of waves moving through my chest to my stomach) each time I took
the road from Paris to Étampes and came across these two words: JEURRE
and BRUNEHAUT (or the reverse, now on the right rather than the left side of
the road when I was traveling back to the city). These two names grace the
facades of two guardhouses near Étampes that are situated roughly one or two
kilometers apart from each other, the former (when one is coming from the
direction of Paris) being rather run down in appearance, the latter less ancient
in mien with its more rigid outlines, its duller materials, and its name written
in letters that are less noble and less warm in hue than the little group of letters
that compose the word JEURRE — in whose sound, at once crude and radiant,
I glimpse the color of hay or ancient gold — inscribed there above a nearly

square window that I now realize lies beneath a stained-glass lunette and is flanked by two other, smaller windows. Squat, but no doubt more spacious than it first appears, this first house is two stories high, the upper one seemingly crushed by a roof whose left side features two terrace-verandas that sit on massive pillars—though I should probably revise and correct these precise details in the light of what further visual inspection of the building might reveal. I take the place to be uninhabited—a humble vestige of an era less distant in time than that of the Merovingians or of the Crusades, or even of the Hundred Years' War, but whose name, so redolent of the industriousness of feudal peasantry yet so ignorant of all the industrial pollution that would follow, I like to imagine as reaching back to an ancien régime far older than the eighteenth century, whose architectural marks the building seems to bear: a block of bricks and stone placed at the entryway to a huge wooded estate, with wide paths leading to a castle and to a fake classical temple, more visible from the train than from the roadside.

Perhaps contaminated by the word BRUNEHAUT with which it seems oddly twinned (each of them at first located at the edge of a tall stand of trees that was then cut down to make way for gas stations and other similar signs of modern excess scattered against the forest background like a colorful jumble of toys), the word JEURRE always seemed to me to be the name of a person rather than that of a locality. A bizarre personal name, because to me it appears to designate the house itself—and not its lord and master, nor the dear creature to which this residence might well have been dedicated like some petty bourgeois villa—and thus confers upon it an ageless individuality as something possessed of an independent existence, like a ship or skiff whose soul can be read in the baptismal name written on its bow or like some household pet who raises its ear when it hears its name mentioned.

As I regularly made my way between Paris and my country home, so deep, despite the insignificance of its source, was the pleasure afforded me by the sight of the word JEURRE and of the solitary building that bore this single syllable as its title that I hesitated at great length before deciding to try set this pleasure down in writing: I was afraid that instead of transforming it from something ephemeral into something durable, the awkward attempt to do so would merely destroy it by imparting to it a form that was not its own, a form that would distort it and thereby ruin even the memory of it beyond redress. But when I finally got down to the task—believing that the matter at hand had matured enough to be undertaken without great risk—I was soon bothered by the idea that I might get things wrong when describing these two guardhouses, so I decided that the best course would be to look them up in the 1972 edition of the *Guide bleu France.* What I discovered in section 22 of the guide ("From Paris to Étampes and Orléans") was that these two buildings were in fact not related but instead belonged to two distinct properties and, what's more, that the names they bore, far from being their own and conferring upon them the status of legal citizens in their own right, were indeed only the names of the two properties in whose service they stood. In the description of the route given by the editors of the guide, one indeed reads that "on its left bank, the route follows the charming Juine valley, bordering on its left the parks of the *castles of Jeurre* and *of Brunehaut.*"

Ever since I discovered this and ever since I decided to paint a more accurate picture of them, I have cast a more attentive eye upon the two guard-houses when I pass by (which has caused me on a number of occasions to modify my description of the first one, a ridiculous attempt at getting things exactly right, for the more I touch up and complicate the design the more the feeling drains away from it, leaving me all the more distanced from it as I try to approach it more rationally), but in doing so I have only caused them to gradually surrender that magical singularity that so appealed to me—the way that they almost came across to me as real-life persons, existing there in tandem, like two dogs by the names of "Jeurre" and "Brunehaut," both satellites of the same master.

JEURRE: a house that expropriated its name and where I have just discovered—the coup de grâce—that its lovely window is decorated with two white curtains that have been looped back, a proof that this ancient edifice that I imagined to be a relic is indeed inhabited, and nothing indicates that it has been freed from serving as the humble guardian of the castle whose entry-way it so accommodatingly graces.

JEURRE: a pleasure that (respecting the deep-seated taboo that held me back for several years) I should have just allowed to quietly live out its little intermittent life, because by trying to put this pleasure into words in order to give it a second life I have merely ruined it, with no other compensation than the meager pride I have taken in providing this (poor and approximate) report.

*

A poppy in a field of wheat.

An oeil-de-boeuf sun in a bank of fog.

A ship leaving port.

A hare stopping on a path between two leaps.

A woman lifting her dress over her head with her two hands and tossing it behind her back.

Riderless, harnessless horses trotting or galloping, their manes like waves.

White upon blue, a long trail of flakes streaming from the faint arrow of an airplane.

A flame flickering back to life and a fountain as it fades.

A moon so huge as to crush houses.

The single star at nightfall or at daybreak.

Great herds of cattle scattered across a field, beyond time.

Ancient flower-patterned paper on the wall of a demolished apartment house.

A beacon flashing at the end of a pier.

In the tropics, the trembling of a hummingbird initially mistaken for a flying insect.

A peacock wheeling and swiveling like a radar dish.

A dog who revolves and then curls to the ground with a heavy grunt.

A lighted train streaking across a plain.

The *cricri* of grasshopper or cricket.

Silence sown with the chirps of birds.

Whatever the place, whatever the season, bursts of casual music.

The scent of tea on London docks and, in the islands, the smell of sugar-cane at harvesttime.

A taste of warm bread that makes you think you're back in a village grade school.

When unclothed, a skin whose marble is so polished one wonders how it came to be so soft.

A narrow road. A tunnel of trees. A fresh dent in a bed.

A dense forest, an isle when seen from without but a bath of chiaroscuro when seen from within.

The discreet breathing of a stream, out of earshot, in the movement of the reeds.

*

In the small hours of the morning, still tucked into my sheets before fully awake, I seem to be prey to a series of treacherous dreams that don't even achieve the level of imagery or (I should say) of thoughts, but hover just slightly above the plane of sensation—a very vague sensation I would label as "anxiety," at least to indicate its insistent throb, unable as I am to describe it more fully.

This takes on various guises, the most basic of which (if I want at all costs to cast things into clear words) involves the repetitive rehashing of things— once I have gotten out of bed and recovered a bit of lucidity as I sit before my cup of tea—that translates itself into a stream of lugubrious musings bitterly flavored with ready-made cliches: the flight of my remaining days; the declining number of friends, carried off one after another to their deaths (so that one's daily mail becomes so impoverished that it now includes only official notices or form letters that arouse not the slightest whit of emotion); the ever more meager future that lies at the disposal of my partner and myself—a future that promises to result in one of us being left behind alone (unless we happen to be granted the exceptional luck of simultaneous death).

Sometimes this malaise I experience—rid of anything that might contribute to its pathos—seems to be grounded solely in the vagueness of the fantasy whose plaything I become and whose indecisiveness tends to highlight the deep anxiety into which I am plunged by the discreet but very proximate presence of two indefinable things I know to be different, if not entirely opposite, despite their apparent similarity and that offer themselves to me as ongoing alternatives, one of whose terms, though more concrete and more fully sensed, might be preferable to the other, even though it be equally faceless.

Often, in the wake of the feelings of disgust that I have projected—God knows how—onto all the odious tasks I have to undertake in the coming days, my obsession with writing haunts my insidious half sleep: I think of sentences to construct (even if this concern with sentence structure is commonly distorted into some singular and intractable problem to be solved or into some obscure ploy that needs to be put into effect); I think of a group of words (a sort of buoy) that needs to be solidly attached to the corpus of the sentence so that everything, and not just the sentence or the book, might be salvaged; I think of the possibility (perfectly utopian, as I come to realize once I have gotten out of bed and cleared my head of cobwebs) of a mutation that might allow my anxiety to evolve into its opposite or, more precisely, that might put it into a position in which (as in judo, the adversary's attack becoming the instrument of his defeat) this recuperated anxiety would have no more meaning than this—to bring into being, now that its venom has been neutralized (a procedure that at the exact moment that I'm here describing was far from literary), the normal wellspring of happiness.

*

Divination, alibi, purification rite: this work from which I expected some rule to emerge but that has helped me neither to establish it nor to establish myself (since it results in virtually nothing other than my ongoing persistence to establish it).

Laboriously calligraphic, this work maliciously consumes me instead of fortifying me (given that its composition has become my major and almost sole occupation).

A narrative, a portrait, or a gloss, this work is nourished by my life rather than providing nourishment in return (since it derives its matter from my life, of which it is but a by-product).

A measure of my highs and lows, a machine running on empty, this work confers no mastery upon me, for I am not even in charge of it (since what gets it secretly done without me is what I do and am without it).

*

Titles, Nothing but Titles:
        Conversations on the Plurality of Worlds.
        The Carcasses of Hunger.
        Having Been.
        Without Having.
        Ever Since When.
        Each One More Than the Other.
        The Ablative Absolute.
        Full Steam Ahead.
        Almost.
        Futile Recourse.
        The Least One Could Say.
        Oh!
        Despite.
        The Ultimate Prothesis.
        Hold Up.

*

Newton's apple, Galileo's chandelier: anecdotal items promoted to the level of emblems.

At the theater, two burning torches and a crucifix honoring a corpse mean *Tosca*, a head on a platter signifies *Salome*, a statue on the move indicates *Don Juan*, a rumored cash box sums up *The Miser*, a skull held in both hands epitomizes *Hamlet*. Not symbols but images that immediately convey the situations or the nature of the characters involved, powerful enough to nearly induce a state of hypnosis.

As I rummage through my life, I would love to be able to discover images of this sort, images that would be to me, if not what the dragon is to Saint George or the Rubicon to Caesar, at least points of reference to which I could firmly hold on.

＊

Filled with a sadness unalleviated by the realization that, everything being in vain, what he had managed to do or not do was without importance, he said to himself that there was not much of his life worth preserving. Failure everywhere down the line: failure as a writer, given that he was nearly incapable of letting go of his own self-regard and therefore had only rarely achieved anything in poetry and, in addition, given his awareness that he was not made of the same mettle as those whose destiny lay in suicide, madness, or permanent departure; failure as a rebel, given that he had never fled his comfortable bourgeois existence and that despite his few intense hankerings after revolution, he had to recognize that his strong aversion to violence or sacrifice meant that he would never measure up as an activist; failure as a lover, given that his love life was ever so ordinary and that his libido had quickly waned; a failure as a voyager, given that being restricted to a single language (his native tongue), he was perfectly incapable of feeling at ease with other people or things, even in his home country. Of his professional work as an ethnographer, there was little concrete to show: specialized research into a Sudanese initiatory language and into ritual possession cults in Ethiopia; derivative work on *art nègre* and other contributions that were antiracist in aim but that despite their noble intentions never made much of a splash; and finally, (his most noteworthy achievement, so he thought even in the blackest of his moods) several articles in which he had urged that the practice of ethnography place itself no longer in the service of Western science but instead in the service of the peoples of the third world—a somewhat naïve ambition, given that the latter have so many other things to worry about . . .

In the deepest depths of his despair, he nonetheless told himself that there was at least one good action that could be registered on his balance sheet: the nonaction involved in not having children. An act of abstention of which he could be very proud in those dark moments, for it demonstrated that even if he had never been a full member of the resistance, he could at least flatter himself for refusing to become a collaborator.

*

Not to hitch your acts to your ideas, but to come up with a system that appeases your conscience by justifying these acts; not to live in relation to what you think, but to think in relation to what you live—this is without a doubt the worst of blots, the stain that sullies so many people, something to be avoided at all costs . . .

If I have held certain beliefs and if I am ashamed that I did not have the fortitude to face up to the dangers these implied, I nevertheless must avoid abandoning all these theories just to justify the deficiencies of my praxis, nor should I find myself challenging them the better to wash my hands.

At least let me delve, without any denials on my part, into the abyss that my weakness has deepened between my thought and my life!

(*One nail drives out another. Only the first step counts. Fall back to leap forward.* The other stain that threatens me: feeling complacent about my confessions, like a Christian feeling absolved just because of all the humiliation he has undergone.)

*

Famous Last Words:

(Rigaut style)	"Don't make me laugh!"
(Bravado style)	"Just a word to the wise!"
(Harpagon style)	"My cashbox!"
(Courtly style)	"Cover your heads . . . !"
(Telephone style)	"Hold the line!"
(Informal style)	"To you and yours!"
(Panic style)	"I've been hit!"
(Philosopher style)	"Better late than never."
(Airman style)	"Bombs away!"
(Casino style)	"Rien ne va plus."
(Statesman style)	"I call this session into order . . ."
(Easygoing style)	"Aw, shucks."
(Complaint style)	"Lady Death! Lady Death! Let me catch my breath!"

*

The English terms *thornproof, sharkskin, herringbone, chalk striped.*

It's natural that the tailor's craft should entail a philosophy, for there is no trade without its own. This is clearly the case with the so-called liberal professions, whose very name indicates that they were freely chosen and thus are the most likely to reflect the world views of those who practice them. There does not exist, so it would seem, any single type of work that (beyond its immediate results) does not set into motion a number of ideas among those who engage in it: every manufacturer (if he's not a swindler) more or less believes in the value of his goods, convinced that they serve a useful public purpose; every salesman aspires to become a psychologist capable of figuring out just what it is his customer needs; every businessman imagines himself to be a tactician or a strategist who draws his lessons from the state of the market, itself a reflection of the way of the world; every leader implicitly or explicitly feeds on fantasies of domination; even the most sluggish of bureaucrats is a firm believer in rules and regulations; like the eloquent gravedigger seen onstage, any garbageman probably has his own opinions about what the trash he collects might reveal about the inhabitants of his district; and it is perhaps only the unskilled laborer who views the materials he has to deal with solely from the point of view of their bulk or weight. As for the tailor, attentive as he is to outward appearances, just as a doctor is observant of how the skin often signals what's going on inside a body, it seems obvious that a man who cuts our clothes in accordance with the idea we have of ourselves (both as we are and as we should be) while at the same time adhering to his particular view of our person and of fashion should be philosophic. Having to observe as he does the fine distinctions between the necessities of conformity and the allowances for free choice, the tailor chooses a field of action essentially located at the dividing line between *being* and *appearing*.

Sheer frivolousness, perhaps? Never has a fitting session with my tailor proved boring . . . I find many of the material details quite appealing: the layout of the temporary stitches he superimposes on our body like some ideal geometric pattern; the sound of a barely attached sleeve that he often rips away with a sudden yank (which gives one the abrupt impression that one is standing there in rags); the way he works like a sculptor, adding a little here and removing a little there; the pins he nimbly inserts into the spacings of the buttons-to-come. Even more appealing to me are the comments he finds it appropriate to make, comments that often allow one to get a glimpse of his philosophy as someone well placed to take the measure of people and things as he accounts for each person's personality and the fluctuations of taste while weighing what might be specific to the individual against what is demanded by fashion, even as he carefully makes sure his suit possesses its own bespoke uniqueness.

A native, I believe, of central Europe but raised in England, a rue Vivienne tailor whose services I relied on in the past so insisted on the dignity and sanctity of his art that his bills or letterheads bore the following slogan in English: *A Bund's suit gives a moral satisfaction*—a motto rivaled by this one: *Patronized by the best gentleman in the city*—as if he wanted to thereby imply that if one were dressed by him one would somehow feel oneself purged of all one's sins and become the equal of all those who, representing the cream of the crop, deigned to put him in their employ. As bourgeois and conformist as these appeals to gentlemanly honor might have seemed, the same Bund never hid his lower-class origins, at the antipodes of the royal court. I in fact remember him telling me how his parents had sent him out to beg in their East London neighborhood, with him rattling his money box and shouting *For the Russians!* as he tried to take up collections to subsidize the émigrés who had fled the reign of the last of the Romanovs (not revolutionaries as I had long thought, but more likely those Jews who, fleeing the pogroms, had largely settled in the East End, as I have learned only of late). As he shared this memory with me (which seemed to amuse him no end and about which I have forgotten how it had made its way into a conversation that had absolutely nothing to do with class struggle), this former Whitechapel street urchin showed (with implicit humor) that he knew how to take the measure of his life and how to view the respectability he had since acquired with the detached gaze of a philosopher, or at least that of a *moraliste*.

A novelist after the fashion of Dickens rather than a precise observer of manners and mores, such was the Irishman Archibald Leahy, who initially had a shop on the quai de Tokyo but then, after having run into severe business troubles, took to working at home, during which period of decline I had recourse to his services. Can I claim that Archibald Leahy confided much of his ideology to me? Certainly not. All I managed to observe was the nationalist fervor of this hyperinsular individual for whom the staff of the ever-so-Parisian and ever-so-long-respected tailor James Pile were nothing but a bunch of *damned Scotchmen*. Nor did he seem to be a good judge of character—one day (speaking to my brother-in-law, a fellow customer), he provided this rather hasty assessment of me: *A jolly fellow! Always smiling . . .* But he was someone whom any student of human diversity would be pleased to observe in real life. He had an odd body, to be sure, darting this way and that with the straight face of a clown or over-the-hill jockey, cutting the figure of a man whom one might have met by chance in a Dublin pub and with whom one might have discussed the odds on the upcoming horse races over a Jameson or a Guinness . . . Perhaps it was his gambling habit—together with his taste for drink?—that had brought about the business troubles that forced him to close up shop; in any event, his financial worries were such that he always asked to be paid in advance, claiming he needed the money to buy the fabric of which one had been shown only a meager sample swatch. On at least one occasion, this ex-employee of the brothers Hill, now living from hand to mouth in his own domicile, sent a moving letter to my brother-in-law, a true Christmas story with a whiff of the pauper: the wintry gloom of his sad abode, his tearful wife, his sweet daughter shivering from the cold, details that led one to imagine him sitting there in his lowly workplace next to an extinguished stove in a room barely lit by a guttering candle, warming himself up with a gulp of whiskey or brandy (if there was any left in the house), and awaiting the imminent arrival of the bailiffs who would cart him off to debtors' prison, where, like some new Pickwick, he would then await the merciful visit of my brother-in-law and me. A perfect disaster when it came to his business dealings (and picaresque enough to have completely vanished one day after having pocketed the money for an order he never delivered), Archibald Leahy was gifted with a kind of genius when it came to his actual trade: the articles of clothing that he cut were so articulately conceived (in that tight-fitting but slightly seedy style that grows only more romantic with wearing) that one would forget the gross spelling mistakes he committed in the process. He even managed to make me a suit—whether because he was distracted or because he was trying to swindle me—whose design (double breasted instead of single breasted as I had stipulated) and whose fabric (selected on the basis of a tiny sample) were not what we had agreed upon but to which I nonetheless acquiesced, given the undeniable talent of this wayward artist.

A more suitable example than Archibald Leahy of the clothes philosophy I have been discussing is provided by another tailor I had heard about: his customers consisted largely of students from the Antilles, and he was proud to claim that he could instantly tell whether a client of his hailed from Martinique or Guadeloupe. Apart from this perspicacity that would make any ethnographer grow pale with envy, I have no idea what skills this tailor might have brought to the field—still to be investigated—of the knowledge of men and things.

Even more illustrative of all this, the statement made by a certain Barrett whose shop I visited upon my return from the Gold Coast (now Ghana) to inquire whether he might create me an outfit from a piece of fabric that I had acquired in Accra and had managed to smuggle through customs with the amiable acquiescence of a British official, an item that in this period of postwar shortages I was as proud to bring back to France as any Mossi or Dogon immigrant might be of the magnificent pieces of fabric into which he had converted the money he had earned in the mines or on the plantations of his colony. *Here we pay no attention to what goes on in the street*, this tailor announced to me one afternoon, thus displaying the aristocratic disdain he felt for that all too vulgar thing—fashion—to which no gentleman should pay attention if he wants to place himself above the common herd.

No less inclined to follow the fashions of the day was the firm of tailors with whom, thanks to my years of patronage, I was on more familiar terms. Johnson and Marié often made mention of the fact that their clientele included—or had included—such personalities as General de Gaulle, M. Marcel Boussac, the secretary of the Duke of Windsor, Ernest Hemingway, and the vicomte de La Panouille. The friend who had recommended them was someone far more experienced than I was, given his age and the renown he had enjoyed back before the First World War as one of the last true boulevardiers, a regular at Maxim's and personal friend of the *vaudevilliste* Georges Feydeau (he would later serve in the war as the leader of a detachment of those African troops who risked their lives at every turn and who were somewhat blithely referred to as the "Senegalese Fusiliers"). Shortly after returning from a visit to London, I remember bumping into this sybarite in the gardens of the Trocadéro (not far from his home near the Musée de l'Homme) and him going on at length about how exactly it feels to take delivery of a tailor-made hat from the firm of Lock and to have two hands place it upon your head like some sacred object, neither too wide nor too tight but perfectly your size, that holds firmly in place with no need to apply manual pressure (he went on and on in this way with a dreamy look in his eye, as if moved to ecstasy by some hedonistic moment of recall). Johnson and Marié spoke admiringly of him, reporting that over the many decades that they had been making his suits for him, they had never altered a single hem nor widened or narrowed the bottoms of his trousers. A standard had been defined for once and for all, and they adhered to it with the same rigor and respect for the rule as this other tailor by the name of Fred Perry whom I patronized when I was a little over twenty and who swore that he would dress me in a manner that *would impress my boss* (understanding as he did that I was a young man who did not have the means to satisfy his thirst for elegance), a rule that was of the same order as the golden ratio or the sculptural canon of a Polykleitos: always the same distance between the notch of the lapel and the breast pocket, the same distance between the latter and the middle button of the jacket (placed exactly at the level of one's natural waistline), and between this middle button and the lower pocket a distance that remained invariable and thus functioned as a module. Neither Sidney Johnson, a pure Englishman whose son had a medical practice in Borneo, nor his cutter, Alfred Marié, a pudgy little fellow who was distinctively French despite his professional training in England and his marriage to an American (who invisibly took care of the books but must have been a fairly striking individual), was a theoretician of the sartorial arts after the manner of Fred Perry. Marié, who was solely responsible for the scissor work, seemed to go about his task in a completely empirical fashion; Johnson, who advised customers on their choices and oversaw the fittings, nonetheless had his own fixed idea: the hatred of what he called "dirty" hues—that is to say, those colors that were not "frank" (because indeterminate in and of themselves or clashing with other colors in a mixed fabric). Of these colors he spoke with a disgusted frown when examining a swatch or a finished suit, as if the very sight or thought of them had sullied him far more deeply than some merely physical repulsion. What he preferred in all things was a classic sense of ease and sobriety, and so observant was he of outward form and of loyalty to his native land that I remember seeing him in his shop with a white shirt and dressed all in black shortly after the death of George VI, looking so crestfallen that I felt I had to offer him my heartfelt condolences. According to his acolyte Marié (who was no more an ascetic than he when it came to fermented beverages), Sidney Johnson above all prized spearmint liqueur, a strange drink for an Anglo-Saxon to like, especially one who so violently detested "dirty" colors . . . Upon retiring, he withdrew to a small cottage that he had acquired—bowing to his wife's wishes—near the cape of Gris-Nez, the nearest point to England on the French coast, and it is there that he died. For some time thereafter I continued to have my clothes made at Alfred Marié's, although the firm (which kept its "Johnson and Marié" name, perhaps because of its British cachet, or perhaps out of loyalty, or perhaps to save on having a new sign made) has now disappeared: to Marié's great disappointment, his son (whom he had sent to Glasgow for his apprenticeship and whom he had hoped would succeed him) instead went into prêt-à-porter. Indeed, the number of young people eager to go into tailoring continues to decline (given the vicissitudes of the trade, what with the rising costs of materials and labor and what with even the poshest of clients often failing to pay), and one doesn't have to listen to Alfred Marié in order to realize that in this field as in many others, industrial production is slowly replacing artisanal labor, just as synthetic textiles are taking the place of more noble fabrics.

I sometimes miss the conversations, however banal they might have been, that I enjoyed with this member of a guild in decline, random conversations with recurring anecdotes about Ernest Hemingway or General de Gaulle. To these my interlocutor would often add frequent allusions to his activity as a Sunday painter: if he did not claim (as a noted Milanese tailor apparently had on his business cards) to be an "architect of the human body," his fondness for watercolors (which he picked up after taking amateur lessons from Bernard Naudin) at least provided a genuinely artistic avenue of escape for this practitioner of a trade that one would have to classify as a minor branch of the decorative arts. A dyed-in-the-wool traditionalist, he informed me that at the firm of Davies and Sons (who were the London partners of his house and whose shop I visited on the ground floor of one of those Georgian buildings that are the glory of British towns) I could ask to be shown an order book dating back to the eighteenth century. In his respect for the past, Alfred Marié (of whose married life I knew nothing) must have been in perfect agreement with his wife, for the latter happened to admit to me, revealing her unsuspected upper-class aspirations over the course of one of our chance encounters, that historical memoirs were among her favorite reading matter.

The fetishistic affection I feel for my clothes, which like my writings represent a feature of my person as it appears to others; the almost oracular authority that I long ago ascribed to the proverb *Kleider machen Leute* when I encountered it over the course of several German lessons at the Berlitz School and which is the exact opposite of our *L'habit ne fait pas le moine*; my somewhat obsessive persuasion that the day will come when I order a suit that death will not permit me to wear (or will barely let me wear); my aversion to getting photographed (convinced as I am that I will not be shown to my advantage and uneasily envisaging the future gap that will separate my actual features from those seized on the fly and abstractly fixed into place); this jealous attachment I feel to my body, which has always nervously kept me from placing it into danger or even allowing it the total freedom to blindly abandon itself to the contortions of lovemaking—all this sufficiently explains why I so strongly tend to believe that the tailor's trade, directly touching as it does on our visible form, is bound to prod one toward philosophy. An act of faith on my part, unproved here by any QED, for if I have demonstrated anything, it's not that tailors are philosophers but rather that they're regular chatterboxes . . .

Coal gray, iron gray, Marengo gray, slate blue, navy blue, *midnight blue.* Or perhaps piebald (were I a horse) or brindle (were I a dog)?

*

A VIP who has no need to insist on his rights and who therefore never has to pull strings, yet who is important enough, even though he doesn't explicitly admit this to himself, to find it normal that he be everywhere accorded preferential treatment. To be dressed very simply but with the greatest of taste, such is his goal: to wear nothing too drab or too businesslike, to avoid loud colors, never to dress to impress, never to dress beneath one's age. Ever gentlemanly but without condescension, ever trying to keep on an equal footing with others, whatever their class, their age, their nationality, or their sex (there being several, given the two homosexualities). Self-satisfied enough with himself to think he doesn't look the part. Detesting vulgarity at its two extremes: starchiness or slovenliness. Keeping an even keel, stoic that he is, and rarely giving in to anger. His countenance (or at least so he hopes) neither too sunny nor too clouded, just conveying that sad serenity of someone who knows enough about things to no longer harbor any worries or illusions. Pensive as one should rightly be, knowledgeable as he is of the human condition and of the miseries of the world. A willing philanthropist. Capable (though hostile to the idea of asceticism) of going without, though only inasmuch as he knows that he could easily have access to more. Happy to be recognized should the circumstances arise, even though arriving unannounced. Not a snob, but someone who disdains having to cultivate connections or having to kowtow to the wealthy; in short, someone entitled but who doesn't need to blow his own horn. "Because I can afford to," as another VIP said to an acquaintance who was surprised to learn that this well-to-do individual would check into very cheap hotels in Venice and elsewhere. Honesty in all things. Unvarnished honor. But how would these qualities fare in an urban disaster situation or in a shipwreck or in front of a firing squad? A perfect gentleman in every respect (even though he doesn't insist on being called "sir"). Cultured enough, but never flaunting his knowledge. A cosmopolitan of course, but reluctant to express himself in another language (not because he is so partial his own, but out of the fear of speaking another idiom poorly). A decent husband, despite a few lapses. Not necessarily a decent father, given that his elegantly disillusioned philosophy and avoidance of responsibility have allowed him to be no father at all.

Observing a happy medium when it comes to funeral ceremonies: not to go overboard nor, just as egregiously, to fall too short; a discreet, functional grave site, but definitely not the potter's field; to avoid cremation, whose protocols are as burdensome and as long winded as a mass; but also to eschew any final foolish jest, such as deciding to get buried in a pet cemetery. An average lukewarm citizen, wavering between his disgust with public discourse and his desire to "do something." A devil of an egocentric, even if he prefers to be retiring and tends to be self-effacing in public. A VIP quite happy that the airline stewardess should add a personal note to her obligatory interaction with him, to assure him that he is not just any old passenger on this flight. A man without decorations. Not a member of the Jockey Club (had he ever dreamed of joining this aristocratic club, he would have been immediately blackballed), nor a member of any academy or any number of learned societies, but freely accepted into various groups or homes for ideas or small circles or associations. Left leaning, of course, for he is not dumb enough to be a reactionary: eager to understand what's going on in the present, eager to look to the future without clinging to the past. An antiracist, who knows that to forever award the first prize to Whites is to give in to family pride and to ignore the fact that no man (or, for that matter, no animal) can be solely judged by their pedigree. Something of a demagogue simply because of his need to be loved and applauded, but seeking general approval only insofar as this does not involve committing himself to anything that might throw his intellectual integrity or clearheadedness into doubt. A sentimentalist, as might be expected (it doesn't look good to be hard hearted), but as allergic to everything touchy-feely as to everything cut-and-dried. A nonbeliever in religious matters, period: obviously not convinced he is possessed of an immortal soul yet refusing to give in to complete despair and believing in progress as a form of Providence, convinced that the world will be one day be better organized than at the present. A social critic in the fashion of Voltaire, he is nonetheless not driven by the crazy desire to see everything crumble before his eyes. A sympathizer by nature, he is no firebrand or hothead. Secretly hoping that things will work out for the best among the well mannered . . . A Very Impotent (or inane or imbecile or innocent or indecent) Privileged person. A signed and numbered limited edition of a book on Holland, Arches, or Auvergne paper (he would have deemed Japan paper too sumptuous). He asks for nothing more, yet still insists on this: his status as a *Very Important Passenger* among the hundreds of millions of those on board the Good Ship Earth.

VIP: a Vapid Immensely Puerile pen tracing a barely disguised portrait of a person passing himself off as a sample of a human life that in fact does not exist because it escapes categorization; a Vomitive Invalid Puler who, when it comes to funeral arrangements, is so obsessed with what will become of his remains that he forgets that it is the common fate of a VIP to die incinerated in an airplane accident, thereby solving the entire problem. But this is just one point of view. What needs to be kept in mind is the following: his remains will be nothing more than a troublesome leftover, representing nothing by which or for which he will have lived.

*

One and the Same:
> *blue stocking,*
> *fine flower,*
> *highness,*
> *idol,*
> *magnate,*
> *mandarin,*
> *movie legend,*
> *nabob,*
> *pontiff,*
> *sâr,*
> *satrap.*

Many of the things he had said, certain that he was hitting the nail on the head but surely without realizing that they should be taken so literally, now came back to him bearing the full bitter fruit of experience. Forty years ago, for example, he had observed: *The poet is in essence someone who feels, who becomes aware, and who takes control by transforming whatever it is that is tearing him apart. Poetry is no dodge: it provides no opium, no land of dreams, but forces us to face up to things and take their lucid measure—a collision from which one can emerge only utterly torn apart (my current condition) or, if one has energy enough, contemptuous (i.e., master) of the world via one's song, a sign of one's pride and of one's victory over those things that, now having been ground down in our mill, can no longer crush us.*

Well, as someone who had wanted to be a poet along these heroic lines, he was soon alarmed to discover—as if fate had played a dirty trick on him—that he was in fact feeling torn apart and that (even worse) it was because of this that he had turned ever further away from poetry, disappointed that it could provide him no opium or means of escape . . .

*

"Poetry," "Revolution"—words as vague as all big words are . . . But convenient as signs that provide a shorthand for what is intended,

on the one hand, by my ever-unslaked thirst for those moments in which life—without ceasing to be what it normally is—appears to me as completely transfigured, either by the effect of a language that might be a spoken language or the instrument of an art distinct from that of common speech, or by conjunctures that are such that a fleeting harmony seems to emerge between the outer world and myself;

on the other hand, by my desire for a world of brotherly love free from poverty and free from all the obstacles of class and race—requiring a transformation too deep-seated to be brought about without violence.

To change life. To transform the world.

There were those of us, including me, who had too blithely believed that it might be possible to make these two imperatives converge—the former Rimbaud's, the latter Marx's. There was for sure no contradiction between the poet's injunction and that of the economist, but it would be absurd to consider them as equivalent. If religion has its rights, it is only to the extent that science falls silent, and the same thing holds for poetry, which—as a drug or as a balm against death or against everything revolution cannot remedy—finds its preferred territory beyond the reach of anything that a social upheaval might achieve.

As radical as it might be, no transformation of the world could change my life through and through, conditioned as it is by my certainty that I am bound to die. There's a part of me that revolution, even if completely successful, will never touch—and it is to this rebellious part of me that poetry (ever an upstart) addresses itself, sinking its roots into its loam.

*

It's not that he felt troubled—as it were by mistakes that would continue to haunt him—by the fact that he had in the past been so utterly dismissive of certain people who had rubbed him the wrong way for no clear reason. To blame himself for having been so unfair, for having so mindlessly lashed out, for having engaged in stunts that were so needlessly vulgar or else sheer bluffs—all this he could live with. What weighed upon him instead was the realization that he now existed in such a state of doubt that he could no longer allow himself to enter into the fray and, even more depressing, that all these debates about poetry and art in which he had so vehemently participated now struck him as hinging merely on questions of personal taste—issues so objectively secondary in importance that he could no longer find any grounds to make a display of his contempt or to argue his position with any true conviction.

*

Because you'd be bored to death by never dying.
Because there's no point in stopping off in a world this absurd.
Because the fallen rain will only rearise as mist.
Because no river would flow unless thrown into the sea.

*

To try to arrive at simplicity (at something, if possible, as dumb as a door-knob) after so many complications whose main (if not sole) benefit will have been to spur my desire to go back to the source and to look at it straight on, without any intervening fog. This act of turning back upon myself is recorded in several entries of my journal, dated late August 1969 and here reproduced in their nearly raw state (even though this dossier, now three volumes and over a thousand pages in length, has not yet reached its close).

. . . The "rule of the game" in the sense that I understand it involves my particular system of values (see Nietzsche) or original choice (see Sartre), which this game must observe in accordance with my proclivities and aptitudes—a game I must play out with rigor and coherence.

. . . If an individual's death leads to no hereafter and the world ends by returning to a state of equilibrium, how can things be taken "seriously"? Which is why one can only call it all "a game."

If everything is a game, that means it is all theater, simulacrum, illusion, etc.—in short, that *all is but vanity.* Convinced as I am by this fact, I could well become a major pataphysician, taking it for granted that all solutions are imaginary and thus equivalent and in the end equal to zero (given that any solution worthy of the name must be the right solution, to the exclusion of all others). Hence the idea that I am only playing my own game—an imaginary solution among other imaginary solutions—according to my own specific system of values or original choice would not bother me a bit. But the fact is—and herein lies my contradiction—that I am overwhelmed by the desire for some sort of objective justification of this subjective system, for a solid foundation that would reach beyond my person and that would provide a license for my actions, which boils down to wanting to transform the game into something serious, into something nongratuitous, and therefore to get rid of all the "fun" basic to any game. What I want, in short, is to play the game for myself as well as for others, to whom I offer the spectacle of my performance like any artist, sportsman, or chess player one might admire; but what I cannot accept is that this game be but a game.

This desire to justify my game, to play it without daring to give myself up to its gratuity, to attempt to moralize it and rationalize it—all this risks becoming a merely *academic* exercise, all the more obviously so because my game is grounded in my activity as a writer and because my need to provide it with a justification encourages me to overorganize it and to round off its edges instead of allowing it to enjoy its own fierce liberty.

. . . What makes my case even more curious (if fairly common) is that my game consists of, precisely, playing a game: the game of letters, far further removed from reality than those games in which actual risks are run (dangerous sports or high-stakes betting, which are real to the extent that they can lead to loss of life or utter ruin). Necessary distinction to be made between game in *lato sensu* and game in *stricto sensu*. In my case, these two senses overlap, which is why my *ars poetica* must at the same time be a savoir vivre (or vice versa). In the end, I see the whole question as coming down to this: How to correctly play the writer game? How to proceed so that this game might provide something on which I could bet my entire life—something that might make it worthwhile? Perhaps my conscience would be clearer (or altogether vanish) if I didn't constantly feel that I was just playing this game, as it were, *with blanks*?

. . . My hope of finding what it is I seek has now been reduced to the hope of finding not even the thing I seek but what exactly this thing might represent. In short, what I am now seeking is *what it is* I'm seeking. (Having given up on understanding the object of my search, I wonder whether it was not the very act of searching that was leading me on as I followed corridor after corridor, my heart continually beating, hoping against hope to come across some lucky find . . .)

As a matter of fact, everything was clear at the beginning, but as I made my way further along I lost sight of my initial goal: wasn't it my original intent to gather those events and facts that had had the greatest impact on me and to examine them in such a way that they would reveal to me that to which— poetically at least—I attach the highest value? From the very outset I knew my choice would lie with poetry, but I still had to figure out the exact relation of this keystone of my system to everything else. Everything got fouled up because I got it into my head to try to define the very thing that—as it were, by definition—escapes defining. Is not the highest value in some way analogous to the *master word*—that sovereign term upon which all others depend, that term that at once provides and escapes all definition, unless it be its own self-definition?

Thus summarized, the thing nonetheless became no clearer. Is it possible to place one's bet on this master word—namely, poetry—without knowing what it means and while declaring that it is useless to make any effort to understand it, thus practically washing one's hands of what one might do under its cover? I no doubt need to account for my path between two opposite errors: to play blindly and to want to define things rationally. A game implies betting—betting on something that escapes us (at least partially). A bet—or a series of bets—to be actively made on the spur of the moment, based on a few clues (often sheer hunches), and of course always more or less strongly counting on luck—thus in a spirit very different from the one that presides over philosophical or scientific reflection, however great the role that intuition might play in these two modes of thought.

Someone who—a pure hypothesis, this—knew how to abolish chance once he had thrown the dice would have no more reason (unless he was willing merely to come out even) to cast them on the table than would the man who had lost his shadow have reason to search for it in his silhouette image or the man whose reflection had been stolen have reason to look for it in his mirror. Thoroughly hindered from taking his chances because he is in a position to win at every throw, he would feel—if dice were his passion—as if he had become a body without a soul, like these two bewitched men above.

But once again I must take back what I have advanced: if I speak as I have just spoken, it's as a man on whom no true misfortune has fallen; were I simply poor or doomed to doing dirty work or looking for a job, I would call anyone who claimed that life was just a game a total bastard or a moron.

*

April 8, 1973 . . .

Toward the middle of this Sunday afternoon, I'm walking the dog just as I do, for his pleasure as well as mine, every day I'm in the country.

We passed by a very large and dark and beautiful farm with a dovecote, a place I know well but that I only recently discovered was the same château du Tronchet where the child Alfred de Vigny used to come—Vigny, far too crowned with laurels and, as far as I am concerned, an informer, since I read how as a civilian he had denounced two soldiers after overhearing them engaged in seditious talk and then even following after them in order to further substantiate his denunciation. Perhaps this is all a calumny, but still—what a blemish on the noble brow of the author of *The Death of the Wolf!*

It's been a quarter of an hour now that I've been bothered by the snow—a very fine snow, almost hail, that has been falling unexpectedly from the leaden sky and that is now whipping my face and my skull and so nipping me with frost that I realize I should have never left home without a hat. I start remembering all those frightening stories about old folks fallen frozen by the wayside on account of the cold.

As we now make our way along a flat road more open to the elements, the snow starts falling harder and harder, and suddenly there is this brief fulguration of a very dry and violent thunderclap, which goes on echoing, followed by nothing further. The dog signals its terror with a wild leap—this dog whom we had boarded at the kennel and who had remained utterly indifferent to the gunshots they would fire off to train the guard dogs, his distant cousins, given that they were all German shepherds, also known as "police dogs."

As we had almost made our way home, an incident: a fight between my dog and a smaller one, across the grille of a gate almost wide enough to allow the two dogs to sink their teeth into each other. Completely surprised by the suddenness of this confrontation, I am unable to hold Typhon back and am able to get him away from his enemy only once the latter's master has done the same. I am completely out of breath after the abrupt ferocity of this encounter, on which I have spent so much effort just to keep the two animals apart.

We are just making our way onto the road that leads to our "Priory" when there is this second incident: a car sideswipes another car, the two vehicles screech to a stop, and coming from one of them I hear the screams of a child—probably a little girl—terrified by the collision but who turns out to be uninjured despite all the fracas.

The dog and I have now reached the courtyard behind our place when I see my wife standing by one of the open doors. Even before we have crossed the cobblestones to the house, she utters these three words: "Pablo is dead."

Two or three days later I will read a newspaper article on the late Pablo Picasso by an art historian who speaks of how crestfallen everybody had felt upon hearing the fateful news of the artist's death on the radio and who compares this to the legend that claimed that the passage from the pagan to the Christian era was signaled by a voice crying out of nowhere: *Pan, the great Pan is dead!*

The end of one world and beginning of another? That is the question, I agree. And I say to myself (torn apart by the loss of this friend, regretting just how reinvigorated I felt by the discovery of all those late works that bore such witness to his fabulous powers of self-renewal) that it is now to our own world—to the world of my wife and me, to the world of all those (now long-lost) other souls—that the fatal *puntilla* blow has been delivered. As if to warn me, there had been this cascade of blows that had boxed my ear:

thunder,
    furious barking,
        cars crashing,
            screams.

*

Having to present myself at the Saint-Antoine Hospital's blood bank (in order to provide blood for the transfusions needed by my gravely ill brother-in-law, now older than normally permissible), I crossed through an open-air Sunday market that was full of life and vivid color. There were people of all races on this street corner: in addition to the Whites (the majority), there were Blacks of both sexes and—vaguely remembered—those Whites (whom many refuse to recognize as such) who are North Africans, as well as a sprinkling of Asians who were not Yellow but more likely natives of India or of some other country between the Near and the Far East.

The gaiety of the marketplace on this sunny Sunday was poorly suited to the sad purpose of my itinerary. As I returned back the same way, it struck me as funny that here I was just a few steps away from the brick building where they had been collecting and distributing different kinds of blood, each bearing its scientific blood type, and that I now found myself among this dense crowd of men and women all busily attending to their shopping while at the same time putting on a display of their large sampling of different bloods (bloods which, unlike those bloods whose deep red hues shone through the plastic pouches in which they were stored for transport, were instead purely metaphorical, on the order of "mixed-blood," "blue blood," "prince of royal blood," "pure blooded").

All that was missing from this global and yet purely neighborhood crowd—a Last Judgment without all the fanfare, played out on a stage at once Parisian and almost provincial—all that was needed to complete this spectrum were a few persons with slanted eyes and a few hippies with their sometimes keen but more often than not vacant gazes.

*

Rather than the red flag—the color of human blood, of mammal blood, of the blood of most of those creatures great and small studied by zoology—it would seem that the black flag of anarchy would provide a more suitable emblem for our species:

black as the boundary that a man traces around himself at a single stroke to distinguish himself from everything else;

black as the night, of which man seems to be sole animal to realize how deeply it envelops him;

black as the *no* he insists on rejoindering to his fate;

black as that cavity of the mouth from which words stream forth;

black as distinctive as those writing systems into which so many cultures decided to project themselves as they emerged from prehistory;

black as the color the impressionists insisted did not exist in nature, thereby evidence of what humanity comes down to in the end—a buzzing fly, trapped in cream;

black as the hole punched in paper or the little hand poking at the clockface;

black as the rage it took to invent fire, which no other species is capable of mastering.

*

Poetically, the hustle and bustle of an airport—a crossroads where I find myself lost among a variegated crowd now branching off in all directions—provides me with a foretaste of death. But on a more practical level I know that my final resting place will be in the empty (or peopled) calm of a library kind enough to concede me my proper footage upon its shelves.

*

When he will have decided to no longer stroll across fields or woods—be it in sun or shade—with his dog, when he will have decided to have someone else walk his animal, someone solid enough to deal with the way he tugs so hard at his collar when provoked by a bird taking flight or a hare scampering away or a fellow canine who doesn't even have to bark or growl to get him going, will those who are close to him, at least all those who are still alive, understand that his days are now numbered?

Far from merely humiliating him, this admission of his decline will snow-ball into a hastening of his senescence, given that he has so arranged his life that the only thing still keeping him in shape are the walks he takes, some-times under clear skies, sometimes under a screen of branches, every time he is presented with the occasion on Saturdays, Sundays, and Mondays, as he overcomes his laziness, eager not to disappoint his dog's quivering and ever more frisky expectations. Once he will have given up on this routine (not without having delayed it from week to week, probably as a result of the hiatus occasioned by inclement weather or because the animal had misbehaved, providing yet another black-and-white example of the fact that it is no longer possible to tell who is the master here and who the slave, or because another stray thorn has pricked his body or soul, thus causing him to cancel his plans), once he will have conceded this ground, a minor matter to be sure, but some-thing that will strike him as the equivalent of surrendering his last bastion, his feet will sink into the mud, his body will become more nebulous, his manner of dress will become more careless, and his words, already ponderous, will feel further weighted down by the state of immobility to which he will have been confined: words now stale and without contour, lacking that humorous twist he liked to impart to them even at their darkest. To listen to him, it will appear that it was his entire person, including his intelligence, that he will have consigned to retirement by having now given up on those ambles through the countryside, every season of which he considered just as beneficial to his daydreams and reflections as to his physical well-being. What, indeed, would his whole mode of behavior come to mean, unless his intention was to wash his hands of everything from here on in and to twiddle his thumbs, no more concerned about appearing as a writer or as an "engaged" intellectual than worried about showing off as the proprietor of a pedigreed dog (nonetheless flattered when people he ran across complemented him on the beauty of his pet)?

If he had been possessed of the requisite courage and complicity, his best tactic would have been, having reached the end of his rope and disheartened by the prospect of taking his walks in the absence of this eager dog, to imitate those ancient kings of the Nile who, feeling that they no longer had the power to respond to the wishes of their people, issued orders that their tomb be dug and that they be laid down therein and that, after their final instructions had been relayed, they be covered by a blanket of reeds . . .

*

Whatever
(a corner of nature, a finely worked thing?)
I can hold on to
without entirely going overboard.
Whatever
even in my absence
might stop my eye
dead in its tracks
and act as
a white blindfold
between me and the void.

*

Marionettes with gestures even less varied than those of the beings they imitate, wooden silhouettes roughly hewn and perhaps merely painted red and blue, the Knights of the Round Table: Sir Yvain, Sir Gawain, Lancelot of the Lake, then Perceval and Galahad—so their names ran in the more scholarly arrangement that allowed me to better understand the old romances that spoke of King Arthur and the quest for the Grail than did the short summaries I had read as a child. My interest in these tales was rekindled in my twenties when I happened upon Apollinaire's *The Rotting Wizard*, a latter-day version of Flaubert's *Temptation of Saint Anthony* but far more unbridled and distantly inspired by the Arthurian cycle—just the kind of mythology that suited me at that point—and this led me to explore the ancient sources Apollinaire was drawing upon (part of my larger desire to clear up all the obscurities in his work) . What Apollinaire, the last great imbiber of stellar spirits, had shown me under the guise of Merlin—that "deceptive and disloyal wizard," whom his lover Viviane, bewitching him with the very spell he had secretly revealed to her, had finally reduced to an absence almost as immense as a death—was the figure of the poet in all its ambiguity, a wizard and a seducer too sensitive to the power of seduction not be its disheartened prey and at the same time the admirable architect of its mirages, a man more wounded than any, but a man nonetheless invested with the highest privilege.

To make one's way across the moors and fallow fields of Brittany, Cornwall, or elsewhere. To ride through the dimness of the forests and below the unsettled skies at land's end, such as in the west of Ireland, where the clouds pile up or dissolve into shreds above a turf whose sod has been striated by the rectangular cuts of the hoe. To sound the horn, to request access to this castle where a trial awaits you, a trial that might seem as benign as a mere chess match with the Lady of the manor but that in fact involves nothing less than facing up to the Gorgon or solving the riddle of the Sphinx. To break lances, to mete out punishment to traitors, to undo magic spells, to make oneself the champion of a damsel with hennaed hair, but also (like Hercules) to have to choose between two paths and become (like that paladin before the age of chivalry) the slave of an Omphale and her spinning wheel. Pure and loyal, Lancelot of the Lake, one of those who seem to be able to triumph over everything, was not without his own failings, given that in loving Queen Guinevere and allowing himself to be loved by her he was thereby betraying the lord to whom he was bound, body and soul, as a liege. The Grail, this chalice (at least according to the Christian version of what must have been an age-old legend) that Christ had sanctified during the Last Supper and in which his blood had been gathered after he had been speared in the ribs on Calvary, the Holy Grail preserved in the castle of Monsalvat (or, according to a different tradition, in an English castle)—this Grail was not brought to life again in all its splendor by Lancelot, because to bring the quest fully to its term one needs to be possessed of a heart and spirit both fearless and spotless.

Merlin (or, more druidically, Myrddhin), the victim of his own witchcraft by a kind of reverse magic, and Lancelot, the chink in whose armor was the openness of his heart, these were the two figures—the former hoisted by the petard of his own mischievousness, the latter of whom one can imagine singing Rimbaud's

Out of delicacy
I lost my life—

with whom I identified far more willingly than with those warriors so blindly devoted to their honor, so willing to act as faithful dogs admitted to the table of their master rather than being thrown scraps, and whose sole fate seemed to lie in gathering themselves about King Arthur (or, more precisely, Artus), a sovereign as grave and rigid as a king in a deck of cards.

Of all these knights who so aspired to be paragons, whatever the errors (or even the sins) they happened to commit, the one who had the most glorious fate—post-mortem, it is true—was Perceval of Wales. This brave and honest Celt (for even if his existence was a fiction, he was rooted in Celtic literature that was later Christianized) was to become the unquestionable jewel of German art, especially after the many changes of skin that eventuated in Bayreuth, which for many represented the new Mecca. His posthumous reputation can be compared only to that of Garin the Lotharingian, who ended his career as the heavy tenor who stars in *Lohengrin* (pronounced "green," not "grain").

It's also not that easy to recognize in the soprano Isolde the extremely medieval Iseut or a barbarian queen on the order of Maeve or Deirdre of the Sorrows. But how discover the clear profile of Perceval behind that of Parsifal, whose strongly emphasized chastity seems to be merely the pharisaical mask of some murky misogyny? The exact opposite of a devotee of courtly love, he rebuffs the Flower Maidens as if they were common whores, and having reached the end of his path to perfection (with the innocence of a half-wit rather than of a member of the elect), he watches the voluptuous Kundry (so naked and knotty under her habit) die like an animal who can be touched only for the purpose of her ritual purification.

Just as much as that false prophet Claudel, my compatriot who had no Ludwig the Moon King as a patron but who was addressed as "His Excellency" or "Maître" while showered with flowers, crowns, and even worse, an official national funeral, another monster whom I (ever the righter of wrongs) would love to slay with my sword is Wagner. Having settled my accounts with their respective pathoses—that sublimity of tone I sometimes find gripping, but never without remorse—would I not feel kin to one of those storybook heroes who, having conquered a plague (the grandeur of this task too great to be believable), now light-headedly realizes that he can not only comprehend but also speak the language of the birds?

However outsize the reputations of these two gentlemen, I see them (almost obsessively) as being marked by a blood spot or oil stain that ruins their work for me, even at those moments when I am most tempted to tip my hat to it. Their preachifying about chastity (which the second of them was far from having practiced, a failing only a Puritan could condemn) seems to be linked to something far more malodorous in origin: a cruelty that is not even sadistic but something mean, something snide, something that takes pleasure in inflicting suffering on those who for some reason belong to the realm of the reprobate. Over the course of the various days of Claudel's long play *The Satin Slipper*, the initial scenes dramatize the transformation (with the help of the Virgin Mary, of various angels, and of Providence) of the noble Don Rodrigue, devoured as he is by a love that disrespects the sanctity of marriage, into a conquistador who gets over his lovesickness by massacring the heathens of America and Asia and then becomes a sort of saint, not because he repents of his crimes as a soldier of the Cross but because (vanity of vanities!) he ends up poor and abandoned thanks to the ingratitude of those for whom he had been constructing an empire. In *Parsifal*—which features the choice (all too standard in chivalric romances) between an honest European forest and a malign and malefic Oriental garden—Wagner opted for pity: now rid of their false magi, let the impure be washed by the cleansing commiseration of the pure! But not content to let Kundry, a spirit condemned to wander the world like Ahasuerus, die (by heavenly grace) in a state of shame barely erased by her baptism, Wagner also allows the knights to display their arrogant conceitedness—whose inhumanity, at least to people of my generation, recalled that of the SS officers trained at the Ordenburger—as they go about punishing their king-priest for having given in to carnal temptation; and it is with questionable insistence that Wagner shows this king tortured (that is, until the hour he is granted his condescending pardon) by the very wound that Christ had received from the spear.

As for Claudel, this chain-mail Christian who ended up in the green uniform of the French Academy, was it his God or his Devil who persuaded him that it was only fitting (while a lowly colonial officer was seizing the reins in Spain to establish fascism) that the anarchists guilty of having set fire to churches be summarily executed? As for Wagner, whose unforgivable sin was his racism, is his past as a young revolutionary in 1848 enough to make one forget how in the process of digging through the German tradition for material for his librettos (literary librettos, more ambitious than the more sketchy librettos of classic operas, but nonetheless so prolix, so freighted with their author's messages that, perhaps on account of my shaky German, I find them to be veritable millstones around the neck of his music), he stirred up the muck of his nation's prejudices by focusing on the theme of accursed gold, a theme that the Nazis subsequently incorporated into their mystique of blood and soil in order to denounce the Jewish plutocracy—with the disastrous consequences of which one is only too aware (a delirium of eugenics that they also projected onto the Gypsies)?

Of these two cronies—the heavyset Picard with his policeman's moustache and the Saxon foppishly wearing a velvet artist's beret—only one of them (in his search for an *absolute* theater as effective as, presumably, the sacred theater of the Greeks) went on his own Grail quest, passing by his own Monsalvat, learning to manipulate sound with genius while taking the high road that would finally dump him down the following trapdoor: to consider himself so seriously as a prophet that (as is the case in *Parsifal*) he would stage earnest simulations of rites and marvels, turning those festive occasions so often celebrated in opera into pious ceremoniousness. In Wagner's case, the phoniness of these scenes, all the more obvious the more edifying they pretend to be, will appear (to those who don't just take their opera in with ecstatic half-closed eyes) as a patent reminder that everything in theater depends on mystification and charlatanism and that one would have to be a fool to swallow it whole. To pedantically rework (as in the case of *The Ring of the Nibelung*) a mythology at once too local and too doctrinally presented as the product of one's ancestral land is to engage in mere antiquarianism, perhaps valuable as a way of reglamorizing the archaic cult of heroes but not effective as a way of imparting (as does Greek tragedy) pity and terror. The initiation of Tamino in *The Magic Flute* brings us far closer to the threshold of the sacred than does Parsifal's, and compared to the epic vision of Wagner's Tetralogy, the verismo of Puccini's *Girl of the Golden West*—sometimes derided as a "horse opera" by the cognoscenti, who forget that the Western is the modern reincarnation of the chivalric romance—leads us into the heart of tragedy. To lend one's credence to an explicit fairy tale or melodrama—without being bothered in the former case by its naïve Manichaeism or Masonic drawing-room mysteries, or in the latter by the biblical echoes of its American gold rush—is far easier than to suspend one's disbelief when confronted by the pretentious gadgetry of Wagner's operas, in which the magister's sermonizing often overrides nearly everything offered to the eye or ear. And if one pursues the matter further and asks oneself (without taking theatricality into consideration anymore) who should be awarded the prize for exemplary musicianship, applying the lesson of *Parsifal*—simplicity and purity as the two sovereign qualities—should one in fact chose Richard Wagner in all his turbulent drapery or rather Erik Satie? Satie, originally a Rosicrucian to be sure, and the author of a *Mass for the Poor*, then a suburban member of the Communist Party, but who remained true to his narrow, solitary path as a humorous Socrates and involuntary follower of Zeno, practicing composition as others might archery.

Placed halfway between history and fiction and no more legendary than all other matters that come down to us from the Middle Ages, the tales of the Round Table delighted me—when I was no longer entirely a child—in a way far differently from my earlier readings of the *Mother Goose Tales* or other stories of this sort, situated in an *elsewhere* that is intentionally left very vague in their references to imaginary kingdoms and in their "once upon a time" evoking a past that has never been recorded.

Back then I cared little if Arthur and his companions had really existed, as did Charlemagne and his barons. What was, however, undeniable was the fact that they possessed a firmness of outline (however fictional they were) that was far more vivid than that of the Marquis de Carabas, Prince Charming, or Perrault's Riquet with the Tuft. Anchored in a more or less evident historicity, these Knights of the Round Table, outfitted in armor like the Dunois or the Bayards, moved about in a fairy-tale world, lending their consistency to the realm of the marvelous, and their various wondrous doings as recounted by the chronicles were all the more convincing because this series of adventures was based on the lives of men (however rudimentary their representation) and not on such imaginary beings as the heroes of folktales or classical mythology.

Equally human were the prophets, the kings, and the defenders of Israel whom I read about while studying the Bible, no doubt because I was taught that their stories, including those episodes involving the supernatural, constituted *history*—something whose truthfulness could not be put into question. The marvels of the Bible were of a consistency far denser than those of fairy tales (the purr of which enchanted me without ever truly coming to life) and were far weightier than the marvels of pagan myth that I began to discover with delight as an adolescent, even though I had been warned that they were associated with the worship of a myriad of false gods and thus to be taken only as fictions. Although both of these shared the capacity to impress themselves upon me, the marvelous realm of biblical history struck me as different from that of the Round Table, not simply because it was filled with figures who were no more real than those of fairy tales or those invented by the Greeks and Romans in the cold light of their Olympus. It was simply because biblical history belonged to the sphere of catechism—a sphere of inculcated belief—whereas the Round Table and the Grail, once I had discovered them, provided me with a treasure into which, unchecked by any iron rule, I could delve to my heart's delight.

Proper names like YVAIN or GAWAIN (almost twinned by rhyme) and UTHER PENDRAGON (Arthur's father, whom I discovered only later) or place-names like AVALON are levers that I merely have to press in order to open the sluice gates of those waters that carry me off like an undefinable wave—a wave that I'll avoid calling *ineffable*, given that this word, pretending as it does to say nothing, ends up saying so much that it ceases to mean anything. "Yvain," the portrait of young and honest man, a daydreamer rendered as stiff as a corpse by his armor. "Uther Pendragon," who in the tempestuous clangor of battle deploys the baroque decorations of his flaming golden banner and whose name could also designate, beyond the warrior, an expert in illusions and magic spells (fabrics shaken to provoke apparitions). "Avalon," as real as those landscapes of Scotland and Ireland that I recently visited and that struck me both as being perfectly suited to me and as translating into their purely earthly nomenclature (whose irrefutable dictionary could even be captured by a series of arid photographs) that transcendence I seek in poetry.

With a power equal to the above words, ROUND TABLE, made of solid wood and cleanly circumscribed, hewn by woodcutters' hands, an earthy ballast for the ideal GRAIL, whose name (at once crystalline and gravelly, like the sacred substance of some special white sugar) does not come to an end but just hovers there in the air, vibrating like a low-pitched diapason or like the faint squeal of a harmonica extending out into invisible drafts of wind. Or again this other name, which also does not end in any closure and which I locate among the knights of Arthur, uncertain whether he belongs to their company but persuaded that he is more or less related to them: BAEDEVER, a name so insistent that I dare to venture (however a philologist might analyze its origins) that it expresses the bizarre dimension of all human existence and that it darkly hints that one cannot go where I want to go, except on the sly (combining, as they might say in an old wives' tales, the courage of a lion with the prudence of a snake); a name, to be sure, with a double register, one that could be equally worn by a scoundrel or a wise counselor, but one that I take in its more noble sense, seeing in it the face of the knight who looks with astonishment upon the following marvel—the emergence of an unknown hand lifting out the water three times in a row the sword that the dying Arthur had asked this knight to cast into a lake. It is, however, possible that I might have mistakenly placed Baedever at the edge of the lake that this uplifted hand seems to have left untroubled by the slightest ripple; the play of assonances would more likely link his name to another, stagnant pool, where no living thing, not even a black swan, lies reflected: ". . . down by the dank tarn of Auber / In the ghoul-haunted woodland of Weir," according to the refrain of one of Poe's most memorable poems. Whatever my mistake—the Arthurian cycle contains tales of different eras that are grafted onto each other rather than perfectly fitted together, creating a whole that is so wobbly that the same character can appear here and there under different names— when I looked up Baedever in the version I own (conveniently shelved next to the *Percival of Wales* prefaced by Apollinaire, not far from Joseph Bédier's edition of *Tristan* and *The Madness of Tristan* as rewritten by the Sade special- ist Gilbert Lély), I in fact discovered that he did not make an appearance, and when I went looking for him in the three other books, he was missing there too. I was all the more disappointed to discover that in my version the knight whom Arthur had asked to plunge his sword into the lake was in fact called (with a somewhat comic slap) GIFLET. Perhaps if I had a copy of *Ivanhoe* on hand (which I read in a condensed schoolboy version around the same time as I was in like fashion discovering the romances of the Round Table), I might be able to meet up with the elusive Baedever, but he would probably be the incarnation (who knows?) of the kind of man completely external to the circle of knighthood.

The dubious death of Arthur. Lancelot a jack of clubs and Perceval transformed into a Himalayan bear cub. Tristan flanked by a greyhound or mastiff and a bagpiper (the folklore substitute for the horn that the here inarguable Wagner proposes to our ear). A shield struck like a gong. The fall of the house of Usher. The storm-tossed trees and dozing heaths of a lordly domain in the Scottish Highlands. Banquo the bloody ghost arrives to trouble the banquet. An Irish ruin signed Cromwell, this reverse Viollet-le-Duc. A megalithic tomb where you have to wriggle and, risking bruises, snake yourself along the narrow passageway through the rock in order to reach the central chapel decorated with spiral ornaments (Père Ubu's Great Gidouille, also visible in Brittany in a cave on the tiny isle of Gavrinis). Enormous royal cooking pots, perhaps transformed into witch's cauldrons and, refined by time, into the Grail, which accompanies the lance, this other attribute of the chieftain (*dixit* Marcel Mauss, here quoted somewhat liberally from one of his courses or conversations).

Following a recipe that might be off-limits to one of those almanacs or chapbooks chock-full of morsels of popular know-how, carefully throw into this admixture, so that the whole dish comes together, measured doses of the following ingredients, listed below using two combined categories—their order of appearance onstage and their affinities:

quasi-immemorial, the Meudon observatory, a stable, reassuring image often present on my horizon, a sort of gray or bluish aerostat whose cylindrical base was anchored into the soil as if—a balloon not merely captive but enrooted—it should never budge or disappoint me;

the forest of Villers-Cotterêts, where I recently wandered—in mistaken memory, it turns out, because it is in the forest of Le Mans where this little drama is said to have played itself out—imagining Charles VI, panicked into a state of madness, being attacked by an unknown assailant who had suddenly leaped out of the bushes and barred his passage by throwing himself at the head of his horse;

the Clamart woods, where our now nearly white-haired friendship first took root and André Masson used to paint as if Oceania lay before him;

the lair of a deified ancestor, Lake Bosomtwe—banked over with mist as I peered at it at the bottom of its warm wooded bowl—in the former Gold Coast, in the heart of Ashanti land;

seen from afar and all got up in white under fair skies, Sacré-Coeur, a Parisian Monsalvat which would be the perfect emblem for my city if (by a stroke of bad luck!) the Eiffel Tower didn't exist;

the Lion Gate that provides an entrance through the cyclopean walls of Mycenae, the two great felines guarding the threshold;

at Youga Dogorou, the cave containing two statuettes made of dried mud, their bodies nearly shapeless but their heads more finely worked, representing two tiny beings who—according to local African tradition—preceded the appearance of man on earth;

in the surburbs of Oslo, the great ramp for international ski-jumping competitions, a toboggan for giants, comparable to a segment of a road whose downward slope spills into a steep upward swoop suddenly cut short to allow a takeoff toward the stars;

not far from Naples and Posillipo, the cave of the Cumaean Sibyl, its deep corridor echoing with oracles;

a structure that appears to the eye as in a hallucinogenic vision, the dizzying castle of Ludwig II of Bavaria at Neuschwanstein, a fake fortress whose appointments are part Wagnerian and part Arabic, with furnishings and household utensils—from the most noble to the most humble—made to order to be one of a kind, because objects fabricated for others or similar to those of others would be unworthy of a sovereign's treasure, however rare or ancient they might be;

in East Berlin, the neoclassical pantheon rather small in diameter and whose cupola is pierced by a round hole that allows the rain to drip down onto the blackish block of rough-hewn marble directly beneath it, the sole monument on this site, which is guarded by two sentries, with only the plaque on the rear wall indicating that this is a memorial for all the victims of fascism;

in the port of Le Havre, in the Compagnie Transatlantique sector, the dry dock—utterly empty—of the SS *France*, so huge, so deep that it makes you a bit dizzy when you lean over to look into it, as if from the upper tiers of the arena of Nîmes or the Colosseum;

in Ireland, the ridiculously wide path that, were it not for the way it snakes upward, would look like it was created by erosion, cutting a great pale scar into the flanks of Mount Patrick, trampled to the bone by centuries of pilgrims climbing to the shrine at the summit.

Without fearing that this might confuse the dish, don't hesitate to spice it up with a Dublin ingredient: namely, the front door of 7 Eccles Street, home of Leopold Bloom, a door I believe to be Georgian in design but that—now transferred to the upstairs floor of the Bailey Bar and hung near the toilets—no longer opens or closes on anything at all. Unless you want to go overboard by adding leitmotifs from Wagner's *Meistersinger* that have been well ground up and sucked to the marrow, top off the recipe with a few sprigs, ad libitum, of those dream castles (true castles in the air) that their inventor Satie would carefully draw in black ink on small cards, supplemented by titles and other calligraphic asides. The pyramids of Egypt, counted among the Seven Wonders of the World; Delphi, so thunderstruck and striking; the Padirac Chasm; the quarries of Saint-Rémy and Les Baux, half natural grotto, half architecture; the Great Wall of China, reeling off all its square guard towers, now deserted; the mysterious circular construction called the "Tomb of the Christian Lady" a few kilometers from Algiers: these are a few further additions that might just be possible. But I'll stop here. If I keep on adding ingredients, I'll just be thinning out the sauce like some devious master chef, and it would entail either speaking of things that have amazed me but that here would be adduced for mere decorative purposes or (by highlighting some of them) simply rehashing everything I have already said over the course of this Long March that can no longer pretend it's even a Grail quest.

These ingredients

—some gathered almost by chance and haphazardly added to the dish as for some potluck supper,

—others carefully chosen and measured out (because for all of them it was their nature, their *quality*, that mattered, and not their *quantity* as expressed by their respective weights or sizes), then filtered down so as to retain merely their fine flower—

I have held on to because they seem to illustrate my sense of the MARVELOUS. Despite their diversity, I recognize their common denominator: they all provoke a feeling of wonder in me. Their comparison should therefore allow one to isolate this quality of the marvelous that they share and, ipso facto, to discern what I include in this word, a word I use somewhat loosely, as if, filled with a meaning that needed no explanation, it were some stored-value card that spoke for itself once removed from one's wallet and plunked down on the table. *Merveilleux*, a luminous word to be sure, but a bit vague, like an image without contours, a word applicable to almost anything if one is not careful, like a blanket of fog veiling (à la Turner) a sun that illuminates it without peeking through but whose brightness nonetheless makes itself felt behind this cloudlet of milk in a cup of tea. If my ingredients come together, the dish I will have produced in my witch's kitchen will have taken this image and turned it into the solid substance of a birthday cake or a *galette des rois*, easily sliced and readily consumed. This successful operation will, however, prove largely theoretical, given that it will have taken place only on the level of abstract ideas; but perhaps it will have opened the path to practical application . . .

Let me point out that all my ingredients, whatever their conscious or unconscious sources, involve monuments or sites or inanimate objects, and even such characters as Lancelot, Percival, and Tristan turn up as motion-less *figures*, addressed only to the eye. One might say that I have included in my realm of the marvelous nothing that might be considered spectacular (for a spectacle is a living, evolving thing), but only items that might emerge from an exhibition hall, a photo library, or an archive—documents that I have temporarily lifted from a museum, without rousing them from their torpor. A comic blunder, for these items are in absolute contrast to my own sense of the marvelous, which for me has to be bound up with life and not be relegated to some abstract realm. A contrast so obvious (and proof of the radical falsity of the entire operation) that I would definitely have to turn in my cook's apron were it not for the fact that, upon examining matters more carefully, I discover exceptions to the aforementioned rules: the forest of Villers-Cotterêts is not a dead space at all but rather a place that every time I have visited I have endowed (as if the thing could have happened only there) with some spe-cial historical event that was rich in repercussions and that seemed to me to perfectly agree with the sweltering heat of these great woods (the Valois king going as mad as King Lear and whose melancholy humor might well have been responsible for the introduction of playing cards in France, and who in turn inspired that other madman Nerval); the ski jump at Oslo is not inert but linked to an action, seeing how it is related to sports, its dimensions tailored to a real event taking place in real time, even if this involve a completely out-of-the-ordinary feat; in fascism's ever-persistent efforts to survive, the East Berlin memorial is not just a temple of memory, for what is so moving about it is that its tragic message, which remains all too relevant, is conveyed (and yet arguable for implying fascism might be eternal) by the archaic quality of this block of marble washed by the rain, so rough hewn and so close to the state of nature that, even more shapeless than the Youga Dogorou statuettes, it seems extracted from primordial magma.

In the light of the above, I have now come to a somewhat different judg-ment of my choices. Yes, I was surely wrong to want to establish some sort of list of the Wonders of the World, rigid in its perspective and no doubt adopted because in my ever more advanced and tepid years I was looking to rely on a certain number of official monuments rather than answering the question "What does the Marvelous mean to me?" or rather than wondering why all this so mattered to me when I was young and hoped to live out the marvelous as intensely as Lancelot or Merlin, even if in other shapes and forms. Instead I had merely mapped the marvelous onto my sixty-eight years: a realm less of perdition or saintliness than of contemplation and retreat, where I might rediscover a hint of that dreamy well-being occasioned by the distant sight of the Meudon observatory during my childhood years. A realm whose role I nonetheless refuse to admit can be reduced to that of Equanil or some other tranquilizer, for if it is to be of any help to me at all it needs to bear the vivid marks (if only in the purely speculative sense) of that dislocation or violation of norms essential to the marvelous. This is, no doubt, why any number of the sites and objects to which I refer are other than they are or other than they were allowed to be considered and why they acquire value in my eyes only in proportion to my inability to confine them to the proper limits of reason . . . An Irish tumulus wearing Ubu's whorl on its belly. A geomorphic accident revealed to be—against all expectations—the simple path trod by the feet of pilgrims. A door from a demolished house, the home of a hero of a novel, with no other function than to introduce the myth of this latter-day Ulysses into a tavern. A royal castle out of some expressionist film, its princely furnishings newer and more singular than any tasteless millionaire could imagine. A forest in the suburbs equaling Oceania. An empty dry dock as the Colosseum. In the Latomie quarries of Syracuse I arrange the rebel mercenary army of *Salammbô*, preparing it for the fatal ambush at the Defile of the Axe. Two sculpted lions become the fantastic guardians of the threshold (armed warriors or samurai) that the young couple of initiates in *The Magic Flute* must traverse as one of their trials, a scene that could well be set in the Roman quarries of Saint-Rémy. By further refraction, the tiny castles—as well as the imaginary blueprints and comic squibs—that issued forth from the pen of Satie reveal to me the kind of astonishing secrets that a harmless-looking little man wearing a pince-nez might harbor in his head as he engages in his private bits of pataphysical fun.

Beyond the large number of antiquities and long-ago memories (the Round Table and the Grail, for starters) that enter into my ingredients—a number ascribable to my attraction to marvels so weathered by time (either inside or outside of myself) as to seem capable of resisting everything and thus providing me with the solid underpinnings I need—what strikes me when re-reading the above list is the fact that it addresses so little that might be deemed erotic, or at least explicitly so, even though any decent person of today might find it child's play to discover the hidden allusions to a realm of the marvelous so unghostly that it could, as it were, easily be seized by bodily force: the womblike chasm of Padirac, for example, or the warm wooded bowl of Lake Bosomtwe, the cave of the sibyl with its receding corridor where the oracle sits hidden, the prehistoric tomb into which one has to make one's way like a snake—these symbols are today utterly without mystery. This huge zone of existence, now consigned to oblivion and of which, like the rope in the house of a hanged man, one would rather not speak, is this what this most tangible form of the marvelous has become for me, a pitiful Parsifal who, no longer having to make the effort to resist the lure of Flower Maidens, just wishes he could also put their voices out of mind?

The sacred realm of eroticism, completely different from anything else, insolently detached from daily life, possessed of the same startling coarseness with which the women in strip clubs (such as the Tabarin, back in the day) would parade their powdered and depilated bodies in front of the noses of their dreary customers, seated there at the tables in their stolid bourgeois outfits. A realm that was off limits and whose most privileged locus was the *maison close*, filled with female nudity and the stench of washbasins, removed from the hubbub or the silence of the street, even though separated from it by the merest of thresholds, a materialization of the taboo surrounding all places of ill repute. A pagan realm, as opposed to the Christian realm of morality, a realm owing less to the Mass than to the witches' Sabbath and belonging to the marvelous not only on account of its astonishing vividness but also because it is a place where rules no longer apply, where prudence is thrown to the wind, where everything pivots into a trance and all lucidity vanishes, opening a rift in the everyday through which that which knows no limits might finally burst.

To defuse matters a bit: when I speak of eroticism (whose marvels spring from the avidity with which we crave them), I approach it via the rather bloodless exemplars of its holy places (thus again returning it to the museum), or if I speak of it in other terms, I do so in very few words—such as those that I have just set down and that have allowed me to drape things in a veil of generality and to keep my rather rhetorical scholia free from references to any precise acts or brief flings. Another area I have scissored out: as concerns love, this fully-fledged region of the marvelous to which the Arthurian tales—with their Ladies of the Lake, their Morgan Le Fays, and their ritual of courtly love often skewing into madness—ought normally to have introduced me, I have not said a word; or if I have spoken of it, it's almost despite myself, by merely alluding to it indirectly or elliptically reducing it to near zero, as when mentioning the Lion Gate I by chance associated it with the couple undergoing initiation in *The Magic Flute*, thereby discreetly letting it be known that I ascribe a great importance to not being one but to being one of two and that I fully recognize the talismanic power of this kind of complicity—which is why I thought it enough to simply cite an illustrative scene from an opera that has always deeply moved me!

I would gladly admit that it was some Myrddhin—or some not necessarily Celtic wizard—who had sworn to bewitch me, distracting me from those

regions I ought to have explored, and who had struck me with blindness or de-
luded me into making silk purses out of sows' ears . . . Need I underscore this
further? This image may be far too literary and misleading, aware as I am that I
was not the victim of any inner or outside interference, but at least it illustrates
the following truth: by setting out from the Round Table and Merlin, I was
following a *Bibliothèque bleue* path that would led me—entranced as I was by
ancient charms—to overlook any real trouble spots and instead direct myself
toward a realm of the marvelous where everything was safe and sound, a realm
that, even if grafted onto the forms of the visible, remains as disincarnate as
any novel, poem, or dream, and not a realm whose flesh and blood is made
up of certain concrete facts that come into play without the master workings
of the imagination.

Having taken note of my deficiency and wanting to explain its mechanics
to myself, I was thus led—my pen guiding me as much I guided it—to recognize that there are two orders of the marvelous, one of which is inscribed
within events, the other created by the imagination. On the one hand, the adventures of Yvain, Gawain, Lancelot, Perceval, or Galahad and the vivid realities that these adventures would have represented for them had these characters indeed existed; on the other hand, that which passes through the heads of
the readers of these tales. This distinction is justified, but it seems insufficient,
because if one wants to follow further down this path, why not also count—
as the third order of the marvelous—the operation that occurred within the
minds of the authors who took constructions more vaporous than clouds and
crystallized them into these tales? To ignore the fact that even though reality
may contain the marvelous within itself, the real is nonetheless not simply
something lifted from the marvelous as found in books and furthermore needs
to be distinguished from the marvelous you just make up in your head—this is
the madness of Don Quixote and Nerval, both having forgotten the boundary
that separates something lived from something imagined, whether the latter
be the product of dream or of conscious creation . . . But this madness, a door
thrown open too wide upon a parade of wonders, represents nothing more
than an extreme obedience to the movement that generates the marvelous:
whether one lives them or whether one knows them to be imaginary, whether
one lives them while infusing them with the imaginary, or whether one lives
them despite knowing they are imaginary, what is involved is an almost love-
struck fidelity to events and facts that are incommensurable with those out of
which ordinary existence is woven. And is not the poetry one writes a response
to this same kind of movement: to capture those incommensurables to which
we willingly abandon ourselves or, inversely, to try to fashion in the very act of

writing those incommensurables that might (at least momentarily) keep us in thrall? The marvelous, poetry, love—all equally arise if I uncompromisingly open myself to something (an event, a living being, an object, an image, an idea) that has been endowed by my desire for the limitless with an aura at once permanent and fugitive.

Can I admit that if he were really battling the monster instead of engaging in a fiction, the storybook hero would be truly experiencing the marvelous, a texture of certain events and not just the lighting one projects on them, or should I instead admit that because the marvelous takes its life from a tale (the one told to me, the I one I tell to others or that I privately tell myself), no marvel can come to fruition without one's having had the leisure to dream of it, even if only for an instant? However unearthly the color of the dragon, our hero will assume—despite the help of magic powers no more efficient than the technical perfection of the arm he wields—that he is committing a brave and meritorious action that is proof of his unmatched qualities but that is as awesomely distinct from the marvelous as taking up arms against some existing enemy who needs to be stopped from doing any more harm (such as imperialism today, long considered a *paper tiger* but still a tiger tout court for those ready to take it on face to face). If the champion of legend truly wants to live within the realm of the marvelous, wouldn't it be when—giving himself over to the enchantments of the fey or (like Siegfried) falling into desperate love with a daughter of the gods—he forgets his heroic vocation altogether and abandons the righteous path of Hercules or Saint George to become *part of the Devil's party without knowing it*, following the example of the true poet, who, according to William Blake, is always on Satan's side? And as for war, whatever its horrors and its upheavals, the rigors of its atrocities do not exclude the marvelous, as witnessed in our day by the way in which Apollinaire (an all too conformist warrior) was unembarrassed to turn its battles into fireworks displays in his songs of praise. (And I, a soldier straight out of some operetta, I remember how I fell into a state of wonder—in the war following his *Calligrams*—finding myself one night on one of the sidings of the Aubrais railroad station while manning a munitions train and having nothing else to do but contemplate, without abandoning my position, the huge shower of sparks that were neither lightning nor cosmic signals in the darkened sky, but rather the stuttered messages exchanged between the stumps of the electrical cables severed by the bombs just dropped by German planes and that were thereby, I imagine, turned into producers of short circuits . . .) But when a soldier is awestruck by the Apocalypse into which he has been plunged is this not precisely because, having taken his distance from the event and hence having split off from himself, he observes this occurrence of the marvelous from the outside, more like some eager spectator than as a combatant in a battle just routinely going about his business as if nothing mattered? The marvelous is a bolt of lightning that erupts between two poles, one of which must be myself, and the other of which is tendered to me by fate, as attractive perhaps as the specific site on which the Taoist chooses to build his temple, although worth nothing if it elicits no answer within me to this offer. To each, therefore, the marvel to which he is ready and able to respond: for Tamino, it is the daughter of the Queen of the Night; for Papageno, the Papagena bird and the tables laden with viands; for Don Juan, who has chosen to risk everything, the marble hand extended to him by the Commander. Whatever the forms it might assume, nothing will appear marvelous if it is not specific to me—as specific as the conscious or unconscious shape of my desire. A marvel in my own image, to my own measure, or at least in proportion to my desire to be someone courageous enough to be thrilled that something of this sort might be happening to him. In the last case, it would be a marvel whose occurrence would no doubt trouble me more than fully satisfying me and that would therefore be a marvel only in the dream that I'm making of it . . .

The marvelous in its raw state versus the marvelous in its distilled form (taking on taste only if processed by my personal alembic). The marvelous that knocks you off your feet versus the marvelous rid of all its virulence (watered down, as it were, and comparable, at least in the realm of ritual practices, to the substitution of dog for human sacrifices, or after the occurrence of a death, the burning of paper figures replacing the burning of humans and their earthly belongings, or polo or chess—from which card games, it would seem, derive—taking over from the bloody jousts of war). The absolute marvelous, in which one can believe only if one does not question it at all, versus the relative marvelous, the wonder of which is that one believes in it without truly believing in it (or, I would even suggest, the effect of whose charm lies in the fact that one should really not be believing in it at all). Less frenzied than the former—which is ever present, ever at a boil, ever in revolt, if not in revolution—the latter would be more evanescent, occasioned by a sudden moment of poetic insight (inevitably contemplative, whether cast in the here and now or in retrospect) or else brought about by those elements in any narrative or work that reveal themselves to be a reflection or an echo or an imitation of this other marvelous, whose wild and immediate reign has no need of any reflection to assume its throne. But if one describes this integral marvelous as an event that by its own tenor and motion makes itself immediately evident, doesn't this also entail defining it as some sort of ipso facto marvelous, inherent in all those events that, independent of ourselves and simply perceived as flagrant violations of the laws of nature, can be classed as miracles only if they are not mere illusions? One might well speak of a nonhuman, transcendent marvelous similar to the one in which religions traffic, but without denying the reality of such occurrences one would nevertheless have to refuse the idea that they were put into motion by some helping hand from above, just as one would have to put aside the explanation that these staggering epiphanies were the products of mistaken perceptions or sudden swerves in the workings of the world and instead accept the fact that because they are unclassifiable they thereby belong to the supernatural, this intellectual catchall term that gathers into itself everything that remains a mystery because unexplained (or inexplicable) to this day.

But even if I had convinced myself that I had gotten to the bottom of the story—to wit, that the marvelous par excellence is nothing other than the supernatural—I was still flailing about in the void, for it turns out that the latter category (which includes, as its name indicates, only that which exceeds the possibilities of natural occurrence) does not account for those things that, in their various ways, cause me to cry out in wonder when I feel the iridescence of their enigmatic impact upon me (as I would describe it, without fearing I was falling into some kind of mumbo-jumbo). The only opposite case: the sensation of crossing to the other side of the mirror that I briefly experienced some thirty years ago while watching a woman friend who, drifting away from us as she breathed her last, now proceeded to sign herself—but in reverse, as if inspired by a demon!—in a gesture so crazy on the part of this nonbeliever that the uneasy amazement it provoked in me felt as if it had descended upon me from the outside, shooting down my nape to the base of my spine. To want to describe the supernatural as the supporting framework of the marvelous would, moreover, be to embrace a notion that is still too bathed in mysticism to be applicable to those occurrences that today are more prudently referred to as "paranormal" (second sight, telepathy, premonition, etc.): things difficult to explain but that, given that they happen, are by definition natural, as is everything that takes place in the world of the senses. As concerns the funereal scene above, the trance that tingled down my spine did indeed give off the clearly visible luminescence of a trail of light, at least as described to me by the friend of mine who was there beside me as she lay dying; I am most intrigued by the utter strangeness of this kind of phenomenon, in which physiological heresy and the marvelous seem to overlap, but what matters to me is not what a spiritist or a metapsychologist might discover in this luminous substantialization of my gooseflesh. I would not have been seized with such a frisson had I not been accustomed to viewing the woman who lay dying before me as the very image of Nerval's *sainte de l'abîme*, a saint of the abyss, and had not my friend (whose companion she was and with whom I had entered into full complicity) been even more overwhelmed than I, the frisson that was flowing through me surely wouldn't have become visible to him (even if only as an imaginary hallucination); absent our shared emotion at the event—to which should be added our sorrow, our fatigue, the beauty of the woman who lay upon her bier before us, the sacrilegious prank that she seemed to be playing (even to our unbelieving eyes) by parodically reversing the sign of the cross—this singular and (apparently) supernatural occurrence would certainly not have have taken place. In and of itself, this surprising materialization of my stupefaction strikes me as nothing more than a bizarre detail, as puzzling as a trick demonstration of physics pulled off in a setting quite hospitable to the whiff of the marvelous: the spectacle of the perfect and beauteous death that our friend apparently wanted to offer us, and the spirit in which we were complying with it, as if taking Communion. I therefore believe that there is no point in wondering about the existence of an ipso facto marvelous, which the marvelous of storybook tales or of our own invention would in turn derive from or mimic: as the architect of science, man is the founder—beyond its walls—of the marvelous, something one can characterize only as a violation of logic or an exception to the rules, for to situate it in relation to those laws which it by definition eludes or to neglect that wave that brings the depths of our feelings or ideas to the surface would be to adopt a merely scientistic view of the marvelous, a contradiction in terms. But the fact remains: more than others, certain things tend to elicit this state of inebriation, be it gentle or brutal, that makes me feel—whether running hot or cold, whether lightning fast or in slow motion, whether possessed or enchanted—as if I am being swept away on a flying carpet.

That which, without necessarily skewing our weights and measure, exceeds the quotidian but cannot be reduced to the utterly outlandish, that which (neither an item to be placed in our mental cabinet of curiosities nor a five-legged sheep) completely exhilarates us, setting our imagination racing into dream or wonder—it is no doubt on these two fields of play (the realms of EFFUSION and REVERIE on a symbolic land registry) that the marvelous takes multifarious root.

When the extraordinary becomes a daily thing, Revolution is at hand—this was basically what the man who before his death embodied the legendary figure

of the guerrillero was saying. In his clearheaded and feet-firmly-on-the-ground
fashion, breathing in the air of his times despite his asthma, Che Guevara was
certainly not thinking of the marvelous when he spoke of how the extraordinary could one fine day be transformed into the everyday. What need did he
have for the standard imagery of Revolution: the angry swarming masses, the
sacking of arsenals, the storming of prisons, barricades, women manning canons or tending to the wounded, soldiers raising their rifle butts, tyrants decapitated or hung on butcher's hooks, statues torn down, monuments defaced? Yet
to refuse to hang on to its folklore does not mean that one is impervious to the
marvelous of the Revolution, a social tipping point that demonstrates—as did
the Greek philosopher who proved the idea of motion by walking—the sudden feasibility of a series of accomplishments previously thought to be lunatic.

Measured against the scale of love or the genesis of Revolution, the bits
and pieces of the marvelous that I have here adduced as examples (or samples,
rather, of those kinds of things that trigger a marvelous made to my measure)
are—except a single one, cited almost by accident—just a gathering of trifles,
almost as futile as a music box, an ornate trinket, or a novelty item. As mental
gadgets or dried flowers pressed into albums or as vehicles of a more weighty
content, none of these items escapes the odor of dilettantism, at least given
the angle from which I approached them, a personal angle in which a thing is
seized upon and posited as a marvel. Between this marvelous that I savor like
a gourmet and the marvelous that (in the full adventurous light of day or in
the penumbra of dream) one takes in without a connoisseur's smacking of the
lips, the distance is immense . . .

Even though my examples might seem quite slight in comparison to that
realm of the marvelous that can't be reduced to the trickery of double-bottomed
suitcases or party favors, I nonetheless maintain that there is a definite reason
behind them: namely, the role played by the void or by absence or lack in
most of these examples. If it had been in use rather than at rest, the Oslo ski
jump would certainly not have struck me as it did (in short, despite its titanic
dimensions, it would not have provided a springboard for my imagination
unless the activity for which it had been designed had not been lacking); the
forest of Villers-Cotterêts was less notable as a landscape than as an empty
stage on which a drama several centuries old was not being performed; what
so moves me in the dry dock of Le Havre is that it fails to be the Colosseum,
just as the woods around Clamart fail to be Oceania; given that something *less*
tends to call forth that something *more* that completes it (just as a void creates
a call for air), I would no doubt not so enjoy the Sacré-Coeur viewed from afar
(less a church than a castle of the Grail with a touch of the palace of Klingsor)

were I not aware that seen up close it's just a bunch of kitsch not even amusing enough to take the place of beauty; at Neuschwanstein, the vertigo is created by the absence of any *true* castle containing any *true* royal treasure; the scar on the flank of Mount Patrick is just a trace, lacking the context that would have allowed me to immediately interpret it; that so little can signify so much, this is the miracle of the two Youga statuettes and of the antifascist memorial in Berlin; as for Lake Bosomtwe, one knows that it is sacred, but this is indicated only by its misty majesty; in Bailey's Bar, it's onto an absence—onto nothing, other than a bare wall—that Leopold Bloom's door opened, attesting to the reality that this fictional character lacked. Finally, to follow up on this idea—namely, that one can be so thunderstruck by a given thing as to discover that it is missing something or that in its perfect absurdity it pulls the rug out from under our feet—I would also invoke the silence of the sibyl's cave (the deserted seat of an oracle bereft of voice) as well as the abyss that in Satie's series of imaginary little castles separates the realistic advertising copy he composed for them from the sheer unlikelihood of the objects he was ironically proposing for sale.

Could it well be that in contradistinction to the marvelous *by excess*, a shattering and overspilling of all limits, there would be a marvelous *by default*, especially destined to appeal to our mental madwoman in the attic: something missing here, something out of whack there, something disjointed, all indicating a certain blurring of the boundaries that mark not so much the frontiers as the outer limits of the real and the imaginary? It may well be that I unwittingly allowed myself to fall back on this more spurious and more slyly argumentative form of the marvelous, preferring it to the violent eruptions of its more explosive upheavals and laying all my bets instead on its altering effects upon the mind (astounded at the great steps it has suddenly taken or flabbergasted at the moment or in retrospect by the swift kick in the shins that reality seems to have taken). In short, does my choice of illustrations (admittedly, naïvely tendentious) prove that what I am searching for today is a nice and cozy marvelous that would lie within reach, even for someone numbed with age, at the mere cost of a bit of mental gymnastics? A cut-rate marvelous, but a marvelous nevertheless, whereas the day will come when there will no longer be any marvelous for me at all . . . Even if he still remained open to a number of pleasures, how could a man whose possessions were being ever more swiftly carted off piece by piece by the frightening bailiffs of old age maintain that mental freedom and alertness on which the lively wingbeat of the marvelous depends? And even if his fever dreams engendered such fantastic scenarios as the metaphysical meandering along the irregularities of a wall or ceiling, or some internal sensation decked out as a theorem with a subtle figure as proof, or the fabulous voyage of a sewer worker or chimney sweep (which I cite as indicative, speaking not from experience but only with a dim sense of foreboding, fearing I would be getting too rhetorical if I went into further detail), an obscure and interminable peregrination that those nearby will interpret as a death rattle, or else engendering other, more nightmarish inventions, such as the menhir-suppository or the lawnmower gravitating down your throat (which are also conjectural fantasies, vaguely analogous to those I experienced when sick but which have left no recoverable traces today, hence my recourse to these equivalents, too visibly concocted for the purpose, I fear), apart from these, what marvel might befall the same individual when his death agony will have shut him up within the little that remains of him, unless it be that final shot of euphoria that will be injected into him as he now nears his end, or (as the last crumb of well-being that his misery will greet as a gift from heaven) the fresh sheet replacing the one he had sweated through?

The two variables of the marvelous: horizontal (how it changes from person to person) and vertical (how for the same person it changes over the years). But that which it must retain as a constant; that which makes it recognizable across all its many avatars; that which demonstrates its meaning, different though its departure points or mechanisms might be. If there is, therefore, one unchanging feature that is inherent to the marvelous and without which it would no longer exist, would it not reside in this sudden élan—an effervescence or vertigo whose source is unimportant—that projects you into another world, not beyond the earth but beyond our usual ruts of thought, a world without grids, onto which you are astonished to have suddenly stumbled, a world of surprise that overlaps with the world of poetry, if it is indeed true that surprise has become the mainspring of poetry, as Apollinaire, that great expert in enchantments both ancient and modern, argued in a text of his that served as kind of manifesto?

Surprise: the surprise of Siegfried upon discovering Brunhild hiding beneath the breastplate that served as her virile cover; the surprise of the man in the street upon realizing that the revolution has changed everything from top to bottom; my own great surprise (even if I had been forewarned) when near the cloakroom of a pub I came across the door painted black that seemed to prove the historical existence of the Dublin Jew imagined by Joyce; my stupefaction (which I shared with my friend) when I witnessed the gesture of the dying woman by our side who by tracing the sign of the cross in reverse seemed to be doubly mocking it. Surprise: a dramatic turn of events, an apparition, a revelation. The surprise I felt at Youga Dogorou as I made my way into a cave and discovered those two unsuspected figures that had emerged out of chaos, and in East Berlin my amazement at the inner arrangement—so simple that it seemed utterly unarranged—of a structure whose pretentiously Hellenic features did not lead one to expect this sober a display. The surprise caused by those two giants, the Oslo ski jump and the Le Havre dry dock, both jaw dropping in scale. The surprise that overpowered me when, passing through Moscow in 1955, I witnessed a performance of *Swan Lake* that was staged (a rare occurrence in our theaters) in its entirety as a silent opera in which the bodies alone are endowed with speech: its star, Maya Plisetskaya, appeared to me in a literal nimbus of the marvelous because she so stood out—a solitary point backed by the brilliant corps de ballet—against a stage setting that was so decrepit and disconcerting that from the very first moment one felt one almost had to rub one's eyes (a background acting as a foil, somewhat like the prosaic desiccation of a modern street suddenly setting off the paradisal enclave of a lush courtyard garden, or like the more nuanced surprise, not heightened by the backdrop of banality or ugliness, offered by the apparent lightness of a work such as *The Magic Flute*, which, with a slight tightening of the throat, one quickly feels is announcing some grave and lasting joy as it slips into depths that were not, à la Wagner, announced on the bill).

One doesn't have to be a genius to realize that in this series of examples surprise is never just a curtain being lifted on realities that are distinct and diverse: what connection is there between the various emotions I have mentioned, the first having to do with love, the second with revolution, the third with pataphysics (provoked by this door at once real and false), others involving the sense of the sacred, and still others inspired (in black-and-white fashion) by the awe of the gigantic, while others are purely aesthetic? What matters—and what possibly inspires wonder—is it the lifting of the curtain, or is it not rather (at least in the short run) what this inevitably surprising unveiling introduces, even if it lasts only a few seconds? To ground the marvelous in this initial moment of surprise would be like founding theater on the conventional raising of the curtain without taking into account what this lift-off announces—a tragedy, an opera, a light comedy, a ballet—and what's more, forgetting that there can also be theater with no curtain. A more radical objection: far from surprise generating the marvelous, is it not the marvelous itself that incites my surprise? To realize that I now find myself in the realm of the marvelous, no longer weighted down by ever-existing constraints, this no doubt constitutes the true surprise, a surprise that will strike me all the more strongly if entirely unexpected and greeted with a certain innocence.

If the marvelous is more than a word (and I remain convinced of this, despite the elasticity of this notion) and if it cannot be defined as solely derived from surprise, what then is the feature that connects and situates those very distinct realities that appear to be its vehicles?

As it goes off behind my back, I am shaken by a surprise gunshot; but this surprise causes only a physical reaction and nothing has occurred remotely resembling the marvelous: I will have been startled for a brief mechanical moment but will have experienced no vertigo. Surprise is no guarantee of the marvelous (witness those many film gags where surprise triggers only laughter): the Meudon observatory, the forest of Villers-Cotterêts, Lake Bosomtwe, Sacré-Coeur, etc., all inspire reveries that draw me to their dizzying slopes, but all this has little to do with my having been astounded when I first encountered them, and if they still seem surprising to me today it's when I consider the power of wonder (a power of unexpected reach) that these bits of mnemonic rubble have so long exercised over me.

Reveries whose slopes I need only dutifully follow in order to wend my way into the marvelous. Reveries . . . But what sort of reveries? And why are they so captivating, in contrast to all those trains of thought that get you tangled up in knots from which you fear you'll never escape?

It's toward distant bluish landscapes (Yvain or Gawain galloping through the dawn mists) that the Meudon observatory orients me, and it is with all those mad kings—whose fate invites us to meditate on such commonplaces as the crown weighing heavily on the head and the mutability of all human fortunes—that the forest of Villers-Cotterêts (like Neuschwanstein) offers me the opportunity for complicity. Like the cave of the sibyl (a magician already alluded to in a children's game I once played, the Oracle of the Sibyl of Cumae, where the reply to the question you had posed was randomly pulled from a deck), Lake Bosomtwe is a sacred site whose appearance is doubled by the various prior readings that the informed traveler brings to it, making it far more than a mere body of water surrounded by thick vegetation and lightly veiled with mist. Sacré-Coeur of Montmartre, whose anachronistic wedding cake whiteness is so foreign to any recognizable era, is far more a symbol of Paris (this Babylon in which I was born) than is Notre-Dame (too trapped in its medieval amber). Though illustrating the power of modern industry, the dry dock calls forth the majesty of Rome as it was taught to me by my history books and my Latin assignments. Mount Patrick, by its name alone, belongs to the land of legend, and at first sight the Oslo ski jump—aggrandized by its very emptiness—propels you into the outsize leaps of the seven-league boots. Maya Plisetskaya's performance during the Russian Revolution (with many in their street clothes at the Bolshoi, which a foreign head of state was nonetheless honoring with his presence) reaches back beyond 1917 to the romantic ballets featuring sylphids and peris and other creatures that can reveal themselves only by wearing out-of-date tutus, and thus her performance twice abolishes time. As for the Clamart woods (where Masson, who was nobody back then, went to paint *sur le motif*) and as for Satie's tiny castles, they are linked to the myth of the artist who, though poor in palaces and Oceanias, is possessed of immense riches; and a further myth of artistic creation (that of the writer who forges realities far more powerful than the real) hides behind this door that opens far more widely onto the genius of Joyce that it does onto Leopold Bloom's private life. And finally, if at the Berlin memorial I was so surprised to come across a block of stone instead of a monument (however modest in size), my surprise (strong as it was) was primarily due to the fact that the place was in its own right sacred and closely linked to a vast and gruesome stretch of history that cannot be reduced to the fake dignity of military glory. How anodyne my surprise would have remained had it not been informed by this larger context to which I was so deeply committed. But had my memory of this not left its limbo like some jack leaping from its box, how academic this fresco of heroes and martyrs might have appeared to me if the moving theme of fascism and the resistance to it had been presented to me in a far more orthodox fashion. And no doubt the same holds true for many of my other experiences, in which the shock suddenly induced by an incongruous thing plays a far from negligible role: is it not because of their astounding enormity that a dry dock, a ski jump, or the traces of footsteps so excited my imagination, the first so large in scale that it seemed to sum up an entire empire, the second giving proof to the existence of a race of men endowed with capacities (if not dimensions) that are superhuman, and as for the third, the trodden flank of the mountain calling up a phantasmagoric procession without beginning or end? How little would I have been moved by the grandeur that was Rome or by the record-breaking achievements of sport or by the Ireland of legend had they entered into me by the well-tended path of rational thought instead of striking me with such unexpected bolts, sparked by all the dazzling associations these spectacles conveyed!

Belief systems barely removed from their distant origins,

the enchantment of storybook tales (where we learn the language of the marvelous),

the wonders of childhood (itself become a tale one has lived),

the looming shadows of history,

extraordinary exploits,

figures to whom I am unconditionally attracted (the artist creating for the sheer joy of creating, the royal madman who proves that madness can never be the province of the mediocre, a modern paladin, perhaps even a utopian champion of liberty and equality),

all these being portions of a mental sphere that normally lies in the shadows but bits and pieces of which a projector occasionally illuminates, catching them by chance, without any deliberate intention on my part, offering mere glimpses or suggestions of them, escaping all geometry, knowing no limits, portending a totality without bounds,

all these being fragments arisen from that jumble of ideas, images, and feelings that has long provided a large and solid base but that, at the sudden moment of surprise, can no longer be clearly labeled, belonging as it does to that zone whose systematic exploration (rather than whose chance discovery) would render forth nothing that would move me as these fragments do, for frozen in the ice of conscious reflection they would be too hemmed in by the sharp edges of their geometries to allow infinity to penetrate them.

Hence the necessity of establishing a reference to this quasi-immemorial base, yet at the same time the impossibility of gaining access to this limitless realm other than by some secret door. *Ad augusta per angusta.* It's the taste of a piece of pastry that revives lost time in Proust, and in Lewis Carroll it's a rabbit hole that leads to Wonderland. To reach the prehistoric chapel of Knowth in Ireland, you have to crawl through a long rock tunnel full of nasty outcroppings. In Hoffmann's "Don Juan," a secret corridor (like the one I followed to pass from the La Scala museum to the hall where *Boris Godunov* was been rehearsed) leads from the dimly lit bedroom of an inn to the brilliant illumination of an opera hall. Had I taken a straight path and avoided all the sinuous detours, would the quest I have undertaken in this *Rules of the Game*, however dilatory it might seem, have had the slightest chance of arriving at the kind of poetic truth that might help me to live my life (or rather to finish my life, for if and when the lightning strikes, how long will it have dragged on)?

Similarly, it is by narrow routes or barely traced paths that the marvelous proceeds in each of these two realities, so different from each other yet both sharing in the myths that instead of being merely dreamed are *lived out* (or at least are lived out by some, even if we are incapable of doing so ourselves): love and revolution. Tiny details (physical features, tone of voice, a chance event acquiring the oracular appearance of an omen, a casual agreement as to something of little importance subsequently taken to be even more all revealing) contribute to making a woman who is not necessarily all that beautiful or talented or outstanding into an elect figure on whom one lays one's bets, a figure one hopes will provide a reply to our desire (or at least a mirror in which we can recognize what it was in the nature of our desire that escaped us) and who will fully satisfy it (so we presume) without ever quenching it. As for the stroke of luck represented by revolution, one that serves to open up perspectives rather than to institute a society following some preexisting plan, when it occurs it's normally after a (never-ending) series of starts and stops, of happy or unhappy results, of bold strokes but also of enormous errors or even bloody failures, following a rough and uneven path that sometimes gets blocked and sometimes opens up again, coming back into sight after having been in hiding, or undergoes deviations before again setting itself straight, with only an ex post facto theorization being able to discern how the unruly and aleatory course it seems to have taken was in fact the shortest and most logical path at hand.

Sometimes (like a dog, inferior to man because unaware it will die and because less garrulous and less industrious, but which can nonetheless provide an image of life more searing than the one provided by the sight of our fellow man) it is the lesser that leads to the greater: less sublime than the Colosseum, the dry dock surpasses it in evocative power, given that it is at once a reminder of the former and all the half-dreamed further associations it provokes at the moment of recall; the fake castle of Ludwig II of Bavaria may well be pure kitsch, but as a caricature it is all the more invested with feudal majesty in that it points us to the nonexisting castle that would epitomize them all; and if in the operas of the titan Wagner the marvelous almost always proceeds at a slow burn whereas Mozart instead causes it to spring forth at every moment—even when playing around with a futile series of disguises in the comedy of metamorphoses and misapprehensions with which *The Marriage of Figaro* closes—it is because the true wonder arises from the mouse giving birth to a mountain rather than the reverse (of which Satie was no doubt aware when he minimized his compositions by providing them with comic titles or commentaries). Or to cast it as an antiphrasis, it's the negative that gives rise to the positive: the deathbed sign of the cross executed in reverse (whether deliberately or not) definitely established the presence of *both* heaven and hell, whereas nothing of the sort would have been felt had this sign been traced in the more orthodoxly pious fashion or had its obvious inversion come from the hand of a resolute atheist who even though she might have been clowning around was bent only on angrily committing this blasphemy. Even more paradoxical was the state of near-panic that overcame me when one day on the Ivory Coast—staying with the Lobi, reputed to be quite backward—I decided to visit the local magician and this humble old farmer led me to the back of his hut, where the heat was unbearable (which only heightened my malaise) and where, now hidden behind a grate, he proceeded to speak in a falsetto voice to imitate the voice of the spirit whom he had supposedly summoned up, this vocal ploy being so obvious as to seem almost farcical and yet nevertheless coming off as a caricature of the marvelous, somewhat cheesy in effect but all the more undeniable because (encouraged by the exoticism of the setting) it was so extremely distanced by the hilarious naïveté of the hocus-pocus that had produced it.

Two people completely in tune with each other, the establishment of a society founded on brotherhood—it is to this that love and revolution both ideally aspire as they trace their wayward paths to their goals. And it would seem, moreover, that the exhilaration associated with the marvelous always involves something good or true that we had dreamed of achieving, a broad horizon opening up in our minds, something extraordinary now accomplished, even if only in oblique fashion or by some ironic ricochet: a response (as unexpected as it was expected) to the fervor of our desire; an orgiastic fusion with a body now become the incarnation of Nature in all its immensity; a subtle operation that transforms our anguish into sensual delight whenever a poetic or musical phrase seems infused with it, whispering to us what its true substance might be; the sight of an object or a locus that (in minds less mechanical than ours) places us in the presence of those idols belonging to the same family as the *tree so thick with every prayer* or the *Christs of other shapes and faiths* that Apollinaire had in his room; a circumstance in which a theme epic in its sweep leaps to mind with no more ceremony than a rabbit being pulled from a hat; the conviction that a given event, however great or small, has found its precise place and formula; the certitude that a given sign has suddenly become completely readable, endowed with a meaning that even the most searching of discourses could never convey. A victory over the improbable with perhaps more victories to come, the infinite embraced in the flesh, a fragment of past history taking on color and relief (in a corner of the woods, say, or in the distorted mirror of some whimsical palace), an Oceania at our doorstep, a Monsalvat in the heart of Paris, a revelation affecting the entirety of the city just as the absurd or disjointed images that interfere with the darkness of our sleep now rouse us from our torpor, the jackpot one has just hit, the hand that has just been extended to us, the cordial that the young prostitute of Oxford Street offers to Thomas De Quincey as he is dying of hunger, everything that seems to prove that despite all indications to the contrary, breaches can open up in the poverty of our condition: manna from heaven, signal favors granted to us by fate, showering us with feast days of the heart, the senses, or the mind when things consent to sustain or heighten our spirits . . . And is this not what unites all the various manifestations of the marvelous, a notion hard to contain within the stolid density of a noun—or, more precisely, within the noun form of an adjective—for to name the marvelous is to forget that this word refers to something that is the very essence of fluidity: a vertiginous realm into which one can only sneak, given that by very definition it excludes regular visits? A blind fate that singles us out, a favor granted to us by destiny, a complicit wink addressed to us by the incommensurable (be it from the heights of Meudon, veiled more by the intervening years than by their distance in space, or else hidden behind the mask of a stage scene) taking on the guise of a lucky bet or fortunate throw of the dice—hitting the right number and enjoying a definite if sometimes intangible reward because it may involve merely the simple guarantee of hope or, more particularly, that obscure sensation of beauty conveyed by the film now being projected within us—this is what the all-too-stable word *marvelous* so poorly designates as we experience it in either joy or anguish or in a combination of both: an incursion into the beyond or rather into that realm deep within us into which we are surreptitiously precipitated by chance impressions that cannot be explained either by the initial surprise that triggered them or by the flabbergasted discovery that we have now been plunged into a world where all barriers have been abolished (the world as it should be, allowing all our desires to reign unchecked, a world we long for without being crazy enough to believe it might be possible), or by our pleasure in realizing that all order begins to falter once the imagination leaps from the given into something altogether different, thus erasing the boundaries of the real and rendering the entire system null and void.

There would therefore be no marvelous if it involved only the interruption of the ordinary course of things (an exception to the rule, a sudden swerve that elicits our astonishment, an unexpected occurrence that would seem to throw all laws into question); no marvelous if it were merely a closed, self-sufficient circuit that did not feed on other roots, slender tubers that possibly pass along a mythology quite distant from the one on which we were raised and that reach far into us (where our true and often uneasy secrets lie, secrets of which we are too confusedly aware to be able to divulge them); no marvelous that does not result from overcoming the odds and that does not announce itself as a piece of exceptional luck from which we hastily benefit every now and then—but would we stand the same chance if we put nothing into the game, if nothing that truly mattered were on the table?

I would probably pay no attention to the small chance factor that, to my great delight, reveals the deep affinity I feel for a woman I barely know if this piece of luck in this particular instance were simply an accident instead of fate's way of approving a choice I have already implicitly made for reasons that would remain obscure even were I to analyze them. And if, when engaging in absolutely unromantic sex with a whore, I can attain the marvelous without these crudest of carnal relations having to be enhanced by some more or less fetishistic form of playacting that would prove that all ordinary behavior had been left at the door, I nonetheless need my partner to offer some kind of response instead of taking our gestures merely to be one more link in an endless commercial chain; the real pros are well aware of this and, this is why, for good measure, they often pretend to feel what they are not actually feeling; my orgasm would suffer and leave me unconvinced that I had been visited by the marvelous if my arousal had not seemed to increase my unknown partner's, with both of us now ascending to a major moment (and as it were, a sign of my predestination) in a climax far headier than the mere capping of some futile escapade. This mad desire to catch further glimpses of predestination would often be fulfilled by the various nods I seemed to exchange with the world, thanks to opportunities exactly suited to me (such as my chance discovery of the apparently especially created locus that would nourish my private mythology), or thanks to my stumbling upon something that might retrospectively prove to be an omen (an event that a later one appears to reproduce under different circumstances, so that the former seems to presage the latter), or thanks to dreams of which I would be proud because they consecrated me as a visionary blessed with revelations—all things demonstrating that I was one of the elect, free from all common bonds, if not so favored as to be spared by death.

The occurrences of the marvelous that life grants us with such disheartening stinginess often remind me of the images provided by art: gratuitous, detached, activating no reference or response, they leave me indifferent and to my mind don't even deserve the name "marvelous." Whereas I am swept up by a great mystery that is about to be revealed when I look at a work like Picasso's *Minotauromachy*, whose dreamlike quality seems to reflect the harsh conflicts that the artist has undergone within himself, and whereas I have always enjoyed the way in which Max Ernst in his collages so surprisingly manages to combine various quaint elements drawn from that period of wonder and disarray when father and mother occupied center stage, by contrast a painting such as the famous Belgian surrealist work whose sole outstanding feature, *a horse galloping on a tomato*, does little more than distort the relative proportions of quadruped and vegetable is something that leaves me neither hot nor cold . . .

The marvelous derives not from an ultimate reality supposedly in hiding behind the scenes but rather from some ideal or carnal desire that has long inhabited us or that suddenly surges forth as from an abyss or from some private bit of folklore long lodged within us, a theme whose obscure ins and outs are braided into a vibrating cord of possibilities. The marvelous needs some fulcrum, but its power does not rest on some highly symbolic meaning that would justify it because of the metaphysical implications to which it points; to consider it in this fashion would mean to make of the marvelous a method of instruction by images or (more modern) an audiovisual technique for introducing us to the secrets of the world—senseless at base, as the marvelous would no longer exist if assigned to fulfill a function. One cannot dissect it, one just has to live it—for its own sake and in the raw intensity of the moment—as a personal adventure that would be far less precious if, based on a reasoned act, it lacked this unexpected intensity that eagerly invites us in. What a poor piece of edification would the Grail quest story provide to the person who, obsessed with its mystical content, would not allow himself to be innocently taken in by all the wondrous events that punctuate this journey as related in the old romances: the idyllic or simply curious encounters experienced by those engaged in the quest, the lovely visions out of illuminated books from which they benefit, the crazy, unpredictable courses of action that prove the valor of those knights with whom one so desperately wanted to identify as a child. Different kinds of luck escort these characters over the course of their journeys, which is why these tales are typically marvelous, just as our own lived encounter with wonder is experienced as a stroke of luck that at once seduces us and encourages us on. (A hypothesis that does not invalidate the existence, at least on the literary level, of a marvelous of the opposite sort—namely, that of the *gothic novel*—for if we want to find sustenance in the antithesis of good luck, malediction, those gloomy heroes who so enthrall us also haunt realms crowded with thrilling apparitions, and in a gamble far crazier than betting on HEAVEN they hopscotch into the square marked HELL, so that facing life under these conditions, even the least rash of them or even (as is my case) those who are the most distraught at the thought of an uncertain outcome and thus the least capable of taking up a challenge must nonetheless navigate their way through unforeseen circumstances and untold temptations, which explains our fascination with these characters whose violent passions lead them (in a supreme act of derring-do) to wager their eternal bliss in a game of chance that they know they will eventually lose but whose immediate payoff they consider to be a marvel.)

To give myself up (immediately and without reservations, throwing all caution to the wind) to something that bewitches me—this (so it would seem) is one of the major implications of the marvelous, arising as it does out of circumstances of which we are not only the spectators or the actors but also in a way the authors, and a similar abandon (tempered though it be by dilettantism) is demanded of us by those works whose cultural (if not vital) function is to instigate the sensation of the marvelous, even if their enchantments will always lack the spark of life.

Whether correct or not, this view of the marvelous as an inner celebration requiring our complete participation whatever the occasion (an activist view of the matter, in which the marvelous depends on a commitment we ourselves have to make) offers no recipe for its occurrence, nor does it (as it would be foolish or dishonest not to remark) allow us to believe that we have gotten to the bottom of the question: in order that we open ourselves to its lightning stroke and be carried away by its enchantment without any reservations on our part, the marvelous first and foremost demands that we be ready to submit to it, and if (be it only for a split second) it releases us from the anxiety that normally weighs upon all our thoughts and actions, this is simply because we have already agreed to be receptive to its impact, having consented to a susceptibility not of our own choosing. What's more, to try to describe the marvelous as a species of enchantment (as I have just done, thinking I had arrived at some sort of conclusion) is to explain one mystery by another mystery (or to explain a mystery by its own mystery), a futile endeavor that involves merely replacing one vague term with a more chameleonic term, a term whose colors vary when applied to, say, the magical operation that endowed Tamino's flute with its e n c h a n t e d powers, or the delight one feels when hearing the e n c h a n t i n g voice of the woman one loves, or the purely aesthetic pleasure provoked by any given concert or a performance that proved to be an e n c h a n t m e n t for its audience.

All those cares that gnaw at us, the worst of which no doubt stem from our fear of death, are held in check by the marvelous, at least as long as its magic lasts or an echo of it persists. A moment that is quickly erased! But like poetry, which owes as much to the marvelous as it takes from it and which, similarly situated *at the limits of life, at the borders of art*, shares with it the equivocal status of both a thing that you can sometimes put your finger on and something that can occasionally assume the quality of fiction (which only increases the difficulty of getting a purchase on the notion of the marvelous or of poetry, for when one speaks of either of them one tends to easily slide between their immediately given form and the form we construct them into, nothing ever being lived without owing something to the imagination and nothing ever being imagined without some visible or secret grounding in life), the marvelous, even though lightning quick, nonetheless has the lasting power to alleviate the torment of life: to be able to say to oneself that despite it all, a door (be it a back rather than a front door) still remains open for moments such as these, moments that you believe have been especially made to measure for you and that allow you to emerge from the deep shadows of your vulnerability—this possibility in effect allows you (without recourse to any religious belief other than this faith in exceptional moments that seem to fall like pennies from heaven) to view your own eventual disappearance or that of your peers with less than total despair. In short, it seems that the marvelous can help you live by suspending your anxiety, but to achieve this you need to be ready to rid yourself of all your worries. A vicious circle not just cooked up in theory but the very one in which we find ourselves trapped as we enter old age: a powerful drug, as strong as the colorful fairy dog Petit-Crû (inspired by Gottfried von Strasburg, according to Joseph Bédier) given by Tristan to Yseut because the lilting of its collar bell was enough to dispel the sadness of anyone who heard it, the marvelous shields and arms us against the fear of death; but this fear, ever more focused as we grow older and lose those on whose presence we relied, blocks the marvelous from suddenly appearing even as we stand in ever greater need of its drug.

The feeling of being utterly overwhelmed, the impulse given to the imagination, sheer luck, enchantment—such are the notions to which I had recourse as I tried to dispel the mists around this word whose luminosity I find blinding: *Merveilleux*. Rather feeble notions for sure, one following upon another in a succession that owes less to a deliberate manner of proceeding than to the need to feel my way forward bit by bit, resulting in an indecisiveness that is perhaps not of my own making but rather inherent in the marvelous itself, as elusive as a will-o'-the-wisp. I have used the word to refer to artistic works whose shared narratives or range of imagery all so radically depart from any kind of realism as to constitute a genre unto themselves, but should I want to extend it beyond this, what definable category of events would it cover? Or it is but mere superlative that points to those various occurrences in my life (including those in my dreams and reveries) that have swept me into spontaneous moments of rapture, moments (however rare and brief) that I hope will continue to offer me the privilege of experiencing them in an act of immediate and complete commitment? As spontaneous as that demanded by love, this act of commitment can result (as it does in love) only from an unconditional choice, a decision not based on the future and operating outside all rules. To limit the field of the marvelous by applying rigid criteria to it would be as absurd as attempting to subject beauty to a series of abstract canons established once and for all. Besides, even if I more or less manage to describe (and even explain) what I feel each time I am overcome with wonder, I would not be able to (usefully) gather all these instances under a single heading, for their variety is such that I would have to come up with a definition so broad as to cover nothing. The only definite family likeness that these moments of experience share (and whose multiple access routes would justify the saying *All roads lead to Rome*) is that, equal in intensity to Proust's celebrated *time regained*, they erase away all the accumulated murk (anxiety, guilty conscience, boredom), allowing one to believe — in the momentary alleviation of all problems — that one has achieved something that approaches Rimbaud's *true life*. The rejuvenated life of which any poet dreams (without necessarily being a mystic or an adventurer), even if it be a life reduced to the nonmetaphysical ecstasies that the glamorous grand bourgeois Raymond Roussel, more greedy than Proust, never could admit were short lived, convinced as he was from an early age that he was someone inspired who was blessed with the visible radiance of *glory* and who later in life — as a final substitute following the wreckage of his illusions provoked by "what Tannhauser dreamt at Venusberg" — indulged in the *euphoria* he obtained from the subtle mix of barbiturates whose doses eventually proved to be deadly.

Other than placing my anxieties within parentheses (a negative analogy, as in the riddle an old Welsh lady once proposed to our household: "How are an elephant and a teapot alike? Neither can climb trees"), my fleeting ecstasies cannot be compared to that proud state of inebriation that Roussel pursued until his dying breath, nor to those sudden resurgences that provided a beacon for Proust's entire life as a writer. I would gladly be able to claim that I have lived under the sign of an experience as forceful as Proust's *time regained* or as illuminating as the *glory* with which Roussel imagined himself imbued, giddily convinced that he was indeed a wonder to be beheld with astonishment by the world. But in fact, rummage as I may for something in my past that might be considered truly fulgurant, I come up only with things that are so scattered, so disparate, and so incoherent that they do not constitute a plenitude but rather reveal how ingeniously I have had to search far and wide to furnish this void: the absence of any major event that would lie at the origins of something that for the rest of my life would take on the authority of a law.

I can no doubt cite a few decisive events that struck me more deeply than they would have affected some merely delighted or dumbfounded onlooker; for instance, the physical revelation of sex that I was vouchsafed at the age of eighteen, and then, much later, the weird funereal scene that I have already related, and, several years later, an occurrence that was neither Dionysian nor verging on the supernatural but rather a public event that (above and beyond the confusion that reigned during the liberation of Paris) marked the onset of the daylight period that followed upon the protracted nighttime of the German Occupation: namely, a solitary man bent over the handlebars of his bicycle, pedaling furiously down the completely deserted quai des Grands-Augustins toward evening's end, shouting out this phrase that seemed to be addressed to everybody and nobody in particular, "The Americans are at the Hôtel de Ville! . . ."—which confirmed the fact that the French troops had indeed entered the heart of Paris, a bit of news that had just been relayed by the ringing of the great bell of Notre-Dame, echoed by the bells of all the other churches and then, vox populi, the raucous singing of "La Marseillaise," followed by the cry of "Liberation" ushering forth from inside the Palais de Justice in a sort of chanted chorus. And yet, however wondrous they were, each after their own fashion, and however intensely I might have experienced them, these three events—from which I have omitted to add two that I have already treated in depth and thus consider (in an act of censorship almost automatic to any writer) to be closed cases: the response that my friend the daughter of Bousbir Khadidja offered to my embrace as if I had thereby joined some Persephone in the underworld, and then in Paris just after the war, when I was taking part in an homage rendered to Max Jacob, who had died a victim of Nazism, reading aloud a special text I had written for the occasion, I experienced an imaginary descent into hell as I faced the black abyss of the theater hall that lay beyond the lights of the stage—all these events that seemed to me to verge on the miraculous in fact remained just what they were, and nothing that followed indicates that any one of them might have had a crucial or durable impact on my subsequent behavior. If they remain so strongly anchored in my memory, isn't it largely because of their illustrative value? Is their real power any greater than that of the news photos on the front pages of tabloids or the exhibits of evidence introduced into a courtroom trial?

Today, numbed out as I am—and given my growing mistrust of everything that presumes to be ever so marvelous in its bright borrowed raiment (a mistrust that goes hand in hand, in matters of art and literature, with my growing preference for a cards-on-the-table sort of realism)—it's often on little nothings that the blaze of the word *marvelous* seems to me to perch. On, say, a scene that proves to be no exception to the rule yet stands out simply because of the fascination it exerts on me in all its usualness. Sometimes when drawn to the transparency of a stream and its bed of rippling weeds, my eyes are washed free of care, and—in another bit of weekend bliss prompted by the walks I take with the companion I call (vain biped that I am) "my" dog—sometimes I feel my brow suddenly wiped free of clouds when grazed by the shade of the nearby woods, or, even better, my eye meets with a stand of trees that seems to have been parceled forth from the plain and just sits there squarely like the forests in the backgrounds of ancient miniatures, offering itself to view like a cake positioned on a plate. A marvelous that is reassuring, as in the soothing folklore of Nerval's *Sylvie* (as opposed to the deliriums of his *Aurelia*, with all their high-tension wonders). A damped-down marvelous, whose discretion rivals that of an actor speaking his part softly to be better heard (for it's not by shouting that one attracts attention). A pure and natural marvelous, distinct from the marvelous generated by a performance that has gone off course or by the vagaries of adventures real or imagined, and distinct from the more properly poetic construction of the marvelous that occurs when words and forms begin to behave like chemical bodies reacting in a laboratory. A marvelous without sleight of hand, involving neither the uncritical acceptance of the impression that some extraordinary thing or event might have made on you nor the desire to hold on to this impression in your memory because it at least will have proved that something unbelievable had in fact happened to you, but rather an impression made by something so ordinary that you are amazed it could produce this extraordinary effect. A marvelous as naked as the hand, rooted in the banality of the real, then leaping forth (depending on the season, the day, the hour, or the weather conditions, be they inner or outer, affecting the light) as all pervasive as that purely imaginary realm into which the shadowy and enigmatic BAEDEVER first introduced me. BAEDEVER, how long I wondered whether I had been mistaken about his name—a name passing by like Baudelaire's *stifled sigh of Weber*, sweeping past sylphs and lakes and then (here I go chasing after echoes) coming upon Ver-en-Valois (visited by Nerval) and, in the Ardennes, reaching Verviers by way of Villers-Cotterêts (whose very sound conjures up a forest scattered with little bundles of sticks and kindling wood gleaming with resin)—until the day I discovered someone by the same name in a book that has now entered our common library but that had previously belonged to my wife's brother-in-law. Far more widely read than I, this Kantian never wavered in his cult of Wagner (the long-standing source of many of our futile arguments), despite his devotion to cubism (of which he became an active supporter from the very outset), despite his taste for objects that were then called *nègre*, and despite his championing of Debussy during his heroic years. His library contained, in addition to an accumulation of art books, a fair number of French volumes, among them those that he himself had published, such as Apollinaire's *The Rotting Wizard* and *The Medusa Trap* by Satie ("with dance music by the same individual"), as well as a collection of books in German (his native language) and one in English. It was among the Anglo-American shelves of his library (which I rarely browsed) that, while looking around for materials relating to the Round Table, I came across a modern edition of Thomas Malory's *Le Morte d'Arthur*, where it is recounted that as he was approaching death the king summoned "Sir Bedivere" to throw his sword Excalibur into the lake, a name mentioned (as I was to discover as I leafed through the book) alongside those other companions of this king "Sir Tristram" and "Sir Pelleas."

Like an addict relapsing into his ersatz ambrosia, I thus return to the magic of these names, so seductive either because of the adventures they evoke or because of their sonority, for their sound alone is often enough to need no further elaboration. Running on these two currents, these names strike me as doubly marvelous, without my being able to figure out—at least in many cases—what matters most: the name as it is pronounced, or what this name sums up (the way a title abbreviates the events of a book once read)? This is clear when it comes to ARTHUR, an old-fashioned first name that even if followed by the patronymic "Rimbaud" still maintains something of its man-about-town insignificance, taking on greater meaning only if linked to that semilegendary king whose distant model was a certain Celtic chieftain who battled the Angle and Saxon invaders of Great Britain. This same thing is true (but in the opposite way) of PELLEAS—whose story I would find far less touching if MELISANDE and he did not share in the sheer music of their unusual names. But things are different when it comes to BAEDEVER, for in him I see different valences of the marvelous coursing together and inextricably melding: the aura surrounding the tale of which he is the protagonist, the strangeness of the syllables that make up his name (whose oddity I have emphasized by substituting the Latinate *ae* for a simple *e*), the string of associations that these syllables generate, based not merely on the empty puns suggested by their overlapping sounds but on the twilit atmosphere of the tale and thus on everything suggested by its events. A confluence, a crossroads, as if the word *Baedever* provided the intersection of several paths down which I might venture (throwing off the shackles of the dictionary) to finally reach what I call the "marvelous" or, just as empirically, what I call "poetry"—that is, everything (now no longer judged in terms of its Goodness or Beauty) that seems to place itself above and beyond all else, everything (now pleasurably released from the normal flow of happy or unhappy days) that can (as I at long last realize) be conveyed by almost anything at all: a reality (however humble, however derisory) whose strangeness suddenly opens onto grandiose or even ludicrous horizons and that, having *nothing in its hands, nothing in its pockets* and referring to nothing definable, presents itself in all the nakedness of its reply to a question that has barely been broached; a dream that offers itself up to be read or a reading as deeply convincing as a dream; a brilliant formal composition (be it verbal or not) drawn across our deepest fibers like a bow; prelude to that delirious explosion of love, that most idolatrous of acts, in which each of the lovers takes aim with their entire being in order to transform themselves into a statue at once sensitive and sensitizing. All these things of course do not automatically generate the marvelous, but they provide it with a footing that renders it possible provided we have made the necessary leap, a leap that (depending far more on our dispositions than than on our desires or decisiveness) we may or may not take. In short, there are lures extended to us, lures upon which we should seize but which we rarely seize at the first go, whether they involve events that have nothing made up about them or artworks that try too hard to make a claim upon us (let it be said in passing that no work can possibly succeed unless it features, even at the level of its execution, something that has happened by chance, foreign to any calculation, and so irreducible to any preestablished model as to defy all analysis).

Whether it be of the order of the real or that of pure image, the field most hospitable to the upsurge of the marvelous is always just that—a field—and it is up to us to put it to work at the right moment, throwing all caution to the wind without the game having been decided in advance, ever astonished that such a thing could happen (the surprise provoked by the most ordinary of things, out of which we make something infinitely more important than it is, all the while accepting it as such, attentive to its powers of allusion but not reducing it to a mere sign standing for some esoteric truth).

It's no doubt the idea of death—a "natural" death, that is, an ebbing away into nature that makes it far easier to accept—that informs the peace I manage to find in the woods, even if they are far more modest than the druidic forest (half light, half dark) near Blarney Castle in Ireland, reminiscent of those majestic forests where the rites of "our ancestors the Gauls" are said to have been celebrated. And if a forest glimpsed from afar succeeds in soothing me, cloaked (to my eyes) in the same mystery as those sacred woods of Africa into which no one uninitiated may enter and that are (so it would seem) the remainders of the primeval forest, the particular locus or fragment of landscape that I'm looking at now reveals to me no arcane message related to death, nor does it distract me from my certainty that I am doomed to disappear: providing neither instruction nor diversion, the spectacle by which I am captivated (with no other business to attend to) is reassuring precisely because the peace that it presents—the silence and quiet of death—allows me to fully absorb this idea of death that normally so frightens me, imparting to it a coloration at once less macabre and more marvelous (a coloration more appropriate to the swaying shadows of an Arthurian forest than to the administrative wasteland of a Parisian cemetery). The fact that an experience this funereal in hue could have granted me the same sense of wonder as my did my early glimpses of the Meudon observatory in the distance or as have, more recently, any of those apparently inviting signs addressed to my attention from the world around me (even humorous ones, such as Leopold Bloom's door decorating the interior of a Dublin bar)—all this leads me to wonder whether what is being shown to me in black-and-white fashion by the calm mystery of a forest is not in fact a characteristic (not always perceptible, yet essential) of the marvelous. Indeed, perhaps a drop of death (sometimes brought on by the play of melancholy or by an atmosphere of violence or of tragedy, sometimes produced more metaphorically, as in the act of love or by whatever gives you the impression you are entering another world) is essential to everything (be it dark or bright) that provokes the sensation of the marvelous—which is not a message we receive from some hypothetical beyond but something that, within the boundaries of the world of the here and now and within the most private of our paths, is imbued with the power to introduce us not into some sacred locus of gnosis and veneration but rather into a place that might be compared not so much to a threshold (such as the one overseen by the two warriors of *The Magic Flute* or that of the Berlin memorial, guarded by two soldiers) as to a cape or a land's end that marks the extreme reach into an immensity one almost believes one can command (but not without vertigo) at a single glance. A drop, a soupçon, or, even better, a shadow of death: just enough for death to make itself present (either explicitly or allusively) on my inner stage, but not so present that I'll thereby fear I'll become its imminent prey—in which case it would truly be a poison and not this pleasant and heady brew which, when the right occasion presented itself, I would be invited to drink. If the marvelous cannot come into being (so it would seem) without the involvement of this little bit of death, and if it is this condition of mortality that confers upon the marvelous its particular dignity (without its having to pretend to gravity), it is nonetheless obvious that if the idea of death is absorbed in too strong a dose, you will kill the marvelous from the very start: if I were totally strangled by my fear of the impending blade of the guillotine, how would I have the heart to take the bullet of the marvelous on the fly?

Thus rendered powerless or irrelevant once things start going badly, is the marvelous indeed that wondrous thing to which I had so madly given credence, or is it simply an aesthete's complacent dream, a topic of conversation to be shared with his peers? If the excitement I felt as a child who had prematurely been taken to see *Lohengrin* and *Parsifal* at the Paris Opera, if the reading of *The Rotting Wizard* as a young man had plunged me into the entire cycle of Arthurian romance, if after these periods of enthusiasm the Grail and all its mystical lore—Christianity grafted onto the Round Table—began to leave me cold (just as I was left cold by occultism, something I never took to be a fountain of truth but the forms of which I found seductive for a certain period of time), the reason for this is twofold: the idealism of these make-believe tales is based on imagery too distant from modern life (or, more specifically, from life as lived by the twentieth-century man that I am), and—an even more serious reproach—their stale aestheticism has only served to nourish those who take beauty to be so crippled as to be incapable of making its way without the crutch of symbols. As I here reach the end of my reflections, I begin to realize that by referring openly or covertly to obsolete matters of this sort, so ill suited to the naked reality in which I would like to be grounded, I am thereby allowing the marvelous (here occasioning insights no less convoluted than those elicited by recognized masterpieces) to lose something of its freshness, as if by placing it under a globe in order to better examine it I had thereby mummified it. There is nothing surprising about this, for in my eagerness to dissect the marvelous and to inspect its workings so as to gain a better purchase on it, I was going against its very nature, which demands that one assent to it outright and at a single go without being held back by questions. Wanting to be punctilious enough not to pull the wool over anybody's eyes and yet at the same time liberal enough to stretch the notion of the marvelous as far as possible to account for all its features, growing more and more annoyed as I engaged in my pursuit (far more extensive than this transcription into writing might indicate), ever more irritated by the realization that the marvelous had long been absent from my life and that if I was trying to account for it by examples that dated back to my past, the reason was simple, I had drifted off course as I tried to find various ways forward and in the space of a few paragraphs had allowed myself to become so despondent as to place the marvelous into doubt, under the weak pretext that there are circumstances so alarming as to be utterly incompatible with it. Given that the marvelous is precisely something to which one needs to give oneself up on the spur of the moment and without second thoughts, my turning it into the object of intricate reflection (or of the divagations of a dilettante who likes to play the philosopher) served only to further distance me from it. And even if it didn't quite become the quintessentialized tribute to everything I wanted to consign to the flames, the fine-tooth comb I was applying to my subject was certainly not the way to achieve the goal I had in mind (without great hope for its success): namely, to live the marvelous at the highest and most accelerated intensity and not just talk about it, to learn how to ring forth notes from its keyboard without lowering them to the level of a mere literary theme. To attempt to lift the veil of this unknown entity with its ever-changing mask was perhaps to commit the same mistake as a Psyche too eager to solve the disguise of Eros or a Princess of Brabant too curious to know the true identity of the Knight of the Swan . . . But by casting things into these terms, am I not in fact drawing on examples that are too archaic in their nobility, thereby lapsing into the very aestheticism that I have just condemned?

Wanting from the very outset to rid my mind of anything that might incline me to speak of the marvelous with an air of homespun profundity or else with tremolos in my voice, I have said a few nasty things about Wagner, notably when I accused him of "passing by his own Monsalvat" with his theatrics. But perhaps I was wrong, for (as rumor has it) by his very manner of death (an adventure that, until the final curtain, is part and parcel of life) Wagner managed to achieve the marvelous, a lived experience that I locate above and beyond everything else and to which as an examiner I would assign the highest grade, but only if this experience is lived not only for oneself but (without so intending) also for those who are or will be able to be filled with wonder that something of this sort had happened at all. It is said that Wagner—this pure bard of the pure Parsifal and someone for whom Flower Maidens (viz., Kundry) were nothing more than devils in disguise—died while undergoing ancillary fellation in the palazzo Vendramin Calergi, today the site of the winter casino in Venice that picks up where the summer casino on the Lido leaves off. Wagner's end, certainly a guilty one, not in and of itself but as a sin against that sexual asceticism he so touted (having made himself the public champion of an ideal of chastity, only to fall so grossly short of it), and nonetheless a scandalous end inasmuch as it betrayed the ultimate message he had wanted to convey in his art while also opening him up to harsh condemnation if interpreted in terms of class warfare (the master getting sucked off by some slave)—in Wagner's death (true, I hope) I see the beautifully ironic hand of fate. What's more, if this rumor of his death is to be believed, it's not impossible to imagine that the destructiveness of this orgasm (his jubilant flesh bursting open the very limits of his being), encountered at the end of his quest for the grail of sexual delight, might have led Wagner (who was also the celebrant of the shared *Liebestod* of Tristan and Isolde) toward the threshold of that realm where, far from the showiness of his mythology and from the sheer muddle of his thought, he finally discovered what he was looking for all the while: the marvelous. This was the same intense realm into which he had first wandered (so one supposes) in 1848, among the barricades of the

Dresden insurrection, and now, at the end of a journey so often brightened by the wonders of romantic passion, here he was (if indeed his actual death coincided with his *petite mort*) once again rediscovering the marvelous in a casual amorous encounter beyond his wildest dreams. Does not the access to the marvelous depend on one's complete innocence, on leaving oneself open to sheer luck? This being the case (and despite all my misgivings about him), I have to admit that Wagner (or his legend) has taught me a lesson, but without his in any sense having played the schoolmaster to me . . .

If, as this rumor has it, this was indeed the way he died, this illustrious protégé of the Bavarian Ludwig II with all his fantasy castles, is it not a wonder that Wagner's final intoxication should have crowned the existence of a man who, drinking from the depths of his own music, had tried to give body to many a marvel through his genius as a composer—a fascinating genius I must admit, repelled as I am by all the horrid ideological blunders that so tarnish the memory of the demigod of Bayreuth? But if Wagner's end might well provide a fitting (and most piquant) conclusion to some comic book version of his life (to his even greater glory), it's obvious that I wouldn't even have dreamed of bringing up the subject of the marvelous in relation to his death if it did not involve someone whose creative powers, whose ambition, and whose renown had made of him an almost mythological figure (the death of the French president Félix Faure while having sex never brought anything similar to my mind).

If something that happens to me succeeds in triggering the sensation of the marvelous, will this sensation—which, unable to define it more explicitly, I in the end associate with the impression of being suddenly liberated from everything that oppresses me—transcend mere euphoria if I am the only one to experience it? If the MARVELOUS is fully to take place (i.e., if this incredible thing that is happening to me takes on the full force of an *event*), does this not require that that boundaries of my own person also be abolished (whether temporarily or for good) and that (whether in flesh and blood or if need be as a phantom in the eyes of others) I leave my habitual isolation behind to assume a completely different mode of being? That another being undergo this experience with me (as during sexual climax). That I be a member of a community that is also living through this (as at the turning points of history). That in the absence of this moment of absolute sharing I communicate my experience via the thing that inspired it in the first place (as Proust does with his *time regained*). That without my necessarily having experienced it as marvelous, the thing in question appear to those who are my admirers or aficionados—a necessary precondition, given that the rich only get richer and that if expected, wonders never cease—as something surprisingly suited to my person (*this could only happen to him*), or, if I were somebody surrounded by the nimbus of legend (and thus no longer a real-life subject) and therefore a permanent instance for the marvelous, that this actual thing (and not its embellishment) take on a privileged place within this legend.

Ideally:

to become a hero—seen from within or without, perceived in the raw or in effigy, be it in those rare moments of luck (shared in person or conveyed poetically) when I manage to free myself from my daily tedium to die a kind of painless death, or be it when others seize upon certain aspects of my life as if they belonged to an imaginary character—a hero of episodes at once so real and so mythical that they allow me to exist on either of these planes, both of which would appear to be, O wonder of wonders, as different from death as they are from life.

Concretely:

—no longer to split hairs about the marvelous, because instead of opening windows, this far too intricate approach (which can also be misleading if one is not wary of all the convenient fluctuations of the meaning of this word) has no doubt led my attention astray from any number of those less spectacular marvels that can fall like manna from heaven upon anyone who has not been utterly ground down by fate;

—to remember that in order to fit him into a mythology and to account for his rumored escapade at the palazzo Vendramin Calergi, Wagner first and foremost had to be Wagner: that is, someone who had accomplished the very task he had set for himself throughout his career;

—to be careful that my wish to live a life whose particulars would be surrounded by a halo of myth (a timid enough wish, given that it includes no call for unforeseen tragedies) not deteriorate into a hunger for sanctification or into the urge to do my Michel Leiris number, but rather that it remain the generous desire to reach a few others through the fusion of my work and my person, thereby creating a complicity far more intertwined than the simple mutual agreement of the head or heart;

—not to seek to live in a fairy-tale world, which would be all the more futile given my age, but to work—even if in this case work might not prove to be sufficient, because no literary undertaking can completely allow you to wash your hands of all the horrors that afflict the world or rid you of all the anxiety that dwells within you—to paint a truthful picture of my life, to which I would nonetheless like to impart (here and there) some of the magic sheen of a fairy tale.

Panoramically:

to cast an ironic eye on how sticking to this goal would in fact contradict the very principle that had justified my autobiographical quest from the very outset: having flattered myself that I was writing in order to discover myself and to point my life in a clearer direction, the decision to give a realistic picture of it occasionally visited by shimmer of the marvelous would entail mistaking the end for something I had intended to use only as a means; instead of writing my life in order to learn how better to live it, this would be to pretend that my life as I have lived it was essentially meant to be written down and that any of the marvels that might have burnished it had primarily occurred to allow me to tell my tale.

Utopianly:

to discover the sources of the marvelous not in what disorients me but in the "naked reality" of life at its most ordinary (not even country life, still too exotic, but life as lived in my city, in my neighborhood, in my house, even in the bedroom where my wife and I together listen—until when?—to time rushing by), for this would mean that no longer sidestepping the issue, no longer disguising it or sifting it out, I had at last admitted the idea of death in all its appalling reality.

*

As meticulous as that perfect housewife ever on the lookout for the slightest speck of dust . . . So middle class in his vigilance!

Always scouring and polishing and tidying up, he was unaware that all this mania for cleanliness was of no use to someone marked by a blemish that was uncategorizable yet indicative of the diminishment to which he might be prey should circumstances arise, a stigma as worrisome to him as scabies.

His irremediable flaw was literary in nature, for such was his major occupation and such was his most frequent occasion for engaging in the most punctilious of sophistry—whose precise functioning dawned on him only late in life when he was traveling to Avignon, over the course of one of those trips that amount to little in themselves but that by breaking your routine allow you to come to fuller terms with things. It was a flaw that was perhaps as portentous as one of those *sins against the Holy Spirit* of which Catholic theology speaks, a sin that illustrated his basic moral shortcoming when engaged in his preferred activity: that is, whatever his claims to the contrary, his need to find a refuge in poetry, to use it as a means of forestalling death instead of availing himself of the wings of language to parachute into space and to speak with the ease of someone who, although not oblivious to death, is willing to place it within parentheses. More damningly, his self-interested need to be a poet only for reasons of mental hygiene or greater comfort, his attempts to achieve a superhuman note even though, distraught as we are despite no imminent threat of catastrophe, we know all too well that calamitous events of our age are now so frequent as to transform all of humankind into subhumans.

A smirch, perhaps indicated only by a dotted line (so nearly virtual is its mark), for fate alone has spared this fastidious individual from having to confront any far more grossly defined blot upon his character. A blemish that long went unnoticed by him but of which he wondered whether it had not always been connected, in his relationships with others, to a lack of spontaneity, to an awkward oscillation between self-control and self-display that, while leaving his image apparently intact, could only heavily mortgage his need not just for admiration but for fervent friendship. In his blindness, perhaps more far reaching than he imagined, was he not in fact the opposite of what he thought he was: namely, an infatuated naïf whose tendency to believe he was the sole person on earth was merely accentuated (rather than remedied) by his paper chase after his unique personal truth, this Sisyphean task in turn providing him with excellent excuses to avoid responsibilities in many minor matters (letters to be written, domestic harmony, consideration to be shown for this or that person)—or, even worse, was he not just like the bore who, by very definition, is too obtuse to be aware of his own boorishness, so obvious to all and so unappealing?

To conduct his private life with graciousness and extreme modesty, to cease playing the bitter jokester or the lunatic whose self-examinations lead only to sullenness—such was the solution toward which he decided to orient himself, if not exactly to erase then at least to partially compensate for the flaw he had discovered in himself. Such was the final stage of all the thoughts stirred up by his brief visit to Avignon, its palace still standing near its broken bridge, for a posthumous tribute to Picasso, that most thoroughly inventive of all creators.

*

"Ici fruit à la tête se dit: là on s'enlise."

It was no doubt my surrealist leanings when it came to dreams or to the inventions of half sleep that caused me to note down the above sentence, which I found myself mentally rehearsing one morning long ago as I dazedly made my way from sleep to waking.

An absurd statement, but one which in its impeccable equilibrium sounded like an obvious verity, seemingly offering up a key like many of those formulas that, similarly symmetrical and similarly peremptory, appeared to ask more of me than I felt responsible for.

That language should speak to me rather than my speaking it, that it should address me in my own tongue (the one in which, without always understanding it, I feel as comfortable as in the one belonging to someone of whom, even though I might barely know him, I could say that *we speak the same language,* so seamless does the communication between us appear)—it is to this that I believe my poetic efforts are primarily directed: to make language speak and, to confirm the validity of its message, to make it speak to others as it speaks to me, sometimes in the decanted language that is occasionally afforded me but more often in a language that I try to concoct for myself in order to slot it into common parlance, an effort that often goes awry, falsifying or destroying what it is I want to capture and share (less my ideas than my inner life), for it is only the former kind of utterance, sibylline yet exact in formulation, that is truly mine, suited to my intellectual being and, despite its obscurity, at least understandable by those few whom I take to be my counterparts.

Fruit à la tête, which I can locate only *ici,* or *here* in my own head, this fruit consisting of those constructions elaborated in my brain, those buddings

and burgeonings (possibly monstrous) so intimately connected to me and endowed with such density and relief that I am tempted to designate them by an
image of something that is commonly edible: a fruit that one would partake
of, just as, in contradistinction to a *rêve* [dream], which is something more
addressed to the eye and thus more of a figure, a *songe* [dream], consisting as
it does of a more substantial lie [*mensonge*], similarly possesses the full weight
of a foodstuff, akin to the red mushroom (the *oronge*, or royal agaric, whose
poisonous variety is called *fausse oronge*, or fly agaric) or akin to the bone—to
follow the curlicue logic I have allowed to proliferate around the first part of
the singular sentence cited above—that one gnaws [*ronge*] to the marrow, perhaps after the dreamy [*songeuse*] fashion of Rodin's *Thinker*, one's chin resting
on one's fist unless, that is, one is actually gnawing at this fist, thereby illustrating, like someone acting out a charade, the expression *se ronger* [be gnawed
by] or (as my mother used to say, associating dark thoughts with something
one kneaded) *se malaxer* [knead oneself into knots].

Passively "to be absorbed" in a task or, more actively, to "ruminate" an
idea, to "devour" a book, "to feed" on depressing matters: all expressions relating to mental activity and all suggestive in their own ways of acts of eating or
being eaten, a reference to the kind of nourishment that I like to associate with
the "inner life," choosing to take these two words at face value, to mean something more than a spiritual life without form or color but rather a life as concrete as the one that plays itself out inside our bodies, sorts of caverns filled with
our entrails and other organs, in the depths of which, through the constant
interchange between inside and outside, what we consume is transformed into
products necessary to our existence. A reduced model of this sort of life, one
that I would want to take in through my own senses, even though it be a life
led only in my head: that hazy mass—neither an opaque object nor a room
with curtains drawn nor a landscape, and yet undeniably real—that I see from
behind my closed eyelids and that casts a red glow when my eyes are turned to
the light. Somewhat lower, at the level of the thorax, another example that is
the product of neither verbal artifice nor allegory: that nauseous sensation of
anxiety of which I cannot say whether it is mental or physical in origin.

Ici ("here," my locus, my place of observation, the site from which I emit
these words)

fruit à la tête (the fruits of my imagination, which take on body through
the act of speech or writing and that form a protrusion I would today compare
to those "balloons" containing the words or thoughts of comic book characters)

se dit: (or "means," indicating the equation established by the median
colon)

là ("there," at a location considered more or less distant from "here")
on s'enlise (one flounders, gets bogged down, gets stuck, gets sucked under).

It's indeed *here* that the head of fruit is located, and it's *here* that I speak
of it, referring to getting bogged down *there*, an adverb that can only function
rhetorically as a parallel to the initial *here*, thus indicating (by way of autocri-
tique) that it is my mental operations, as manifested by their oral or written
fruits, that risk leading me down the wrong track or getting me stuck in the
mud, but a *there*—placed as it is in radical opposition to a *here*, thus cutting
the sentence into two segments, each of which is focused on an apparently
distinct location—that I had initially interpreted as if the threat were situated
beyond and not within the orbit of this *here*, the inner cave inhabited by what
I shall shamelessly label "my very own self": in other words, what I feel and
what I feel myself to be. If *fruit à la tête se dit . . .* , one has to understand that
the two parts of the formula separated by the colon are interchangeable (or in
agreement as to their goal) and that to arrive at its single overall truth I can
just as well base myself on the "fruit in the head" as on the "getting bogged
down." To me, the truth that this sentence (despite its ambiguity) so obviously
expressed and whose implications I merely had to tease out ran as follows: that
on the one hand there are the fructifications of the imaginary and on the other
there are the dangers of the outside world, and that the inside that provides
us with a home and the outside that threatens us are in fact an opposing pair,
much like a poison and its antidote or the two pans of a scale. No other alternative, then, but to bring my imagination to fruition, to devote my life to this
game and find a way to exist within it or else, unable to abstract myself from
an all too real life that (even if all its pitfalls were surmounted) is sure to end
in death, to risk being snared by the anxiety created by all the traps laid by the
outside world.

Here (or so it seems to me) is how the sentence invited me to make use
of the illusory convexity of *fruit à la tête* to fill in the abyss that so inexorably
opens beneath me with every step I take. Indeed, if I have occasionally been
tempted to think—as when I noted down this other adage: *a poet is a speaker
of a fruited tongue who tastes his words and offers them on to be savored*—that
poetry, this thing after which we so hunger, is basically a beautiful fruit, and
if I have sometimes dreamed of simply *singing* instead of wearing myself out
on this laborious piece of work, which, having been initially born of the vague
desire to learn how to flawlessly play the game set by my ideas, has become less
the rulebook than the actual playing field of this game and, directed toward
an illumination that demands an ever-renewed series of questions, is perhaps
now little more (except for brief breakaways) than the belated chronicle of

a depressing pursuit of a mirage, yet nothing prevents me from embracing a strategy that would be the exact opposite of my getting drunk on my own words: to take the bull by the horns, to stand up to the vicissitudes of the world out there, and to commit myself to a life of action with my eyes wide open. In their day, this was the purpose served both by the travels I undertook under the banner of humanism and by those periods when I worked hand in hand with activists on the left or extreme left. Need I cast doubt on the efficacy of these remedies, given that they provided me only with stopgap measures? To be honest, I have to admit that remedies never work for the person who only half applies them—which is my case, partially because of my lack of initiative and partially because of the difficult (or, I would say, insoluble) questions that these activities caused me to ask myself. How, for example, be an ethnographer (whose vocation attracts one to traditional cultures) and yet someone who is impatient, out of friendship for those whom one has refused to study as mere insects or rare plants, to see them finally equipped to make themselves heard (or in other words, to help these peoples become more "modern" and thus lose the very attributes that so attracted us to them in the first place)? How, in one's fight against racism (including the need to root out the slightest traces of this insidious disease within oneself), not to be embarrassed when, having freed oneself from all prejudices (even favorable ones) about people of another color, one finds oneself having to deal with real pains in the neck among them whom one has to put back in their place, even at the risk of being considered racist? How, if one believes in the necessity of revolution (if only to shake the so-called elites, be they defined by race or class, out of their complacency), conceive of an organization that before or after the revolution would function with all the requisite efficiency without, however, sacrificing the liberty of individuals to the smooth running of the machine? Anyone who dares venture into these territories out of his hatred for inertia is thus exposed to any number of setbacks and misguided actions, if not outright stalemates.

Like the devil, the ways in which one can get bogged down are thus legion. Indeed, they are so multifarious that their menace is felt *here* perhaps less harshly but just as perniciously as *there*. And this is why I now have doubts about the accuracy of my analysis, doubts that may well turn into certainties upon further examination: was it in fact my voice that had uttered this sentence whose import had so impressed me that I judged it to be "crucial" upon transcribing it onto an index card long after having first noted it down and then appending an initial commentary on it? It was without a doubt I who was speaking, for I am not naïve enough to think that this message was addressed to me by some supernatural power. But who exactly was this I who was now speaking, and am I not mistaken in identifying this I with the one who can produce his ID upon request, the I who blithely cultivates his *headful of fruit* for fear of getting utterly bogged down in outside matters? On second thought, it seems to me that this voice that arose from the depths of half sleep was at the same time mine and not mine—that is, a voice that had traveled from so far away, from some hidden recess of my cave, that it was almost foreign to me—and that I was therefore wrong to have interpreted the word *here* that was placed at the outset of the message as designating the very place I occupy when moved to utterance in my daily life. "Here": is this not precisely the remote location that belongs to me but over which I have no control—that is, the place from which this voice speaks to me, a voice to which I cannot listen as I would to the voice of an interlocutor, whose act of saying "Here" does not exactly coincide with my perspective, given that it belongs to him alone?

Ici (this obscure location which is a "here" only for the voice that speaks in me)

fruit à la tête (what I happen to imagine at a level less deep and what I exteriorize by articulating it)

se dit: (is to be judged as will be specified)

là (in this "headful of fruit," as seen by the voice that speaks but that is not absolutely my voice)

on s'enlise (one flounders, one gets stuck in shifting sands).

This adage, which I initially took to be an encouragement to engage in what Nerval calls a "second life"—namely, to pursue this work that colors all my days, that protects me from the fear of what their succession might hold, that carries me beyond words by its very words, that frees me from my daily life without functioning as a diversion, involving as it does the mental reworking of materials drawn from this very life (be it diurnal or nocturnal) and treating them from a point of view that, escaping from the restless searchlight of everyday thought, is located on the far side of existence or that has managed to sneak its way into death, were it not for the fact that (returning back to zero) death implies the erasure of any point of view whatsoever—well, this adage has undergone a complete reversal of meaning: it now stands as a warning about getting bogged down in my private elucubrations and not as a warning about the all too obvious risks of real life, and rather than advise me to turn toward my inner life and make an effort to render it perceptible, it addresses an indirect call to me to open myself to the outside, even if (as I was later to think when adapting this adage to one of the great problems I was unable to solve) this didn't necessarily entail political commitment on my part, a difficult ordeal for anyone who agrees to sacrifice his sense of self as far as possible but who, come what may, is unable to fully suspend his critical capacities. As for the question of inside versus outside, I am grossly exaggerating when I categorically place these two fields of action in opposition: what I am thinking inside passes to the outside in the form of the sentences that I utter or write, and the options offered to me from the outside oblige me to engage in reflections in which I can get just as lamentably lost as in the constructions I build up without any outside pressure. And there's more: what would I think about within my head if it weren't nourished by the outside, and what would I do on the outside if not driven by inner desire or if not guided by the few ideas in which I truly believe? When, forgetting all their exchanges, I speak of this inside and this outside as opposites that exclude each other and between which one has to choose, I am probably lapsing into my long-standing tendency to stage my problems in theatrically contrasting terms and to turn them into the subject of a drama à la Corneille: pleasure versus duty (in a neat antithesis like love versus honor in *The Cid*, at least as it was taught in high school), contemplation versus action, reason versus unreason. Be it a result of my schooling or a permanent disposition, to proceed in this manner is to subscribe to a puerile Manichaeism that—by excluding all dialectics—wants Good to be located here and Evil to be located there, each comfortably settled into its place.

Ici (the seat of the tribunal that deep within me renders its verdicts)

fruit à la tête (the various sophisticated notions, be they intellectual or moral, that I find far too seductive)

se dit: (translates as)

là (in all those behaviors I need to avoid)

on s'enlise (I lose my way, get flustered, struggle in vain).

In the end, the content of this sentence reveals itself to be quite harmless, even though I almost got bogged down in my interpretations of it, having understood only late in the game the double dangers it was warning against. To stop beating around the bush, to distrust baroque amplification, to stop splitting hairs, this is what this message is advising me to do, not only in the matter of verbal creation but also as relates to active political commitment, both equally rejected, without any assurance that the former could be fruitfully played off against getting bogged down in the latter and thus without any indication that I should choose one over the other. As trenchant in its form as the blade of a guillotine, this elliptical sentence which at first sight seems so full of hidden meanings enjoins me not to choose between two different kinds of activities but rather (reluctant as I am to deny myself the conflict that provides one of the motors of my personal life) to pursue both at the same time, however thorny their coexistence might prove on the levels both of theory and of praxis. What it provides, in short, is a wise invitation to generally behave with a bit more common sense and spontaneity and to avoid indulging in the multiplication of those meanderings that guarantee that any path one feels one has to follow ends up being only a dead end. How could I have been so mistaken as to believe that this sentence was the bearer of a revelation, whereas under its oracular veil the most banal of truths lay ready to be deciphered?

What I now realize is that in trying to determine what the sentence meant, I had proceeded to interpret it by substituting what it said with what it suited me to hear it say: an apology for the imaginary, then a call to action. Assigning it these two meanings in turn before arriving at the version that now appears to me to be its *ne varietur* edition, I took the same liberty with this adage as one does when making use of those emblems that without any visible change in form often undergo surprising variations in content over the course of time: the red flag that before becoming the emblem of revolution (or, for that matter, the signal of roadwork or of a dangerous truck load or of a sea too rough to swim in) was the banner flown by the royal troops when engaged in firing on rebels, thus a sign of insurrection but seen from the other side of the barricade; the Red Cross, today a symbol of aid to the sick and wounded, but originally worn by the monks of the order of the Templars, the gendarmes of conquered Palestine, as a mark of their fealty; the swastika, an ancient ideogram of life, adopted by Hitler as a rallying sign for what eventually turned out to be an atrocious industrialization of death; the Gallic cock, now baptized, perched on the top of a church steeple. Like these emblems whose forms are fixed but whose contents are fluid, many adages, subject as they are to various elucidations, change their meaning without losing any of their authority and perhaps even become all the more esteemed the more interpretations they attract. Take the examples of those semilegendary philosophers Heraclitus and Lao-tzu: wouldn't they be far less fascinating if many of their sayings did not present themselves as enigmas open to any number of conflicting commentaries? In addition to its concision, it was no doubt its hermeticism and its promise of different translations that made this sentence so valuable to me when it suddenly appeared in my head one morning like a freshly grown piece of fruit, a sentence that I long let rest (as if wanting to await its ripening) before returning to it in order to turn it this way and that, without foreseeing that all it would yield to me was a poor and fragile bit of truth. Am I even completely sure, now that I have stripped it down to its core, that it is bidding me to be far more natural, or should I on the contrary conclude that the risk of stalemate is the price one has to pay and that to retreat from this eventuality is to deprive oneself of the possibility of fruit in one's head, which is to say that fearing to go astray, one ends up engaging in self-sterilization or self-castration?

To rush forth. To vacillate. To twirl about. To capsize. After several advances followed by second thoughts, the examination of this sentence has led me to conclude that even if its grammar can be correctly read, it remains obscure and grows ever more so if I try to extract a watchword from it instead of merely accepting it as a detached observation. Having articulated itself independent of my volition, the sentence was certainly dictated to me; but now it is I who am dictating to it the meaning I find most pertinent to me, which means that although it was initially heard as a warning issued from the beyond, the sentence has simply become the changing reflection of my opinions concerning the question that it raises without, however, indicating how to go about resolving it. Having stepped down from its pedestal, it now proves of no use on the terrain across which I had hoped it would lead me; because its masterfully poetic form had encouraged me to read it as if it were the statement of some golden rule, I had ascribed to it more power than it actually had, thus causing me to cast doubt on the validity of those *oracular utterances* that I have occasionally felt resonating within me, heralds of truths marked by the seal of eternity but also so fragile that they cannot survive their translation into everyday language. Creating a burden of doubt that nearly cripples the (visceral) credit I ascribe even to the most elaborate of poetry, this gradual unmasking of the inconsistency of a sentence whose diamantine limpidity had so won me over at the start now revealed just how deceptive this contrapuntal mode of thought can be, even as the message it conveys—more sensed than understood—seems to burn with a gemlike flame.

And yet, despite the shock of this realization, one thing remains certain for me. If, given my nagging qualms, I am intellectually inclined to waver between *for* and *against* in a state of constant oscillation, and if both inside us and outside us things wear down so quickly as to leave no solid ground underfoot, my sole recourse is to try to give myself over to the sheer movement that occurs in the simultaneity of affirmation and negation: continuously renewed acts of aesthetic creation, contributions to a social revolution that must always be taken up again and carried further. This is, of course, a program to which I have long subscribed, as it were instinctually and without finding any need to provide proofs of my commitment. Yet merely subscribing to it is not enough, and it's here that the difficulties begin, even were I to chose one of the sides (as if the dice were not already cast for me) and decide to be either a tireless inventor or an authentic revolutionary . . . To ward off the specter of failure that once again haunts all the hallways of my house while clanking its chains, where can I discover a fallback position that might fill in for a magic circle?

Let the various means I have at my disposal—first and foremost, my writings, poetic or other—be of help (in however fragmentary or specialized a manner) in the creation (however embryonic) of this utopia, a fruit I carry within my head, as do many other companions both known and unknown for whom the word *revolution* entails not just a strategic view of things but a desire for the complete liberation of humankind: to move as soon as possible beyond this madhouse we inhabit into a civilization where tasks and goods would be equally distributed, where investments would serve the convenience of the people and not their exploitation, where with the end of racism, the sexes would also be equal, without either abolishing or encouraging their difference, where, if the other is of age and willing, all forms of love would be permitted, where elective affinities would supplant institutionalized family ties, where the exercise of the imagination, available to all and inviting all to live on different wavelengths, would count as much as the formulation of scientific research hypotheses, where death, seen as a simple counterpart of birth, would be considered less a tragedy than a normal conclusion to life, nothing more than something one would simply want to delay as long as possible. To know that through the good times and the bad my poorly tuned efforts have been of some use in envisaging the above, to know that all the sentences I have so tirelessly dispersed here and there were not just so many soap bubbles—this is something that would reassure me, at least somewhat. Convinced that I have been nothing but the distorted reflection of my age, I might well imagine that it was precisely through my various contradictions, my weaknesses, my false starts, my headlong plunges (and not always ironic ones) into futility, and my back-and-forthings between the dry observation of the real and the random launching of flares that I have made my small contribution to the arrival of a world rid of its stink, even if I have personally washed my hands of too many things out of fear or boredom and even if I have not avoided, here and there, the stain of blood by the enormity of the mistakes I made . . .

Yet is all this worth more than a belief in the beyond, this distant, unverifiable hope from which I can derive no precise rule, a hope (given the dark times we are going through in the present and the darker ones no doubt to come in the immediate future) that might seem as pure moonshine as a bit of science fiction or one that in the end reveals itself to be nothing more than a blind bet on a paradise so dismal as to make one want to kill oneself or throw bombs, and yet nonetheless a hope that provides me with a frail cane as I move on in years, allowing me to view my life as it nears its end from a perspective that just might save it from absolute meaningless?

A worthy place to end, to which (illusion upon illusion) I would, however, like to append this confession: in addition to flattering myself for having
helped (ever so infinitesimally) inaugurate the possibility of an egalitarian society to come, I wish that the drop of water I might have contributed to this
eventuality (if luck so has it) be recognized as *my* drop by (let us say) the few
readers in whom (absent yet audible) I might awaken an echo and whose
attachment to me (rooted in something finer than mere reason) would keep
my first and last names (symbols of my person not yet utterly drained of blood)
from getting stuck in the sands of general indifference, a fate it would be foolish to prefer to utter oblivion.

*

Between my two long-standing proclivities—poetry and political engagement, two forces whose confluence point I would have liked to locate, given that there is no incompatibility between privately trying to raise reality to the level of myth and joining up with others who wish to transform the myth of a free society into a reality—the battle has not been the classic case of the iron pot shattering the clay pot, but rather one in which two clay pots collide, the match ending in a draw, leaving both combatants in pieces . . .

And yet (whatever I might claim), for me poetry has the last word, seeing as how I immediately try to remedy this disaster by providing an image for it, here and now.

*

With the collapse ever more evident, I now write like a singer who has so lost his voice that he no longer feels the desire to perform, less and less confident that he can rely on the technical proficiency that in the past allowed him to believe (at least for himself) in the illusion.

A voice now hoarse, flattened, and deadened—such is the condition of the instrument that this artist barely dares to play, inevitably hitting false notes as he tries to produce a decent musical sound from his throat, requiring efforts as great as any day laborer's. And each note that he misses is felt by him as a deviation from or an alteration of his person, each one tearing at his guts more than at his ears, each one causing him as much worry as the irremediable sin that the true believer is convinced will cost him his salvation.

Even on his better days, he will have to draw upon his voice as best he can, much like an alpinist drawing his climbing companion out of a crevasse with a rope. Having been so laboriously retrieved from the glacial darkness of the abyss, how can this voice, which can warm itself up again only by struggling like a madman, pretend to the Truth?

*

January 11, 1975 . . .

My brother lies in the hospital, where, as his wife just phoned me, he did not survive the major malaise he had been experiencing for several hours, even though earlier this very week he had seemed on the way to recovering from the effects of a terrible accident not far from his home (in which he was knocked over by car that had skidded up onto the sidewalk, no doubt because the street was so slippery that morning and because its driver was going too fast for the weather conditions).

A hideous image, which the final dressing of the deceased will materially assuage, replacing it with one that is more harmonious and more conventional and that will mark a kind of return to normal or indeed a painless passage into a new state—the feigned timelessness and symmetry of a body apparently lost in marmoreal sleep—but an image that despite this piously fraudulent attempt to mend the irrevocably broken link on a higher plane I will never be able to get out of my mind: its face turned to the wall, its knees gathered up under a rumpled sheet, the skinny frame of a dog or other household pet discovered dead in its corner, completely cut off from us, now no more than an inert packet of indefinite matter, now utterly silent, lying there beyond all pity . . .

But at this very moment, don't I likewise want to proceed with the dressing of my own corpse and, in the hope of rendering the thing more palatable, to take up my pen to impose an order on this nameless horror?

*

In this final volume, rosy at moments but where (what can I do?) black tends to predominate, I have been free and easy when it comes to the staggering of dates or to well-thought-out construction. Often placing those things that came *after* as if they had happened *before*, often approaching the snows of yesteryear through my present cast of mind, removing them from their drawers or storage boxes in order to mix them up with things occurring today or barely yesterday, sometimes involving an old story or a former idea, sometimes (for want of a better word) involving a "poem" or a piece of writing that suddenly or gradually took shape over the course of the journey. But can one ever achieve the vantage point of eternity by thus mixing up the dates or multiplying the points of view or varying the tones as one pleases?

It all comes down, if you will, to a question of arrangement, the way the Japanese traditionally arrange—ever so patiently, without seeking to bunch them into the profusion of a bouquet—a small number of flowers to provide pleasure, or peace, to the eye, while leaving certain things unsaid.

A florilegium, then, or an anthology shaped less by its deliberate choices than by its unforgivable omissions: everything I was unable to detect or formulate, everything I was loath to bring to light.

MICHEL LEIRIS (1901–1990), born in Paris, was an early surrealist, a published ethnographer, and an influential author of poems, essays, and, most important, the four-volume, thirty-five-year project of autobiographical and linguistic self-reflection *The Rules of the Game*, of which *Frail Riffs* is the fourth and final volume to appear in English.

An emeritus professor of English, French, and Comparative Literature at New York University, RICHARD SIEBURTH has published award-winning translations from the French of Nostradamus, Maurice Scève, Louise Labé, Gérard de Nerval, Charles Baudelaire, Michel Leiris, Henri Michaux, Eugène Guillevic, and Jacques Darras; and from the German of Oswald von Wolkenstein, Friedrich Hölderlin, Georg Büchner, Walter Benjamin, and Gershom Scholem. He has, in addition, edited a number of Ezra Pound's works for New Directions and the Library of America.